M000200508

RAWLS AND RELIGION

RAWLS
AND
RELIGION

EDITED BY

Tom Bailey and Valentina Gentile

p 240 — Voluntarism

Columbia University Press   New York

Columbia University Press
Publishers Since 1893
New York   Chichester, West Sussex
cup.columbia.edu
Copyright © 2015 Columbia University Press
All rights reserved

Library of Congress Cataloging-in-Publication Data

Rawls and religion / edited by Tom Bailey and Valentina Gentile.
pages cm
Includes bibliographical references and index.
ISBN 978-0-231-16798-7 (cloth : alk. paper)
—ISBN 978-0-231-16799-4 (pbk. : alk. paper)
—ISBN 978-0-231-53839-8 (e-book)
1. Rawls, John, 1921–2002.   2. Religion.

B945.R284R39   2015
200.92—dc23   2014015955

Columbia University Press books are printed
on permanent and durable acid-free paper.
This book is printed on paper with recycled content.
Printed in the United States of America

c 10 9 8 7 6 5 4 3 2 1
p 10 9 8 7 6 5 4 3 2 1

Jacket design by Noah Arlow

References to websites (URLs) were accurate at the time of writing.
Neither the author nor Columbia University Press is responsible
for URLs that may have expired or changed since the manuscript was prepared.

CONTENTS

PART I. REINTERPRETING RAWLS ON RELIGION

FOREWORD

Sebastiano Maffettone

John Rawls played a pivotal role in the development of contemporary liberal political philosophy—indeed, it might even be said that political philosophers live in "the era of Rawls." But his sensitivity to religion is often neglected and his own treatment of it often misunderstood. His recently published undergraduate thesis, *A Brief Inquiry Into the Meaning of Sin and Faith,* and his later autobiographical remarks, "On My Religion," speak to his personal sensitivities. And his idea of a well-ordered society inspired by liberal democratic principles and bringing together religious and nonreligious citizens represents a sort of "reconciliation" between the moral realm and that of politics.

Importantly, the "reconciliation" that Rawls proposes differs from the liberal "standard view." For traditional liberals, religion is an obstacle to peace and stability, and this suspicious attitude leads them to confine religion to the private sphere. Rawls's attitude is different. For him, religion is a constituent part of the liberal democratic res publica—his examples are such religious liberals as Abraham Lincoln and Martin Luther King Jr. So, rather than privatizing religion, Rawls proposes a way to make it fruitful for the whole population.

If religion and politics are reconciled in Rawls's work, their most important encounter is provided by his theory of public reason. This inclusive theory considers religious people as active participants in the life of the liberal democratic republic. In only a few matters of extraordinary political importance—Supreme Court decisions, parliamentary voting, and so on—religious citizens are asked to reformulate their religious arguments in terms that all other citizens can understand. This "proviso" does not apply unfairly to religious citizens, as some have alleged, since it applies equally to all "comprehensive" doctrines, including Marxism, utilitarianism, Kantianism, and even Rawls's own account of justice as fairness. And its appeal to a kind of mutual respect among citizens of different value orientations is notably less demanding of religious citizens than many competing liberal theories.

Rawls's theory of public reason nonetheless implies a form of priority of the political over the religious. When matters of basic justice are at stake, it asks that religious or "comprehensive" arguments be reformulated in terms that all citizens can reasonably accept, but it does not ask the opposite, namely, that shared matters of justice be reformulable in religious terms. The reason for this reflects the liberal problem of justifying political coercion: nobody should be coerced for reasons dependent on "comprehensive" views. Even we Italians would not want Catholic doctrine to be enforced by the *carabinieri*! One might therefore object to this priority of the political over the "comprehensive" as an unjustifiable imposition of liberal democracy on religious citizens and communities, as some critics of liberalism have. Some radicals might even maintain that in Rawls's liberalism not all communities are treated in the same way: the justification for a political community is taken for granted, whereas other communities, and particularly religious ones, have to justify their very existence.

It is the merit of *Rawls and Religion* that it finally reveals and explores a new and persuasive understanding of the place of religion in Rawls's liberal framework. Tom Bailey and Valentina Gentile's introduction offers a clear and insightful account of the background debates, showing that Rawls's liberalism offers rich, and sometimes neglected, resources for accommodating religions in the political life of liberal citizens. The contributors then explore a range of crucial philosophical, practical, and theological issues regarding Rawls's idea of public reason and its implications for the role of religion in public life. The volume thus makes important contributions to the academic and intellectual debates that have emerged in recent years over Rawls's treatment of religion. I have rarely read a book that combines so well the clarity of the subjects treated with the philosophical acuity of its arguments, and I am sure that readers from various fields and at various levels will learn much from it.

ACKNOWLEDGMENTS

The editors would like to thank Péter Losonczi, Sebastiano Maffettone, and Aakash Singh Rathore for their invaluable advice and assistance in preparing this book. The editors also thank them, Domenico Melidoro, the administrations of LUISS University and John Cabot University, and the International Research Network on Religion and Democracy for their assistance in organizing the conference "Between Rawls and Religion: Liberalism in a Postsecular World," at which Christopher Eberle, James Gledhill, Peter Jonkers, Micah Schwartzman, Robert Talisse, Johannes van der Ven, and Paul Weithman were invited to present drafts of their chapters. Alessandro Ferrara, David Rasmussen, Will Kymlicka, David Held, Neera Chandhoke, and Richard Bellamy also provided very helpful advice on the book's structure, themes, and publication. Finally, the editors would like to thank all the contributors to the book for their support and cooperation in bringing the book to completion.

ABBREVIATIONS OF RAWLS'S WORKS

BG   "The Best of All Games," *Boston Review* 33 (March 1, 2008).

BI   *A Brief Inquiry Into the Meaning of Sin and Faith, with "On My Religion,"* ed. Thomas Nagel (Cambridge, Mass.: Harvard University Press, 2009).

CP   *Collected Papers*, ed. Samuel Freeman (Cambridge, Mass.: Harvard University Press, 1999).

IPRR   "The Idea of Public Reason Revisited," in *LP* 129–80, or *PL* (exp.) 440–90.

JF   *Justice as Fairness: A Restatement*, ed. Erin Kelly (Cambridge, Mass.: Harvard University Press, 2001).

LHMP   *Lectures on the History of Moral Philosophy*, ed. Barbara Herman (Cambridge, Mass.: Harvard University Press, 2000).

LHPP   *Lectures on the History of Political Philosophy*, ed. Samuel Freeman (Cambridge, Mass.: Harvard University Press, 2007).

LP   *The Law of Peoples, with "The Idea of Public Reason Revisited"* (Cambridge, Mass.: Harvard University Press, 1999).

MR   "On My Religion," in *BI* 259–69.

PL   *Political Liberalism* (New York: Columbia University Press, 1993). A revised paperback edition was published in 1996, and an expanded edition in 2005. References are to the first edition unless indicated by "(pbk.)" or "(exp.)."

TJ   *A Theory of Justice* (Cambridge, Mass.: Harvard University Press, 1971). A revised edition was published in 1999. References are to the first edition unless indicated by "(rev.)."

RAWLS AND RELIGION

Introduction

TOM BAILEY AND VALENTINA GENTILE

Religions pose special challenges to liberal ways of justifying political authority. For while liberals generally wish to allow the utmost freedom to religions, they often also wish to justify political authority by the (at least hypothetical) consent of those subject to it, and thus to uphold certain more distinctive ideas of freedom and equality. But religions need neither share this peculiar liberal concern nor provide justifications that agree with liberal ones—they may prioritize doctrine over reason or illiberal hierarchies over equality, say. Indeed, the wealth of different religious sensibilities, voices, and demands present in contemporary liberal societies makes these challenges particularly urgent. In the United States, for instance, while strong Christian forces have persisted, neo-Protestant movements and an unprecedented array of other new religious groups and sensibilities have also emerged. In Europe, while the traditional Christian churches have declined, they have been replaced not only by more "secular" cultures, but also by new forms of Christian and other religious influences, including the oft-emphasized Islamic ones.[1] While liberals may wish to embrace these religious phenomena, they are often also wary of their potential for destabilizing liberal structures of political authority, whether by disturbing these structures directly or by upsetting consensus over them.

This book explores these challenges by reexamining perhaps the most sophisticated, influential, and controversial liberal response to them, that of John Rawls. Particularly in his second book, *Political Liberalism*, Rawls recognizes that citizens of liberal societies inevitably hold a plurality of religious and other moral worldviews. But he argues that citizens can nonetheless reach a consensus over a shared conception of political authority by means of a particular kind of "mutual respect" independent of these moral worldviews. And he claims that this shared conception ought not only to inform the constitution and political institutions that citizens share, but also to guide citizens' public deliberations and decision-making. This appeal to an independent "respect" is standardly read as reflecting liberals' wariness of religions by excluding them from political or public life, and it has thus been much criticized, both by those who think that liberal concerns imply a more extensive accommodation or restriction of religions and by those who question these liberal concerns themselves.

Yet it is our contention, and that of most of the contributors to this book, that this standard critical reading of Rawls is mistaken, and that he rather offers rich, neglected resources for accommodating religions in liberal political life. In particular, he envisions consensus over political authority as emerging internally and dynamically from citizens' various religious and other moral worldviews, such that religions and engagement with them are crucial to his conception of liberal political life.

In this introduction, we briefly present Rawls's treatment of religions, the criticisms that are standardly made of it, and the various alternative approaches that have been proposed. We then set out a defense of Rawls against these criticisms and alternatives. We conclude by situating the chapters in light of this defense and in terms of their contributions to the three main themes around which the book is organized, namely, the reinterpretation of the "respect" and "consensus" involved in Rawls's treatment of religions (the first part of the book), the exploration of the means he proposes for accommodating nonliberal religions in liberal political life (the second part), and the reevaluation of his liberalism from the "transcendent" perspectives of religions themselves (the third part).

RAWLS ON RELIGION

Rawls admits that the freedoms characteristic of liberal societies inevitably produce a plurality of "comprehensive doctrines," or general moral and ontological frameworks of convictions about what makes lives worth living. He also admits that these doctrines strongly influence how citizens live and relate to one another, whether they be religious, such as Christian, Islamic, or Buddhist, or nonreligious, such as socialist, perfectionist, or utilitarian. But he insists that citizens have no overarching way of judging between them. In societies in which citizens inevitably hold different comprehensive doctrines, therefore, to justify political authority in terms of any particular doctrine(s) would be to impose political authority on at least some citizens without their consent—something that Rawls considers unacceptable, given liberal commitments to freedom and equality. Thus, while admitting that comprehensive doctrines such as religions proliferate in contemporary liberal societies, he denies that political authority can be justified exclusively in terms of any such doctrines.[2]

Rawls nonetheless considers political authority to be necessary, since it represents the stable rules that are essential for social cooperation. He therefore argues that, rather than of comprehensive doctrines, citizens may consent to political authority on the basis of a further notion of "mutual respect," insofar as this is reflected in the rules of their social cooperation.[3] He also refers to this mutual respect in terms of "fairness," "reasonableness," "reciprocity," "civic friendship," and a "duty of civility" among citizens, and he regards it as implicit in the political culture of liberal societies.[4] From it, he considers it possible to derive a conception of political authority that citizens may share independently of their different comprehensive doctrines—a conception that he therefore considers to be distinctively "freestanding," or "political." In his first book, *A Theory of Justice*, he argues particularly for a conception of "justice as fairness," which emphasizes two basic principles, one regarding citizens' equal basic liberties and the other the fair equality of opportunity and the equality of resources and responsibilities among them.[5] In *Political Liberalism*, he argues that citizens' shared conception of political authority, rather than their different comprehensive doctrines, ought to guide not only their constitution

and political institutions—what he calls the "basic structure" of a society—but also their public deliberations and decision-making, at least
in contexts of special political significance, such as when considering
constitutional issues as officials, candidates, or voters. In his terms, in
these contexts "public," or "political," reasons ought to take priority
over reasons reflecting citizens' comprehensive doctrines.[6]

Crucially, however, in *Political Liberalism* Rawls also argues that
reasonings based on comprehensive doctrines may be admitted into
the "freestanding" framework of political authority in two ways.
First, he argues that each citizen may consent to the shared conception of political authority for different reasons, based on his or her
own particular comprehensive doctrine. In his terms, there may be an
"overlapping consensus" on the political conception among citizens'
different comprehensive doctrines.[7] Second, he argues that reasons
which reflect citizens' comprehensive doctrines may be employed in
public deliberations and decision-making, as long as supporting reasons which reflect citizens' shared conception of political authority
can be provided "in due course." He thus endorses what he calls a
"wide" view of the admissibility of reasonings based on comprehensive doctrines in public life.[8] While insisting on a shared conception
of political authority based on a shared notion of respect, then, he
also holds that reasoning according to citizens' other, different comprehensive doctrines may be consistent with respectfully sharing
this conception.

Rawls thus develops a sophisticated liberal response to the proliferation of religious and nonreligious worldviews in contemporary
societies. This response acknowledges the pluralism and force of these
worldviews, while nonetheless insisting that political authority can be
justified by citizens' consent in terms of a particular sense of mutual
respect among them.

CONTESTING RAWLS

Rawls's treatment of religions has been extremely influential, both
within the academy and beyond. But it has also been much criticized.
The criticisms made of it can be divided into two broad kinds. Criticisms of the first kind allege that the restrictions which Rawls places

on citizens' reasonings over political authority or issues are overly demanding of religious citizens, while criticisms of the second kind allege that these restrictions are insufficiently democratic and thus inappropriate for contemporary liberal societies.

Criticisms of the first kind generally allege that Rawls's restrictions are overly demanding of religious citizens in one or more of three broad ways. First, to exclude religious reasons from the justification of political authority and from public deliberations would appear to be simply alienating for religious citizens. For this exclusion may be so strict as to infringe on their moral integrity or so controversial that they could not accept it, even were their own religiously based conclusions to coincide with those made according to it.[9] Second, and relatedly, the exclusion of religious reasons seems to involve an overly negative estimation of the contributions that religions make to society. For it seems to presuppose that religious reasonings necessarily cause political conflict, such that stability can be maintained only by restricting citizens to nonreligious reasonings, or at least to deny that religious reasonings make valuable contributions to political society—for instance, in terms of citizens' participation in politics, their shared allegiances to the state, or their reaching consensus over issues.[10] Rawls's exclusion of religious reasons thus seems to place him in a long tradition of liberal philosophers overly wary of the dangers of admitting religion into politics. Third, the liberal ideas of freedom and equality inherent in Rawls's basic notion of "respect" are often considered insufficient to justify his exclusion of religious reasonings. For these ideas might perhaps be upheld without accepting these restrictions—Rawls may overestimate the importance of consensus, say.[11] It is even alleged that these ideas themselves constitute a particular moral perspective, such that they cannot provide for a genuinely shared conception of political authority and, in particular, that they will not be shared by some religious citizens.[12]

Criticisms of the second kind can also be subdivided into three distinct forms, since Rawls's restrictions are generally alleged to be insufficiently democratic in one or more of three broad ways. First, his exclusion of comprehensive doctrines is alleged to make public reasonings too indeterminate and thus controversial. Debates regarding abortion or same-sex marriage, for instance, seem to be irresolvable without appeal to comprehensive doctrines, including religious ones.[13] Second, it is often argued that genuine democratic deliberation ought to extend beyond basic constitutional issues among officials, candidates, and voters to other, equally "political" or "public" questions and functions. Again, legislation regarding issues such as abortion or same-sex marriage might be considered a legitimate object of democratic deliberation, particularly by citizens with religious convictions on these matters.[14] Finally, rather than being too exclusive of religious reasonings to be democratic, it is also often claimed that Rawls's restrictions are too inclusive of them. That is, it is often thought that religious reasonings should be excluded from democratic deliberation altogether, in order to ensure that both religious and nonreligious citizens can comprehend, deliberate over, and consent to the decisions made. Seen in this light, Rawls's admission of religious reasonings into citizens' "overlapping consensus" and their public deliberations and decision-making, however qualified, would seem to threaten the possible participation and consent of nonreligious citizens.[15]

Such criticisms of Rawls have motivated a wide range of alternative proposals, from attempts to accommodate religions more extensively in liberal politics to claims that liberal politics must exclude religions entirely. Among the "accommodationists," some argue that liberal citizens need not share the same reasonings in order to agree sufficiently on political life, and therefore that no special restrictions on religious reasonings are required. It is claimed, for instance, that through deliberative processes citizens may converge on political rights and policies for different personal reasons, that liberal ideas of freedom and equality require all reasonings to be equally admitted in citizens' pursuit of just policies and agreement over them, within a framework of basic liberal rights, and even that liberal politics ought to actively promote a diversity of values and thus a diversity of reasonings.[16] Other "accommodationists" argue that cultural contexts are necessary for the exercise of liberal freedoms and therefore that, when it is necessary to protect such contexts, members of religious and other cultural groups may be given special rights—special educational, economic, or decision-making privileges, say.[17] Still others emphasize citizens' democratic responsibility to engage with the variety of religious and nonreligious views now present in contemporary societies, at least in deliberations outside institutional contexts. By doing so, it is supposed, citizens learn to consider issues from one another's perspectives and thus extend the justificatory scope of their deliberations.[18] Thus liberal philosophers have proposed more open and dynamic attitudes toward religions in public life than Rawls appears to provide, echoing broader political calls for a distinctively "multicultural" politics and society and for the special recognition of religious identities and groups.

In contrast, others have taken the supposed failings of Rawls's treatment of religions to reflect a fundamental incompatibility between religions and liberalism, the impossibility of accommodating religions in liberal politics. Among these "exclusivists," some liberal philosophers argue that, since only "secular" reasonings can be shared by all citizens, liberal ideas of freedom and equality can be upheld only by excluding religious reasonings from the political sphere.[19] Such concerns often also underlie broader political calls for the reassertion of the "secular" or "neutral" nature of modern societies and liberal politics, as well as fears of the inflammatory effects of new religious influences. But other "exclusivists" have taken issue with liberalism itself, arguing that liberal ideas of freedom and equality, and associated senses of consent, justification, pluralism, and respect, conflict with genuine religious practice and belief. For these philosophical critics and those who adopt similar positions in politics, political life ought instead to be based on other, openly religious grounds.[20]

RECONSIDERING RAWLS

However, it is our contention, and that of many of the contributors to this book, that these critical responses to Rawls's treatment of religions ignore crucial and fruitful elements of it. Indeed, in our view, his "exclusion" of religions is extremely limited and qualified, such that he provides for an extensive accommodation of religions in political life, and the notions of "respect" and "consensus" on which his "exclusion" is based are much more subtle, open, and flexible than his critics suppose.

Regarding the extent of Rawls's "exclusion" of religions from political life, there are six reasons for not considering this to be objectionable in the ways that his critics have claimed. First, his exclusion applies only to particularly significant institutions, issues, and contexts, such as the consideration of constitutional issues by political officials or voters. This leaves an extremely broad range of other deliberations entirely unrestricted—those conducted in what he calls the "nonpublic" and "background" culture of society.[21] Second, as already mentioned, Rawls holds that religions and other comprehensive doctrines may be employed in the public, political realm as long as supporting reasons that reflect citizens' shared political principles can be provided "in due course." Although he does not explain precisely when and how supporting reasons are "due," this need not be interpreted narrowly. Indeed, he remarks that it is to be "worked out in practice," presumably according to the particular practices of a society. As examples, he refers to Abraham Lincoln's arguments against slavery, which, he claims, rightly appealed to religious ideas with equivalents in other comprehensive doctrines, and to Martin Luther King's arguments for civil rights, which, he claims, rightly employed religious arguments to support "political" reasonings and thus showed how an "inclusive," rather than an "exclusive," approach "best encourages citizens to honor the ideal of public reason."[22] Third, Rawls encourages reasoning from comprehensive doctrines that are not one's own, with a view to showing how they might support the shared conception of political authority—what he calls reasoning by "conjecture"—and he even allows that reasonings based on religious and other comprehensive doctrines which cannot be supported "in due course" may nonetheless be heard in political spaces: he refers particularly to the "witnessing" of such excluded reasons.[23] Fourth, his exclusion of religions from politics applies only to reasonings, and thus leaves undisturbed other ways of expressing and practicing religious and other comprehensive doctrines. Fifth, insofar as he excludes religions from political life, Rawls does not discriminate against them, since his exclusion applies equally to all comprehensive doctrines and does so on the same grounds. That is, he considers all comprehensive doctrines to be equally "metaphysical" and controversial, and thus equally problematic bases for deliberation over political authority and policies.[24] And, finally, his exclusion of religious and other comprehensive doctrines from political life need not render political reasonings objectionably indeterminate or narrow in scope, insofar as citizens' shared conception of political authority provides a framework of considerations for reasoning.[25] In the light of these six considerations, then, it seems implausible to suppose that Rawls's restrictions on citizens' reasoning need be profoundly alienating for religious citizens or deny the contributions that religions can make to politics in his narrow sense, or, indeed, that they need affect in any way the range of other "political" activities in which religious citizens may engage.

The reasons Rawls gives for this extremely limited "exclusion" of religions—his concerns for respect and consensus, and the senses of freedom, equality, and pluralism that they express—also need not be objectionable. As mentioned above, his concern is to justify political authority by the consent of citizens in contemporary liberal societies. Since such societies are marked by a plurality of comprehensive doctrines between which there is no overarching way to judge, he claims that consent to political authority can be based not on any particular comprehensive doctrine(s)—which need not be shared by all citizens—but rather only on a further notion of "respect" among citizens with different comprehensive doctrines, on the basis of which they can derive a shared conception of political authority. Insofar as Rawls places restrictions on citizens' political reasoning at all, then, these restrictions are intended to be the least demanding necessary to ensure respectful consensus in contemporary contexts of moral pluralism. This respectful consensus, like the senses of freedom, equality, and pluralism that it expresses, does not discriminate against religions or presuppose negative evaluations of their contributions to society, since it applies equally to all comprehensive doctrines. It is also minimal enough that it need not be alienating to citizens with religious commitments, although it may be unacceptable to some.[26] Indeed, Rawls's treatment shows how liberal senses of freedom, equality, and pluralism can be upheld without requiring citizens to forgo religious reasonings for the sake of a substantial "secular" conception of political life. Instead, it is sufficient that both religious and nonreligious comprehensive doctrines be excluded from a narrow "political" realm, while being left entirely unrestricted in other political contexts.[27] And, finally, Rawls's minimal sense of respectful consensus also suggests that, insofar as his "exclusion" of comprehensive doctrines from this narrowly "political" realm renders reasonings in it indeterminate or narrow in scope, this ought to be accepted for the sake of the mutual respect, or the associated commitments to freedom, equality, and pluralism, that it expresses.[28]

Admittedly, this understanding of Rawls's liberal approach to justifying political authority, and of the minimal senses of respect and consensus involved, differs substantially from those often attributed to him by his critics. For, in our view, Rawls's argument appeals neither to substantial "liberal" moral values or cultural practices nor to a substantial "liberal" conception of political principles, one emphasizing, say, a strong notion of "autonomy," the value of diversity, or the priority of the "right" over the "good."[29] Having excluded such "comprehensive" senses of liberalism, he is concerned simply with how shared principles for the narrow "political" realm can be elaborated from among the diverse moral values of a society in mutually respectful ways.[30] Citizens' "overlapping consensus" on political principles therefore need reflect no particular moral or political limits besides those of mutual respect, and will vary according to the particular moral context of a specific society and the particular ways in which citizens employ and interpret this context. Indeed, even the distinction between this context and the principles, or between the non-"political" and the "political," will be determined by these principles. Rather than abstracting from moral worldviews in the name of a "social contract" applicable to all citizens and times or a theory of political "rightness" or "rationality," then, Rawls envisions a much more contingent and dynamic consensus.[31] He requires only that this consensus be mutually respectful in contexts of moral pluralism, and thus "reasonable" or "legitimate," and that it be sufficiently "stable" to facilitate social cooperation, in the sense that citizens assure one another of their commitment to a shared conception of political authority whenever their inevitable moral differences call this commitment into doubt. In his terms, the consensus that he envisions thus neither reflects a "comprehensive" liberalism nor is a mere "modus vivendi" among citizens.[32]

In this light, it is unsurprising that Rawls insists that non-"political" reasonings—those of the "nonpublic," "background" culture—be entirely unrestricted. For only in this way can citizens come to recognize the plurality of different comprehensive doctrines in their society and find and endorse shared political principles to guide their social life in respectful ways.[33] Indeed, here his remarks about Martin Luther King are again telling, in emphasizing how when there are deep divisions over citizens' shared political conception, religious reasonings may provide principles that subsequently become part of that shared conception.[34] It is also unsurprising that Rawls encourages citizens to engage in "political" reasonings not so much from supposedly universal "liberal" values as from their own different comprehensive doctrines, by employing the opportunities offered by the "in due course" condition and such methods as "conjecture." For only by reasoning in terms of an "overlapping" agreement among these doctrines can citizens express and renew their respectful consensus over a shared conception of political authority based on it. And it ought to be equally unsurprising that Rawls later presents the conception of "justice as fairness" that he had proposed in *A Theory of Justice* as just one of the possible conceptions of political authority that citizens might thus agree on.[35] For the overlapping consensus present in any specific society will vary according to its particular moral resources and how they are elaborated by its citizens.

If such a reading of Rawls is right, he provides a novel liberal response to the proliferation of religious and other worldviews in contemporary societies, one that appeals to a minimal sense of mutual respect, rather than strong "liberal" presuppositions, and one that envisions a consensus which depends on and varies according to a society's particular moral context, rather than abstracting from it. The contributions to this book critically explore the rich resources for accommodating religions in liberal political life—a sophisticated alternative to both "accommodationist" and "exclusivist" approaches— that this response offers, and that both Rawls's sympathizers and his critics have neglected. In particular, the chapters consider three main themes, according to which the book is divided, namely, the reinterpretation of Rawls's senses of respect and consensus and his associated argument for "excluding" religions from political life, the exploration of the particular means that he proposes for accommodating nonliberal religions in a liberal consensus, and the reevaluation of his liberalism from the "transcendent" perspectives of religions themselves.

CONTRIBUTIONS

The first part of the book, which focuses on Rawls's senses of respect and consensus and their role in his "exclusion" of religions from political life, begins with a bold restatement of the criticism that Rawls's exclusion cannot be justified by liberal "respect." In "Respect and War: Against the Standard View of Religion in Politics," Christopher Eberle considers Rawls to exemplify what he calls liberalism's "standard view" of religions, namely, the view that officials and other citizens may not appeal to religious reasons in advocating coercive policies because such reasons cannot be sufficient to justify such policies. On the standard liberal argument that Eberle sets out for this view, this is because citizens are treated with respect only if they can share the justification for coercive policies and because, in the morally pluralist contexts of contemporary societies, only nonreligious justifications can be so shared. Eberle objects to both premises of this argument, using the advocacy of war as a representative case. First, he argues that citizens may support the same policy without having the same reasons for doing so. And second, he argues that religious reasons are no more or less shareable than nonreligious ones, insofar as the justification for them may satisfy or fail to satisfy the same epistemological, moral, or sociological criteria. Eberle concludes that liberalism ought therefore to abandon the Rawlsian claim that if citizens are to be respected, then the justification of any coercive policy must be shareable by those subject to it. For Eberle, then, the admittance of religious reasonings into political debate is not disrespectful toward other citizens. However, in specifying this accommodationist position, he also rejects an alternative such position, according to which citizens may "converge" on policies for different reasons. In his view, not only would this still preclude religious reasons from justifying policies; it would also preclude justification to some basic liberal rights that, on his own accommodationist position, constitute the only legitimate limit to liberal democratic politics.

Robert Talisse's chapter, "Religion and Liberalism: Was Rawls Right After All?," takes up Eberle's challenge to defend the Rawlsian claim about respect and the shareable nature of justification. Indeed, Talisse also defends the Rawlsian claim against the broader worry that, by excluding appeals to strictly religious reasons as disrespectful toward other citizens, the claim itself disrespectfully violates a basic liberal right that Eberle rightly insists on, namely, the freedom of conscience. Talisse focuses on Eberle's accommodationist claim that liberal respect need require only that citizens conscientiously *pursue* shareable reasons and not that they refrain from advocating policies for which they fail to discover such reasons. To this, Talisse replies first by arguing that if this were so, then in some cases some citizens would be required to accept the advocacy and implementation of policies whose justification they could not accept—a disrespectful, illiberal requirement of them, and one more demanding of religious citizens than the "standard" one that Eberle rejects. Talisse then argues that Eberle's position conflicts with a crucial sense of shared liberal citizenship, according to which requirements can be made of citizens only for reasons that they can accept, reasons regarding such things as freedom, equality, and civil peace, and not such things as religious faith or doctrine. Talisse thus defends Rawls's vision of an overlapping consensus that excludes unshareable reasons from the justification of coercive policies. Crucially, however, he does not equate this exclusion of religious reasons with the "standard view" that Eberle rejects. For he defends Rawls's limitation of the exclusion to "basic" and "constitutional" issues, by arguing that, since laws vary in the severity of their coercion and the "irretrievability" of their effects, finding shared reasons is more urgent the more severe or irretrievable the policy concerned. He also defends the potential indeterminacy of shareable reasons, on the grounds that justificatory liberalism requires only that debate in terms of them be exhausted before other considerations are introduced. By reading Rawls's "exclusion" of religious reasonings as limited and as based on a minimal sense of respect implicit in liberal citizenship, then, Talisse presents Rawls's vision of overlapping consensus in the inclusive and thin manner that we have proposed.

The third chapter, Paul Weithman's "Inclusivism, Stability, and Assurance," further explores the grounds of such a reading of Rawls's treatment of religion. Weithman has criticized Rawls in the past for overly excluding religious reasons from political life, arguing in particular that Rawls overvalues mutual respect among citizens and underestimates the contributions that religions make to liberal political life.[36] But in his chapter here he argues that Rawls instead gives novel reasons for adopting what Weithman calls a "qualified inclusivist" attitude toward religious reasonings in political life. Weithman proposes that this derives from Rawls's concern with the rationality of obedience to political authority, understood in game-theoretic terms. In particular, he claims, Rawls is concerned with each citizen's assurance that others will obey political authority, an assurance that is necessary if his or her own obedience is to be rational. Simply excluding religious reasons from political reasoning will not provide citizens with such an assurance, Weithman argues, because differences over especially controversial political issues will tend to raise doubts about citizens' commitments to obey their shared conception of political authority. For Weithman, the necessary assurance can be provided only by allowing citizens to employ religious reasons in political deliberations and decision-making, while requiring them to explain them in terms of shared "political" reasons if doubts arise. This conditional embracing of religious reasonings, or "qualified inclusivism," is what Weithman takes Rawls to mean when he claims that citizens may employ "comprehensive" reasons only if "in due course" they can also give "political," or "public," reasons to support them. Weithman thus shows that Rawls does not exclude religious reasonings from liberal political life by appeal to alienating or discriminatory claims about the "uncivil" character of religions or their bad consequences for institutional stability. Rather, on Weithman's reading, Rawls appeals merely to the need for consensus over political authority in morally pluralist contexts, a need that leads him both to embrace religious reasonings in political debates and to require that they be supported by shareable reasons when dissensus arises.

In the final chapter of this first part of the book, "Rethinking the Public Use of Religious Reasons," Andrew March argues that a more fine-grained conception of the possible forms and functions of religious reasoning than Rawls and others employ can also help to explain when such reasoning should be admitted in political debate. March first argues that a piece of religious reasoning need not assert or imply that coercive laws be justified by religious authorities; rather, it may simply express a moral doctrine, commitment, or insight associated with a religious tradition. For Rawls to classify all religious reasoning as the expression of a "comprehensive doctrine" of moral justification is therefore misleading. March then argues that religious reasoning relates very differently to different kinds and objects of political debate, in ways that Rawls's distinction between "constitutional," "basic," or "public," matters, on the one hand, and the "background culture," on the other, does not adequately grasp. In particular, March distinguishes between debates over individual freedoms, debates over the interests of those who are not or cannot be represented by the state or in the public sphere, debates over the value of collective institutions and undertakings, and debates over the character of society itself. He also insists that the acceptability of religious reasoning is not limited to Rawls's concerns with mutual respect and consensus, since it depends also on whether the relevant reasoning advocates appropriate interests of appropriate agents or entities in appropriate ways, where the relevant sense of "appropriate" is a democratic one. March proceeds to bring out the implications of these various extra-Rawlsian considerations by considering some specific examples of religious reasonings. In particular, he argues that religious reasoning should not be admitted in debates over homosexual marriage because marriage is an institution that bears on basic individual freedoms and equality. In contrast, he argues, even appeals to religious authority may be admitted in debates over social welfare, since welfare is a collective institution and religious views of it tend to be other-regarding and not demeaning or paternalistic. Religious reasonings may also be admitted in debates over the status of "noncitizens" such as enemy combatants and the environment, he argues, since such issues concern the expansion of moral consideration beyond existing terms of political debate. However accommodating Rawls may be to religious reasoning, then, March claims that a better understanding of when and why to admit religious reasoning into political debate can be achieved by discriminating more carefully among kinds of religious reasoning and kinds and objects of political debate.

Both March and Weithman refer to the possibility that citizens lack a shared conception of political authority: March by proposing that religious contributions might reform existing terms of political debate, and Weithman by suggesting that dissensus over these terms will be especially widespread in societies that fail to fully endorse and realize justice as Rawls conceives it, such as contemporary liberal democratic ones. The challenges posed by the religious rejection of liberal principles in such non-"well-ordered" contexts, and the resources that Rawls offers for accommodating such nonliberal religions within liberalism, are the focus of the chapters in the second part of the book.

The first of these chapters, Patrick Neal's "The Liberal State and the Religious Citizen: Justificatory Perspectives in Political Liberalism," argues that these challenges lead Rawls to adopt a significantly different justificatory perspective. Notably, by claiming that the sense of respect which Rawls requires of a conception of political authority is a demanding one, Neal reads Rawls in precisely the "exclusivist" manner that Eberle, Talisse, Weithman, and we have criticized. Indeed, for Neal, when Rawls takes the respectful perspective of a liberal state or public official in arguing for his own conception of political authority and its exclusion of comprehensive reasonings, he considers citizens who reject it to be unjustified, or "unreasonable," simply by definition, since they simply lack the required sense of respect. But Neal's innovative claim is that Rawls does not consider his sense of respect to provide an overarching justification for his or any other conception of political authority, such that it must always take priority over religious and other comprehensive doctrines. For when considering the possibility of citizens endorsing his conception, Neal claims, Rawls adopts not the perspective of a liberal state or public official, but that of a citizen deciding whether to affirm or reject such a conception for his or her own comprehensive reasons and relative to competing conceptions of political authority, or the perspective of an observer contemplating how citizens thus reason over political authority. From these alternative perspectives, Neal argues, Rawls does not take the justification of his conception for granted, as if the respect that it expresses possessed an intrinsic, independent value. The possibilities for consensus rather depend on how citizens' comprehensive doctrines themselves might be elaborated so as to affirm respect, and thus the conception of political authority that Rawls bases on it. On Neal's account, then, while appreciating that some common conception of political authority is required for political life and that any such conception will impinge on some comprehensive doctrine, Rawls sees his particular conception's success in winning religious citizens' endorsement as depending entirely on the content and interpretation of the religious beliefs that they hold. This makes the achievement of an overlapping consensus a highly contingent, dynamic, and, indeed, daunting task. Neal nonetheless concludes optimistically, by briefly imagining a Christian theology that might support Rawls's sense of respect by emphasizing our epistemological limits.

The following two chapters pursue Rawls's concern with the elaboration of religious citizens' own "perspectives" on liberal principles by developing the notion of "reasoning from conjecture" that Rawls briefly mentions in his late essay "The Idea of Public Reason Revisited." As reasoning that aims to show how an apparently conflicting comprehensive doctrine may in fact justify, or at least not reject, giving priority to a shared conception of political authority, reasoning from conjecture offers a possible, albeit partial, contribution to resolving conflicts between religious and liberal reasonings in morally pluralist contexts. It thus provides a crucial means of elaborating an "overlapping consensus" among religious and other moral worldviews in the respectful, contingent, and dynamic manner which we have suggested that Rawls envisions.

In "Reasoning from Conjecture: A Reply to Three Objections," Micah Schwartzman defends reasoning from conjecture against the suspicion that it may be disrespectful to holders of religious doctrines and explores its limits as a means of cultivating consensus. He first argues that conjecture is not insincere or manipulative, and thus not disrespectful, insofar as conjecturers make clear that they do not endorse the comprehensive doctrine from which they argue and whether they believe that their conclusions really follow from it. Nor must the attempt to convince others with reasons that conjecturers are not convinced of themselves display a lack of respect, since it is only in this way that a shared conception of political authority can be established in morally pluralist contexts. Schwartzman then argues that conjecture also does not represent an external, "imperialist" imposition on holders of the comprehensive doctrine in question, since it is based on reasons internal to that doctrine. It is therefore no more precluded by holders' internal resistance to criticism or by conjecturers' external status than internal criticism is precluded to holders of the doctrine themselves. Finally, Schwartzman considers the epistemic authority that a conjecture might achieve, admitting that this presents daunting epistemological challenges. But he argues that in some cases the failure to demonstrate the epistemological authority of a conjecture will be attributable to the "unreasonable" unintelligibility of the doctrine in question and that reasoning from conjecture will thus always be limited by the moral resources of the comprehensive doctrine concerned. Undertaking such reasoning may also be politically inadvisable if the moral resources available are sufficiently opposed to those of a respectful consensus. While showing how reasoning from conjecture can be respectful, then, Schwartzman also makes evident the dependence of the consensus which conjecture aims to cultivate on both the moral resources of a specific society and citizens' ability to elaborate them.

If Schwartzman's chapter considers how conjecture might be employed to reason from an ostensibly nonliberal religious doctrine to a given liberal consensus, the final chapter in this second part of the book, Johannes van der Ven's "The Religious Hermeneutics of Public

Reasoning: From Paul to Rawls," demonstrates how conjecture might also operate in the opposite direction. That is, holders of a religious doctrine that is excluded from a given consensus might respectfully reelaborate that consensus by conjecturally reinterpreting not only their doctrine's own moral resources, but also those of the consensus itself. Van der Ven proposes this by means of a close examination of Paul's address to the Athenians as reconstructed by Luke in the New Testament. There Paul is presented as convincing his Athenian accusers of Christianity's acceptability by reinterpreting Christianity in terms of their own Hellenistic religious commitments. He thus develops a "common ground"—an understanding of God that both Christians and Hellenistic Athenians can share. Crucially, this reinterpretation does not only elaborate the resources for consensus offered by Christian doctrine, providing Christians with a new self-understanding in shared, Hellenistic terms. It also reelaborates the resources of the Hellenistic consensus itself, leading to an "overlapping" agreement among Athenians and Christians that had previously been lacking. For van der Ven, Rawls requires religious and nonreligious citizens to adopt analogous strategies in contemporary societies. Since these societies are marked by a functional differentiation that precludes a Pauline appeal to a shared moral worldview, religious or otherwise, the "common ground" that Rawls invites citizens to pursue is rather a shared conception of political authority. Yet van der Ven argues that, in this distinctively pluralist context, Rawls nonetheless calls on religious and nonreligious citizens to pursue strategies analogous to those of their Christian and Hellenistic counterparts—that is, to reinterpret their own and each other's moral worldviews so as to develop shared terms of understanding. Van der Ven's hermeneutic reading of Rawls thus demonstrates how religious doctrines excluded from a given consensus might themselves contribute to respectfully reelaborating that consensus in more inclusive terms, and again emphasizes that a respectful consensus must depend on the particular range of moral resources available in a society and on how citizens elaborate them.

Following van der Ven's lead, the chapters in the third and final part of the book consider Rawls's treatment of religions, and particularly his senses of respect and consensus, from the extra-Rawlsian, "transcendent" perspectives of religions themselves. In so doing, the first two of these chapters raise novel questions about the "religious" character of Rawls's own liberal project. In the first, "E Pluribus Unum: Justification and Redemption in Rawls, Cohen, and Habermas," James Gledhill claims that, rather than proposing simply to convince religious citizens to accept his liberal framework, Rawls ought to reflexively recognize this framework's own religious form. In particular, Gledhill argues that Rawls is ultimately concerned with the moral redemption of the human individual, and that the differences between his conception of justification and those of his major critics, G. A. Cohen and Jürgen Habermas, ultimately lie in their different senses of such redemption. Beginning with Cohen's analogy between a just society and a free jazz band, Gledhill emphasizes how by treating citizens' ends as antecedent to their social cooperation and as realizable independently of it, this analogy implies a transcendent, "God's eye" perspective on principles of justice. Gledhill argues that, in contrast, Rawls's own analogy with an orchestra treats principles as ends that citizens can have and realize only as participants in the relevant cooperative activity. Gledhill traces this sense of redemption to Rawls's undergraduate senior thesis, *A Brief Inquiry Into the Meaning of Sin and Faith: An Interpretation Based on the Concept of Community*, but he finds it to be particularly evident in Rawls's later account of the overlapping consensus by which citizens "sublimate," and thus "redeem," their particular religious and other comprehensive doctrines in shared terms of political deliberation. Yet Gledhill argues that the analogy with an orchestra also reveals how Rawls's justificatory framework implies a further, transcendent source for political principles, a "conductor" for the social "orchestra." To illuminate this, he employs another of Rawls's analogies, that of a game. This, he argues, reveals how Rawls treats principles of justice not as merely regulative of the social "game," but as constitutive of it, just as rules are constitutive of a game such as baseball. Rawls consequently insists that citizens can and must agree to principles of justice simply as participants in social cooperation, without "regrets" or "reproach," and thus implies a transcendent source of these principles which he cannot explain. For Gledhill, only Habermas's treatment of principles of justice as ideal yet immanent presuppositions of citizens' communicative practices—as revealing a "transcendence from within"—could save Rawls's account of political redemption. Gledhill thus suggests that, even on the minimal, flexible account that we have proposed, Rawls's vision of "mutual respect" among citizens may unjustifiably "transcend" the religious and comprehensive doctrines that it is intended to accommodate.

Peter Jonkers also argues that there is a transcendent moment in Rawls's treatment of religions in his chapter, "A Reasonable Faith? Pope Benedict's Response to Rawls." Jonkers does so by exploring Pope Benedict's engagement with Rawls, and particularly their differing positions on the role that "truth" or "reason" may play in resolving political conflicts in a morally pluralist society. Jonkers notes that Pope Benedict insists on a divine truth for politics and Rawls on a deliberative one, and that in this respect each misrepresents the other—Rawls in identifying divine truth with authoritarianism, and Pope Benedict in reducing deliberation to an agreement based on citizens' particular interests. But Jonkers argues that, from these different perspectives, both Pope Benedict and Rawls ultimately arrive at a Kantian sense of "faith." This "faith" consists in affirming what cannot be theoretically verified but must be postulated as the regulative referent for human reason in a pluralist politics. According to Jonkers, Rawls expresses this with his "reasonable faith" in the possibility of a just constitutional politics, while Pope Benedict expresses it with his proposal that nonbelievers in pluralist societies act "as if God exists." By comparing these different "faiths," Jonkers concludes that, while Rawls's "faith" reveals Pope Benedict's to be overly demanding of a pluralist society, Pope Benedict's "faith" reveals Rawls's to be insufficiently demanding, leaving political conflicts inadequately regulated. Like Gledhill, then, Jonkers presents Rawls's treatment of religions as inevitably "transcendent." But rather than proposing that this transcendence be explained, as Gledhill does in turning to Habermas, Jonkers suggests that it must be inflated if Rawls's framework is to resolve political conflicts in morally pluralist contexts.

A different religious perspective on Rawls's liberal treatment of religions is taken in the concluding chapter of the book, Abdullahi An-Na'im's "Islamic Politics and the Neutral State: A Friendly Amendment to Rawls?" There An-Na'im develops a liberal distinction between the state and politics on Muslim grounds, and argues that this distinction is preferable to Rawls's own liberal distinction between the "public," or "political," on the one hand, and the religious, on the other. By emphasizing the inherently human and fallible nature of the interpretation of Sharia, An-Na'im raises both the problem of identifying a singular "Islamic" perspective in political thought and that of the unlikely fit between a state's general policies and Muslim citizens' interpretations of their obligations under Sharia. If a state is to achieve legitimacy in the eyes of its Muslim and other citizens, he proceeds to argue, Muslims therefore must accept the modern separation between the state and religions, while being allowed to employ Sharia-based reasonings in political debate, with a view to contributing to a broader "civic" consensus acceptable to all citizens, whether Muslim or not. An-Na'im considers this distinction between a religiously neutral state and an inclusive politics to be preferable to Rawls's exclusion of religions from public reasoning because, unlike Rawls's treatment, it avoids discriminating against religions and recognizes the potential for critical reasoning within and among religious and other comprehensive doctrines and thus Islam's possible contributions to a broader consensus. Furthermore, although these claims might seem to correspond with our own, more accommodating understanding of the consensus that Rawls envisions, An-Na'im objects that even this understanding excludes religious reasonings from some political debate and treats religious and other comprehensive doctrines as if they were sealed against criticism. His conclusion is that a liberalism acceptable to Muslims can be developed only by transcending Rawls's framework entirely and engaging with Islam itself.

The chapters in this last part of the book thus open Rawls's liberal treatment of religions to extra-Rawlsian, religious considerations. Perhaps Rawls himself would have welcomed this, just as, on our reading, his vision of a political consensus welcomes the respectful revision of both those included in and those excluded from it.

Notes

For their valuable comments on a draft of this introduction, we would like to thank James Gledhill, Peter Jonkers, Sebastiano Maffettone, Aakash Singh Rathore, Johannes van der Ven, and Paul Weithman.

1. On this "return" of religions to liberal democratic societies, see particularly José Casanova, *Public Religions in the Modern World* (Chicago: University of Chicago Press, 1994); and Pippa Norris and Ronald Inglehart, *Sacred and Secular: Religion and Politics Worldwide* (Cambridge: Cambridge University Press, 2004).

2. See *PL* (pbk.) xvi–xviii, 36–38.

3. See *PL* (pbk.) 122, 139, 156–57, 303, 319, 337–38, and 369.

4. On the "criterion of reciprocity," see *PL* (pbk.) xlii–xlv, xlvii, xlix, liii, and 16. On "civic friendship" and the related "duty of civility," see *PL* (pbk.) xlix, 157, 320, and 322. For the claim about implicitness, see *PL* (pbk.) 13.

5. See *TJ* (rev.) 47–101.

6. In his later work, Rawls also gives notably less emphasis to the two principles of his conception of "justice as fairness" than to the general notion of a shared conception of political authority and its constitutional expression in basic liberties. We suggest his reasons for doing so below.

7. See *PL* (pbk.) xvii–xxx, 15, 36, 39–40, 65–66, and 133–67.

8. See *PL* (pbk.) xlix, l–li, l, and 225, and *IPRR* 462–63.

9. For examples of this criticism, see Nicholas Wolterstorff, "The Role of Religion in Decision and Discussion of Political Issues," in *Religion in the Public Square: The Place of Religious Convictions in Political Debate*, ed. R. Audi and N. Wolterstorff (Lanham, Md.: Rowman and Littlefield, 1997), 105 and 116; Wolterstorff, "Why We Should Reject What Liberalism Tells Us About Speaking and Acting in Public for Religious Reasons," in *Religion and Contemporary Liberalism*, ed. P. Weithman (Notre Dame: University of Notre Dame Press, 1997), esp. 176–77; Christopher Eberle, *Religious Conviction in Liberal Politics* (Cambridge: Cambridge University Press, 2002), 140–48; Robert Talisse, "Dilemmas of Public Reason: Pluralism, Polarization, and Instability," in *The Legacy of John Rawls*, ed. T. Brooks and F. Freyenhagen (New York: Continuum, 2005), 110–12; and Bryan T. McGraw, *Faith in Politics: Religion and Liberal Democracy* (Cambridge: Cambridge University Press, 2010), 126–43.

10. Examples of this criticism include Paul Weithman, *Religion and the Obligations of Citizenship* (Cambridge: Cambridge University Press, 2004), esp. chaps. 5 and 7, and Talisse, "Dilemmas of Public Reason," 113–16.

11. For this criticism, see, for instance, Paul Weithman, "Introduction," in Weithman, *Religion and Contemporary Liberalism*, 19; Weithman, *Religion and the Obligations of Citizenship*, 201–6; and James Boettcher, "Public Reason and Religion," in Brooks and Freyenhagen, *The Legacy of John Rawls*, 142–43.

12. See, for example, Jeremy Waldron, "John Rawls and the Social Minimum," in *Liberal Rights*, ed. J. Waldron (Cambridge: Cambridge University Press, 1993), 250–69; Wolterstorff, "Why We Should Reject," 164; Wolterstorff, "Why Can't We All Just Get Along with Each Other?," in *Religious Voices in Public Places*, ed. N. Biggar and L. Hogan (Oxford: Oxford University Press, 2009); and Eberle, *Religious Conviction in Liberal Politics*, 81–151.

13. This criticism is made in, for instance, Michael Sandel, "Review of *Political Liberalism* by John Rawls," *Harvard Law Review* 107 (1994): 1791; John M. Bohman, "Public Reason and Cultural Pluralism: Political Liberalism and the Problem of Moral Conflict," *Political Theory* 23 (1995): 259; Philip L. Quinn, "Political Liberalisms and Their Exclusions of the Religious," in Weithman, *Religion and Contemporary Liberalism*, 149–52; Boettcher, "Public Reason and Religion," 143–44; and Richard Bellamy,

Political Constitutionalism: A Republican Defence of the Constitutionality of Democracy (Cambridge: Polity, 2007), 99–103.

14. See, for instance, Jürgen Habermas, "Reconciliation Through the Public Use of Reason: Remarks on John Rawls' *Political Liberalism*," *Journal of Philosophy* 92, no. 3 (1995): 129–31; Habermas, "'Reasonable' Versus 'True,' or the Morality of Worldviews," in *The Inclusion of the Other: Studies in Political Theory* (Cambridge, Mass.: MIT Press, 1998), 81–84; Habermas, "Religion in the Public Sphere: Cognitive Presuppositions for the 'Public Use of Reason' by Religious and Secular Citizens," in *Between Naturalism and Religion: Philosophical Essays* (Cambridge: Polity, 2008), 120–35; Habermas, "'The Political': The Rational Meaning of a Questionable Inheritance of Political Theology," in *The Power of Religion in the Public Sphere*, ed. E. Mendieta and J. VanAntwerpen (New York: Columbia University Press, 2011), 25–28; and Weithman, *Religion and the Obligations of Citizenship*, 182–85.

15. See Robert Audi, *Religious Commitment and Secular Reason* (Cambridge: Cambridge University Press, 2000), 86–100; and Stephen Macedo, "In Defense of Liberal Public Reason: Are Slavery and Abortion Hard Cases?," *American Journal of Jurisprudence* 42, no. 1 (1998): 22.

16. For the first of these three claims, see Gerald Gaus and Kevin Vallier, "The Roles of Religious Conviction in a Publicly Justified Policy," *Philosophy and Social Criticism* 35 (2009): 58–62. For the second, see Wolterstorff, "The Role of Religion," 177–81; Wolterstorff, "Why We Should Reject," 176–77; Wolterstorff, "Why Can't We All Just Get Along with Each Other?," 35; Eberle, *Religious Conviction in Liberal Politics*, 58–61; and Jeffrey Stout, *Democracy and Tradition* (Princeton: Princeton University Press, 2004), 10. For the third claim, see William Galston, *Liberal Pluralism: The Implications of Value Pluralism for Political Theory and Practice* (Cambridge: Cambridge University Press, 2002), 39–47.

17. See, in particular, Will Kymlicka, *Multicultural Citizenship: A Liberal Theory of Minority Rights* (Oxford: Oxford University Press, 1996), 107–30.

18. This approach has been developed particularly by Jürgen Habermas. See, for instance, Habermas, "Religion in the Public Sphere," 128–35; Habermas, "An Awareness of What Is Missing," in *An Awareness of What Is Missing: Faith and Reason in a Post-Secular Age* (Cambridge: Polity, 2010), 20–22; and Habermas, "The Political," 23–27; and Eduardo Mendieta, "A Postsecular World Society? On the Philosophical Significance of Postsecular Consciousness and the Multicultural World Society: An Interview with Jürgen Habermas," *Immanent Frame*, 2010, http://blogs.ssrc.org/tif/2010/02/03/a-postsecular-world-society, 1–2 and 9–12.

19. See, in particular, Robert Audi, "The State, the Church, and the Citizen," in Weithman, *Religion and Contemporary Liberalism*, 54–63; Audi, *Religious Commitment and Secular Reason*, 145–79; Audi, *Democratic Authority and the Separation of Church and State* (Oxford: Oxford University Press, 2011), 59–103; Richard Rorty, "Religion as a Conversation-Stopper," in *Philosophy and Social Hope* (New York: Penguin, 1999), 168–74; and

Rorty, "Religion in the Public Square: A Reconsideration," *Journal of Religious Ethics* 31, no. 1 (2003): 141–49.

20. See, for instance, John Milbank, *Theology and Social Theory: Beyond Secular Reason* (Oxford: Blackwell, 1990), esp. ch. 1; Stanley Hauerwas, "The Democratic Policing of Christianity," in *Dispatches from the Front: Theological Engagements with the Secular* (Durham: Duke University Press, 1994), esp. 92–93 and 101–6; and William T. Cavanaugh, "The City: Beyond Secular Parodies," in *Radical Orthodoxy: A New Theology*, ed. J. Milbank, C. Pickstock, and G. Ward (London: Routledge, 1999), 182–200.

21. See *PL* (pbk.) 212–22, 220ff., 227–30, and 382n13, and *IPRR* 441–45. On this, see also Patrick Neal, "Is Public Reason Innocuous?," *Critical Review of International Social and Political Philosophy* 11, no. 2 (2008): 134–38 and 147–50; Neal, "Is Political Liberalism Hostile to Religion?," in *Reflections on Rawls: An Assessment of His Legacy*, ed. S. P. Young (Farnham, Vt.: Ashgate, 2009), 156 and 157–58; and Sebastiano Maffettone, *Rawls: An Introduction* (Cambridge: Polity, 2010), 274–82.

22. *PL* (pbk.) 247–48. See also *PL* (pbk.) 249–54; Neal, "Is Public Reason Innocuous?," 132–34; and Neal, "Is Political Liberalism Hostile to Religion?," 155–56. On the significance of Rawls's remarks on King, see Leslie Griffin, "Good Catholics Should Be Rawlsian Liberals," *Southern California Interdisciplinary Law Journal* 5 (1997): 318–21; and David A. J. Richards, "Ethical Religion and the Struggle for Human Rights: The Case of Martin Luther King, Jr.," *Fordham Law Review* 72, no. 5 (2004): 2151–52.

23. See *IPRR* 466n57. Andrew March gives an extensive account of reasoning by "conjecture" and how it might be employed in engaging with Islamic comprehensive doctrines in March, *Islam and Liberal Citizenship: The Search for an Overlapping Consensus* (Oxford: Oxford University Press, 2009), 17–22 and 53–96. See also Griffin, "Good Catholics," 321–22; Mohammad Fadel, "Public Reason as a Strategy for Principled Reconciliation: The Case of Islamic Law and International Human Rights Law," *Chicago Journal of International Law* 8, no. 1 (2007): esp. 4–19; and Fadel, "The True, the Good and the Reasonable: The Theological Roots of Public Reason in Islamic Law," *Canadian Journal of Law and Jurisprudence* 21, no. 1 (2008): esp. 30–50.

24. See Griffin, "Good Catholics," 313–14.

25. Samuel Freeman defends the "completeness" of citizens' conception of political authority on Rawls's account, in Freeman, "Public Reason and Political Justification," *Fordham Law Review* 72, no. 5 (2004): 2053–65.

26. In "Is Political Liberalism Hostile to Religion?," 172–74, Neal emphasizes that, for Rawls, citizens must evaluate respect on their own comprehensive grounds, which in some cases may not allow for its affirmation. On its minimal nature, see also Fevzi Bilgin, *Political Liberalism in Muslim Societies* (London: Routledge, 2011), 37–40 and 49–50.

27. See *IPRR* 452–55 and *CP* 618–20.

28. See *PL* (pbk.) 240–41 and *IPRR* 478–79. For a reading of these and other passages, see Neal, "Is Public Reason Innocuous?," 138–44; and Neal, "Is Political Liberalism

Hostile to Religion?," 160–64. See also Andrew Williams, "The Alleged Incompleteness of Public Reason," *Res Publica* 6, no. 2 (2000): 209–11; and Micah Schwartzman, "The Completeness of Public Reason," *Politics, Philosophy and Economics* 3, no. 2 (2004): 209–14.

29. Galston rightly points out that the commitment to the heterogeneity of values need not preclude Rawls's giving some values, like liberty, a lexical priority over others. See Galston, *Liberal Pluralism*, 31. Thus Rawls presents the shared conception of political principles that he envisions as only "broadly speaking" liberal, insofar as "it protects the familiar basic rights and assigns them a special priority." *PL* (pbk.) 156–57. See also Weithman, *Why Political Liberalism? On John Rawls's Political Turn* (Oxford: Oxford University Press, 2011), 28–32.

30. On Rawls's distinction between "comprehensive" conceptions of liberalism and his own "political" liberalism, see *PL* (pbk.) 154–58 and 195–200.

31. Notably, at *PL* (pbk.) 53 Rawls limits "rationality" to private reasonings.

32. On Rawls's notion of a "modus vivendi" as a consensus that lacks the required mutual respect and stability, see *PL* (pbk.) 143–49.

33. On this, see particularly Rawls's discussion of the "morality of the association" in *TJ* (rev.) 409. See also *CP* 619–20; Nancy Rosenblum, "Civil Societies: Liberalism and the Moral Use of Pluralism," in *Civil Society and Democracy*, ed. C. M. Elliott (Oxford: Oxford University Press, 2003), 107–14; and Stephen Macedo, "Why Public Reason? Citizens' Reasons and the Constitution of the Public Sphere" (August 23, 2010), http://ssrn.com/abstract=1664085.

34. On this, see Macedo, "Why Public Reason?" Relatedly, in *BI* 7 Rawls emphasizes how religions provide frameworks for developing relations among individuals.

35. See *PL* (pbk.) 226 and (exp.) 439.

36. See the references to Weithman in notes 10 and 11 above.

PART I

REINTERPRETING
RAWLS
ON RELIGION

1

Respect and War

AGAINST THE STANDARD VIEW
OF RELIGION IN POLITICS

CHRISTOPHER J. EBERLE

The last several decades have witnessed a vibrant discussion about the proper political role of religion in pluralistic liberal democracies. An important part of that discussion has been a dispute about the role that religious and secular reasons properly play in the justification of state coercion. For various reasons, a veritable pantheon of contemporary political theorists (including John Rawls, Jürgen Habermas, Richard Rorty, Martha Nussbaum, and Thomas Nagel) as well as an accompanying chorus of editorialists (Richard Cohen, E. J. Dionne, and Andrew Sullivan, for instance) and even politicians (most prominently, Barack Obama) have endorsed a restrictive understanding of the justificatory role available to religious reasons. As I understand it, the "standard view" advocated by the members of that pantheon, and by many others as well, includes two claims, namely, that religious reasons cannot play a decisive role in justifying state coercion (what I will call the "Principle of Religious Insufficiency") and that citizens and public officials in a liberal polity should not endorse state coercion that requires decisive religious support (what I will call the "Doctrine of Religious Restraint").

This is the key. What does he mean by "decisive" here?

I doubt that there is any compelling reason to accept general restrictions of this sort. Of course, I do not deny that various other constraints delimit the justificatory role of religious reasons, such that certain religious reasons cannot decisively justify state coercion or such that citizens and public officials should not employ certain sorts of reasons as a basis for endorsing state coercion. Rather, I am skeptical about the standard view's restrictions on religious reasons as a class, restrictions that apply to any and all religious considerations, to religious reasons as such. My main aim in this chapter is to motivate this skepticism regarding the standard view. I will try to achieve this aim by reflecting on what I take to be the paradigmatic case of state coercion, namely, the use of military violence in war. This somewhat unusual focus provides an opportunity to bring to bear on the topic a vast body of literature on what makes for justified military violence, and also enables us to avoid the fixation on contentious domestic issues like abortion and homosexuality that has often obfuscated the main issues of principle at stake.

THE STANDARD VIEW OF THE RELATION
BETWEEN RELIGION AND COERCION

I will begin by articulating what I take to be the core commitments of the standard view. In order to do that, let me identify an assumption held in common by both its advocates and its critics, namely, the claim that there is a general presumption against coercion. This is a very plausible and widely affirmed claim. It seems particularly compelling with respect to the most brutal kind of coercion, the use of military violence in war. Given that waging war obliterates soldiers, terrorizes civilians, dehouses populations, orphans children, and so on, each and every community has powerful reason to refrain from waging war. Consequently, many have argued that we should understand the dominant Western conception of justified war—the so-called Just War Tradition (JWT)—to include the claim that each and every war is presumptively wrong.[1] But, of course, this presumption applies more broadly. For example, when the state incarcerates citizens who refuse to comply with a duly enacted law, it deprives them of the goods of friendship and familial belonging that are an important component of human fulfillment. There is always reason to refrain from depriving human beings of such morally important goods, and so the state always has presumptive reason to refrain from threatening citizens with incarceration. Similarly for other coercive measures: the execution of criminals, the banishment of traitors, even the imposition of fines. All of these are presumptively wrong.

The presumption against coercion is not an absolute prohibition. It will not uncommonly be the case that weighty normative considerations count in favor of coercion in particular circumstances. In some cases the use of military violence is just, and in some cases the state must incarcerate criminals. So, while there is a general presumption against coercion, coercion is sometimes permissible, and thus the presumption against coercion is sometimes overcome.

But what makes it the case that the presumption against coercion has been overcome? Here we have a crosscutting and disharmonious blizzard of options. In order to keep this discussion manageable, consider the manner in which advocates of the JWT answer that question. According to that tradition, the presumption against war can be overcome only if a number of substantive conditions are satisfied: a political community must have just cause to wage war, legitimate authorities in that community must authorize war, those legitimate authorities must do so with the intention of securing a just peace, waging war must achieve an acceptable balance of relevant moral goods and moral evils, and so on. At least some of these requirements specify the kinds of consideration that can overcome the presumption against war. So, for example, the just cause requirement seems best understood as a condition that specifies the kinds of reason that can and cannot overcome the presumption against war: certain kinds of moral wrongs, such as unprovoked military attacks or massive violations of human rights, provide a community with sufficient reason to respond with military violence, but other kinds of wrong, such as insults to communal honor or delinquency on debts, do not. So the JWT includes a specific set of restrictions on the kinds of reason that can justify a particular kind of coercion.[2]

Advocates of the standard view of religion in politics take a similar approach: they assume that state coercion is presumptively wrong and propose a very broad set of constraints on the kinds of consideration that can overcome that presumption. But the constraints they favor tend to be far more capacious than those incorporated into the JWT—the restrictions they favor apply to *all* instances of state coercion and to a *very* broad range of justifying reasons. One such restriction is particularly relevant, namely, that religious considerations cannot play a decisive role in overcoming the presumption against coercion.[3] To put it a little more precisely, when the coercing agent is the government in a liberal polity, religious considerations cannot decisively justify coercion. Although religious reasons can corroborate (certain kinds of) secular reasons that are by themselves sufficient to overcome the presumption against coercion, state coercion that would not be justified "but for" some religious reason is morally impermissible.[4] This restriction applies irrespective of the content of a given religious reason. Let us call the claim that religious reasons cannot decisively justify state coercion in a liberal polity the "Principle of Religious Insufficiency."

Distinct from, but closely related to, the Principle of Religious Insufficiency is a familiar claim about the duties of citizens and public officials in a liberal polity. Presumably, citizens and public officials ought to do their level best to refrain from endorsing morally impermissible state coercion. But, if the Principle of Religious Insufficiency is correct, religious reasons cannot suffice to overcome the presumption against coercion, and so state coercion that requires a religious rationale is morally impermissible. Consequently, citizens and public officials have a moral duty to restrain themselves from endorsing state coercion that requires a religious rationale. This is what I call the "Doctrine of Religious Restraint."

The Principle of Religious Insufficiency and the Doctrine of Religious Restraint capture an important component of the standard view: that religion should be subject to some important political restrictions in a liberal democracy. More precisely, they capture the assumption, crucial to the standard view but often unstated, that religious reasons are subject to restrictions that do not apply to all secular reasons. These claims are related in the following way. Advocates of the standard view are liberals, not anarchists, that is, they are committed to the claim that the presumption against state coercion is sometimes overridden. Because religious reasons cannot decisively do so, it is presumably the case that at least *some* secular reasons can, and do, suffice to overcome that presumption. Nearly every advocate of the standard view accords to at least *some* secular reasons a justificatory potential that they deny

to *any and all* religious reasons, namely, the capacity decisively to justify state coercion. This kind of asymmetry between religious and
secular reasons is deeply embedded in a great deal of contemporary
political theory.[5]

But why accept this kind of discriminatory treatment? Given the
coruscating diversity of religious considerations, given the varying
properties possessed by distinct religious reasons, given the widely
divergent intellectual virtues (and vices) possessed by different religious adherents, given that secular reasons exhibit an equally bewil-
dering diversity of sociological, substantive, and epistemic properties,
how could it be the case that no religious reasons can even in principle
decisively justify coercion, but that some secular reasons can?

THE ARGUMENT FROM RESPECT

Advocates of the standard view regularly answer this question by
appealing to some variation of the "argument from respect." Fundamental to that argument is the claim that human beings possess
a distinctive moral status—equal dignity, worth, or sacredness. The
worth of a human being is a function of the fact that she is a moral
agent who has her own distinctive aims and aspirations. Due respect
for the worth of our fellow human beings forbids us to treat them as
mere playthings, objects to be manipulated at will, mere means to our
ends. Now, very plausibly, if respect for the worth of human beings
implies that human beings ought not be treated merely as manipulated objects, then proper respect grounds a presumption against
coercion. To subject a human being to coercive measures for which
there exists no compelling rationale is to disrespect that human being.
So far, advocates and critics of the standard view need not disagree.

But advocates of the standard view argue that due respect for the
worth of human beings implies a further constraint on justified coercion. They claim not only that the presumption against coercion must
be overcome by some objectively sound rationale, that each coercive
measure must *be* justified, but also that each coercive measure must be
justified or justifiable *to* those who are coerced. For a coercive measure
to be justified to the coerced, the coerced must *see for themselves* that
the measure to which they are subjected is legitimate. Presumably,

this condition is satisfied only if the coerced have access to what *they* regard, or would regard on due reflection, as a decisive rationale for the relevant coercive measure. So, due respect requires that each coerced human being have, or at least have access to, some rationale that each would on reflection regard as providing a sufficient justification for the coercive measures to which they are subject.

Thus far, the argument from respect specifies a broad constraint on what makes for justified coercion, and so for justified state coercion. It says nothing explicitly about the justificatory role of religious reasons. But the implications of the argument from respect are easy to draw out when we make explicit the relevant social and political context. A well-functioning liberal democracy just is a kind of political structure that effectively protects a number of rights that allow citizens to decide for themselves what to believe about religious matters. That is, any liberal democracy worthy of the name effectively protects the right to religious freedom and thereby the right of each citizen to decide for him- or herself which religious tradition, if any, to embrace. But, as John Rawls and Rodney Stark have both argued, when human beings have the freedom to determine for themselves what to believe about religious matters, they will inevitably reach different and often conflicting conclusions. As a consequence, then, of its constituent normative commitments, one of the defining features of a liberal democracy will inevitably be a pervasive pluralism of religious belief and practice.

In that pluralistic context, only certain kinds of reason can satisfy the required constraints on justified coercion. As Charles Larmore has argued, reasonable and respectful citizens resolve their differences by retreating to common ground—shared premises that provide some deeper basis for resolving the disagreement at hand.[6] So the only kind of rationale that can justify coercion in a pluralistic liberal polity are reasons that are shared by, can be shared by, or are accessible to a diversely committed population.[7] Michael Blake articulates this position with admirable clarity.

> Liberalism is motivated, at heart, by some idea of moral dignity and worth of persons. What makes liberalism distinctive—as well as attractive—is this notion that individual moral agents deserve to be treated with equal concern and respect. . . . Reciprocity offers a means by which we respect these notions of

moral equality. . . . Reciprocity, as I use it here, means simply the methodology of justifying political power with reference to principles acceptable to all those affected. . . . The methodology begins with what we already share—with the reasons we are already presumed to find motivating—and uses what is shared to provide us with reasons to support and defend principles of political justice. These principles are then used to justify and criticize those political institutions we share. Thus, political power is justified with reference to reasons we already share and accept.[8]

But here is the crux. The only shared or sharable premises are secular: only the secular is the universal, natural, and common; the religious is invariably particular, sectarian, and idiosyncratic. Religion always divides; the secular can unite. Hence, coercion in pluralistic liberal polities cannot be justified on decisively religious grounds. Thus the Principle of Religious Insufficiency: only the secular can decisively justify state coercion in a liberal polity, never the religious. Of course, given that principle, citizens and public officials should restrain themselves from endorsing state coercion that cannot be justified absent some religious rationale. That is, the social role of citizen and public official in a liberal democracy is partly constituted by a moral requirement to comply with the Doctrine of Religious Restraint.

FIRST OBJECTION TO THE ARGUMENT FROM RESPECT

What should we make of the argument from respect? I will begin by laying out two objections, each of which requires a drastic, and fortuitous, revision in the standard view. This will lead to a brief discussion and evaluation of a more capacious and inclusive alternative. Although I reject that "convergence conception" of the standard view as well, I regard it as a serious competitor to the even more capacious position I favor.

As I have shown, the argument from respect moves from the claim that respect for human worth requires coercion to be justified to those who are coerced, through the claim that justifying state coercion to the coerced in pluralistic liberal democracies is possible only by recourse to shared or accessible reasons, to the conclusion that religious reasons cannot decisively justify state coercion in liberal democracies. But I believe that the second premise in this argument—the claim that state coercion in liberal polities can be justified only by shared or accessible reasons—is false. Moreover, that claim is false for reasons that have nothing in particular to do with its implications for the political role of religious reasons.

It is possible to see why by reflecting on a case of state coercion in which religious considerations do not even purport to play a justificatory role. So, imagine a possible world very different from the one we actually inhabit. In that possible world, the United States invades Afghanistan, American citizens and public officials fully endorse that invasion, and they do so for fully secular reasons, but they diverge radically as to why the United States is justified in doing so. For convenience's sake, focus on three stylized profiles:

> Citizen A is an advocate of the JWT, and believes that the invasion is decisively justified as an act of righteous punishment for the wrongful attacks on September 11, 2001, but denies that the invasion is justified as an act of liberation, or to spread democracy, or to further US security interests.

> Citizen B is a utilitarian who denies that war may be waged merely to punish prior wrongful attacks or to further the narrow self-interest of particular nation-states, but believes the invasion is justified by virtue of its excellent consequences—the promotion of democracy, free markets, religious freedom, the liberation of women, and so on.

> Citizen C is a realist about war who thinks that invading Afghanistan is absolutely crucial to the long-term security of the United States, but denies that moral reasons are even relevant to the justification of military violence and so denies that the invasion could be justified on the basis of either punitive or humanitarian considerations.

In this case, A, B, and C have what each regards as a compelling secular reason to endorse a coercive act of considerable brutality. Nevertheless, there is no shared reason that each regards as decisively supporting the invasion and they do not retreat to common ground. This is because there *is* no common ground to which they could retreat, given their fundamentally incompatible conceptions of the morality of war. Here we have an act of coercion committed by the government of a liberal polity that each citizen has a secular reason to endorse absent recourse to anything like shared reasons.[9]

Now it seems that the (highly unlikely) state of affairs I have sketched need not involve a jot or a tittle of disrespect. Given that each citizen has what each regards as decisive reason to believe the invasion justified, neither A, nor B, nor C can justifiably claim to be treated as a manipulated object. Each is treated with due respect despite their disagreement as to why the U.S. invasion of Afghanistan is justified. So it seems that due respect provides no reason to prefer state coercion justified by some "ecumenical" secular reason over state coercion justified by a diverse spread of "sectarian" secular reasons. Of course, we could easily expand the example to include a more diverse and exotic spread of reasons. We could, for example, include citizens who take the invasion to be justified on religious grounds, such as the idea that the invasion would improve the conditions of oppressed coreligionists. No matter—so long as each of the coerced has what each takes as decisive reason, none must be treated with disrespect. It follows directly that due respect does not require that state coercion be justified by shared reasons.

The implication of this claim about what makes for justified coercion has direct implications for the duties of citizens and public officials. At least with regard to the requirements of respect for human worth, there is no morally relevant difference between a citizen or public official who articulates one reason that convinces A, B, and C to endorse the invasion of Afghanistan and another who articulates three distinct, incompatible, and highly sectarian arguments that severally provide A, B, and C with what each regards as decisive reason to endorse that invasion. So long as each ends up with what each regards as a decisive reason to endorse the invasion, and therefore is not forced to go along with a policy she rejects, how could it be that the norm of respect provides us with reason to require citizens or public officials to achieve that end by one means rather than another?

We might be skeptical. After all, respect for persons forbids us to manipulate others, and a citizen or public official who tries to justify an act of coercion like the invasion of Afghanistan on the basis of a spate of sectarian reasons, many of which she must regard as defective, might seem to manipulate her compatriots in a manner that disrespects them as moral agents. For example, if the realist supports the invasion merely in order to further the security interests of the United States, but can persuade fellow citizens to support it by appealing to high-minded ideals like the liberation of oppressed women and the promotion of democracy, hasn't she merely manipulated her compatriots?[10]

Here, I think, we should not be excessively high-minded. The realist need not manipulate her compatriots so long as she makes clear, or so long as it is clearly understood, that she does not regard as decisive the reasons that she hopes her compatriots will regard as decisive. This is, in fact, a very common practice in political discourse regarding the morality of war. So, for example, pacifists often object to the morality of some particular war, not on the basis of the reasons that persuade them to object to waging war in general, but on the basis of normative principles that the vast majority of their compatriots regard as marking off just from unjust wars. This is entirely sensible and hardly a matter of secrecy: well-known pacifists have implored advocates of the JWT to refrain from endorsing the U.S. invasion of Iraq by appealing to the justificatory constraints constitutive of that tradition, even while making it clear that they disavow the JWT. So long as they make clear their own reservations, so long as it is understood that they are appealing to commitments that they disavow but that are affirmed as a matter of moral principle by their compatriots, they surely need not disrespect their compatriots.[11]

A SECOND OBJECTION TO THE ARGUMENT FROM RESPECT

Suppose that advocates of the standard view persist in affirming the claim that only shared or accessible reasons can decisively justify state coercion in liberal polities. That claim has the desired implication—that religious reasons cannot decisively justify coercion—only if no religious reason counts as shared or accessible in the relevant sense. Here again, I doubt.

Again, it is helpful to reflect on a particular case. Consider certain considerations that are, I believe, relevant to the justification of military violence. According to the JWT, the presumption against war can be overcome only if the relevant goods to be achieved by a given war are proportionate to the relevant evils associated with that war. Given this proportionality requirement, the U.S. invasion of Afghanistan was justified only if the following claim is true:

(P) The normative goods to be achieved by securing the just causes that count in favor of the US invasion of Afghanistan are proportionate to the evils that will occur as a direct consequence of that invasion.[12]

I take (P) to be a kind of reason that plays a decisive role in justifying war and so in justifying the most brutal kind of state coercion. This is certainly the manner in which proportionality judgments are regarded in the JWT: as ordinarily conceived by advocates of the JWT, war is unjust when disproportionate. On the plausible assumption that (P) is a secular consideration, (P) plays a justificatory role disallowed to any and every religious consideration. So, then, inquiring minds will want to know: What is so impressive about (P)? What is so defective about the infinitude of possible religious reasons? That is, what is it about secular (P) such that (P) can play a justificatory role that is disallowed to any and every religious consideration?

I very much doubt that there is a principled and otherwise defensible answer to that question. My suspicion is that (P) differs in no relevant epistemic, sociological, or moral respects from at least some religious claims, and so the differential treatment of religious and secular reasons presupposed by the standard view lacks a principled basis. So, for example, it seems doubtful that proportionality judgments like (P) possess any epistemic excellence unavailable to any and all religious reasons. Frankly, this is because (P) is not very epistemically impressive, even if it is true. After all, vindicating a proportionality judgment like (P) requires that we possess factual information about temporally distant events that is exceedingly difficult to acquire, much less to verify, that we weigh many barely commensurable normative considerations, that we identify a disparate spread of goods and evils relevant to the moral permissibility of war, and so on.[13] Put more concretely, even if we could uncontroversially identify all of the relevant goods and evils to be engendered by the U.S. invasion of Afghanistan, the epistemic status of the overall judgment that that invasion was "worth it," all things considered, is exceedingly murky. Put even more concretely, if we grant that the U.S. invasion has prevented some future unjust attacks by Al Qaeda, established even a very fragile democracy, and provided all manner of educational possibilities to a previously oppressed population, it is exceedingly difficult to show in a principled manner that the achievement of those goods is worth the suffering engendered in the population by many years of low-intensity conflict, the perception that the United States has imperial aspirations, the destabilization of nearby countries, and so on. Perhaps this is in fact the case, but our basis for believing it seems "subjective" and contentious in ways that cannot but remind us of the manner in which believers form some of their religious convictions.

Clearly, if we can be epistemically justified in believing that (P) is true, we will not be so justified to anything like the degree to which we are justified in believing that something exists, or that torturing innocents is generally morally bad, or the like. And this will be true not only of (P) in particular, but of proportionality judgments in general. But consistency requires that whatever epistemic status a reason must possess in order decisively to justify coercion, that epistemic status cannot be more demanding than the status that (P) and other proportionality judgments enjoy. Given (P)'s rather pedestrian epistemic credentials, then, it is likely that at least some religious reasons will pass muster. Otherwise put, when we appreciate the tenuous epistemic hold we have on some of the secular reasons, like (P), that are crucial to the justification of military violence, it seems hard to believe that *no* religious reason enjoys the normative credentials needed to play a decisive role in justifying coercion.

Reflection on proportionality judgments like (P) thus suggests a general argument. Any plausible version of the standard view must grant that some secular reasons can decisively justify coercion, but it is extremely implausible to suppose that all secular reasons can do so. Secular reasons are a mixed bag, sociologically, morally, and epistemically. So if the advocate of the standard view is to show that no religious reasons can decisively justify coercion, she must articulate some criterion that isolates coercion-justifying secular reasons and then show that no religious reasons satisfy that criterion. But *whatever* the criterion that isolates coercion-justifying secular reasons, some religious reasons satisfy that criterion: there just is no relevant property that all coercion-justifying secular reasons possess and all religious reasons lack. This is in large part because many of the secular reasons that are relevant to the justification of coercion are not all that impressive, epistemically or otherwise. Consequently, there is no good reason—it is arbitrarily exclusionary—to grant that some secular reasons decisively justify coercion but to deny that any religious reasons can do so.[14]

A CONVERGENCE CONCEPTION
OF THE STANDARD VIEW

I believe that the two objections I have articulated constitute a decent prima facie case against many popular versions of the standard view based on the argument from respect. To be sure, there are other creditable arguments for insisting on shared or accessible reasons. But here I would like to reflect on a more capacious version of the standard view, one that replaces recourse to shared, common, or accessible reasons with an appeal to a "convergence" of disparate reasons.[15]

This convergence conception incorporates the claim that due respect for human worth requires state coercion to be justified to those coerced, such that only those coercive measures pass moral muster for which each citizen has what he or she takes to be a decisive rationale. But it lays down no general, substantive constraints on the kinds of reason on which citizens may rely when determining whether a given coercive measure is acceptable *to them*. Most particularly, it does not require that state coercion be justified on the basis of shared or accessible reasons, though of course it might be so justified. So long as each citizen has access to what each regards as decisive reasons, it does not matter whether those reasons are widely appealing or intransigently particularistic. Any reason counts—Hindu or Habermasian, Christian or Kantian, Utilitarian or Unitarian. *Convergence* on policy is required, not *consensus* as to why that policy is required.

The implications of this capacious conception of justified coercion for the justificatory role of religious reasons are far reaching. Why? If state coercion must be justified to the coerced on grounds that the coerced regard as decisive, but the coerced need not have recourse to shared or accessible reasons as a basis for evaluating a given coercive measure, then it follows that state coercion must be justifiable to religious believers *as religious believers*. That is, if a citizen or public official has what she regards as a decisive religious objection to some coercive measure, then that coercive measure cannot be justified to her, in which case it would be disrespectful and so impermissible to impose it on her. So the convergence conception of the standard view accords to religious citizens and public officials a potentially decisive role in determining the legitimacy of state coercion: should a citizen or public official have what she takes on due reflection to be a decisive religious objection to some coercive measure, then that measure would lack legitimacy, even if it would be legitimate absent her religious objection.

It seems to me that the convergence conception of the standard view should be attractive to religious believers for at least three reasons. First, many religious believers have a deep distrust of government. So, for example, there is a venerable, broadly Augustinian tradition of theological reflection for which the state performs morally and religiously important functions (serving as a "straightjacket for sin"), but is also a perpetual danger, competing with God for loyalty, and used by the proud to oppress the humble, and so in need of severe limitation. Those who self-identify with that broad Augustinian tradition may very well find attractive a conception of justified coercion that allows religious convictions to play a decisive role in undermining the legitimacy of state coercion.

Second, many believers are politically active, not because they aspire to impose their religious convictions on an unwilling population, but because they want to protect a way of life that they take to be under assault by an ever more intrusive state. They want to be left alone, not to dominate the world. They want to raise their children as they see fit, not to ensure that everyone raises their children as they do. But as anyone who has children knows, it is extremely difficult to raise your children well without going to bat against the harebrained schemes of local, state, and even federal officials, much less a popular culture that revels in self-satisfied indolence and gratuitous violence. The convergence conception comports well with the political objectives of those for whom religiously guided political activity is primarily needed to defend an embattled community against a regulatory state guided by normative commitments hostile to an unpopular way of life.

Third, the convergence conception does not treat religious reasons with the sort of invidious discrimination to which many advocates of the standard view seem attracted. Precisely because religious and secular reasons can play the same decisive role in defeating state coercion, the convergence conception does not need to involve anything in the vicinity of the claim that religious reasons are epistemically defective, morally substandard, or otherwise normatively disreputable. Given its implicit commitment to the equal status of religious and secular reasons, the convergence conception should be far more attractive to religious believers than those versions of the standard view married to the claim that there is something defective about religious reasons as such—to such dubious claims as that religion is a conversation-stopper, that religious folks are particularly prone to intolerance, that religious claims are inaccessible, unreplicable, uncriticizable, whatever.

CRITICISM OF THE CONVERGENCE CONCEPTION

In significant respects, the convergence conception is far more inclusive than more familiar formulations of the standard view: it accords to religious reasons a far more robust justificatory role than its consensus-oriented competitor. Nevertheless, not everything goes. For it is still a version of the standard view. How could that be? If there is nothing to be said from any secular perspective that decisively justifies some coercive measure, and if the only plausible rationale for that coercive measure is a religious rationale, then there will inevitably be some secular citizens to whom that coercive measure cannot be justified. According to the view under consideration, such a coercive measure would be disrespectful and so illegitimate.[16] Thus secular citizens too can undermine the legitimacy of otherwise justified coercion. So this version of the standard view maintains the core conviction that religious considerations cannot decisively justify state coercion in pluralistic liberal politics and thus includes as a necessary constituent the Principle of Religious Insufficiency. The implications for the duties of citizens and public officials are direct: they must restrain themselves from endorsing state coercion when they know that their compatriots reject the religious considerations that they regard as decisive and lack access to

> Except this would hold for any comparable secular reason, wtf.

any other reasons that they regard as decisive. That is, citizens and public officials must comply with the Doctrine of Religious Restraint.

Despite its considerable attractions, there is good reason to be skeptical of the convergence view. Although it is quite permissive in its treatment of religion, it is still overly demanding in its conception of what makes for justified coercion. Why? Given the pervasive pluralism endemic to a liberal democracy, some coercive measures crucial to a liberal democracy cannot be justified to some citizens, even for different reasons. But then liberals have good reason to reject the convergence conception of justified coercion: better to jettison the conception of justified coercion that undermines measures central to a liberal democracy than to deny the legitimacy of those measures.

Why think that coercive measures crucial to a liberal polity cannot be justified to some citizens? Few claims are more central to liberalism than the claim that each human being has great and equal worth and should be treated accordingly. Liberal polities express their commitment to this claim by limiting what government can do to citizens. For instance, by institutionalizing a right to religious freedom, we prevent government from tearing down churches and forcing citizens to attend meetings of Fundamentalists Anonymous, thereby violating them in pretty fundamental respects. But respect for human worth does not only ground policies that limit what government can do to citizens by way of coercion. Although coercion is dangerous, a failure to coerce can be just as dangerous. After all, "there are two kinds of injustice," Cicero tells us, "the one on the part of those who inflict wrong, the other on the part of those who, when they can, do not shield from wrong those upon whom it is inflicted."[17] Given that there are various nongovernmental actors who intend to violate their fellow human beings, the absence of governmental coercion can be just as morally troubling as its presence. Consequently, liberal polities must protect the innocent from those rights-violating nongovernmental actors. Most particularly, they must arm police with guns and authorize them to kill the murderous, and they must arm soldiers, sailors, and marines with weapons systems and authorize them to repel aggressors. These protective measures are absolutely crucial to the overall liberal aim of treating human beings as befits their great worth: given the broken world in which we live, we cannot effectively protect citizens from violation unless government authorizes some of us to kill others. Liberalism is a killing creed.] Surely this is contestable

But some citizens believe that it is never morally permissible for one human being to kill another, and so oppose any measure that authorizes any governmental agent to use lethal violence. We can see this by reflecting on the figure of the "agapic pacifist," a citizen who takes Jesus's command that we love our neighbors as ourselves to forbid the lethal use of violence and therefore war.[18] According to the agapic pacifist, for any human being to use lethal violence is for her to violate a divine command to love her enemy-neighbor as herself. Consequently, it is never morally permissible for any human being to intentionally kill another human being, even if doing so is required to prevent egregious violations of human rights. From the perspective inhabited by the agapic pacifist, compelling theological reasons count against coercive measures that are in fact absolutely essential to the effective protection of basic liberal rights. Lethal violence is apostasy.

No doubt agapic pacifists are an exceptionally small proportion of the population. But that is precisely why they might be so attracted to the convergence conception: that conception requires that state coercion be justifiable to them, and they have principled objections to any and all lethal violence and so to any and all wars. To be sure, their objections depend crucially on contentious theological claims. But for the convergence conception, this is unproblematic: state coercion must pass muster before the agapic pacifist's sectarian convictions, no less than before the normative commitments of the just war theorist or the realist about war.

The moral of this story is rather straightforward: liberalism cannot survive the convergence conception of justified coercion. Judged before the bar of that conception, all manner of commitments that are crucial to a liberal democracy lack legitimacy.[19] Because the liberal commitment to human dignity and rights cannot be effectively implemented absent the state's willingness to use lethal violence (in war and otherwise), and because pluralistic liberal democracies will always include citizens who have excellent reason from their own perspective to reject all lethal violence, liberals have excellent reason to reject a conception of justified coercion that would allow these citizens' reasons to render impermissible the state's use of lethal violence.[20] ✳

That said, liberals are not the only ones to have excellent reason to reject the convergence conception of justified coercion.[21] As I have noted, I am interested in reflecting on how the morality of justified military violence is articulated with the conceptions of justified coercion that constitute the heart of the standard view. I am an adherent of the JWT and I take it that advocates of that venerable tradition should also reject the convergence view. How so?

I have been exclusively concerned with the justification of state coercion to the citizens of a liberal polity. In so doing, I have followed the self-understanding of every advocate of the standard view with whose work I am familiar. But it is hard to espy any principled reason to limit the scope of the convergence conception to domestic coercion. And advocates of the JWT cannot in good conscience deny that due respect for human worth should govern the manner in which military violence is employed. After all, the principle of noncombatant immunity—the wrongfulness of direct, intentional military violence directed at those who do not participate in any unjust military attack—is an absolutely essential component of the JWT and seems to depend on the claim that the dignity of the members of any political community imposes potentially severe restrictions on the military violence directed at them by outsiders. So if advocates of the JWT must respect the worth of any and every human being, if respect for human worth requires that state coercion be justified to those coerced, and if waging a war is a paradigmatic act of state coercion, then respect for human worth requires that military violence be justified not only, or even primarily, to the citizens of the political community that wages war, but also, and most importantly, to those against whom that violence is directed.[22]

But it is implausible to suppose that this requirement could actually be satisfied. Given familiar details regarding the vastly different ways in which the members of warring communities are socialized, their differential access to relevant information, the competing normative traditions regarding the morality of war that are dominant in distinct cultures, and so on, the members of warring communities will often rely on vastly different evidential sets when they reflect on the morality of the military conflicts in which their community is involved. Given their dependence on such vastly different information and normative principles, the members of warring communities will often, and perhaps typically, be in a condition of what Vitoria called "invincible error" regarding the justice of the wars their community wages: they will wrongly evaluate the justice of the wars they fight no matter how responsibly and conscientiously they evaluate the available evidence.[23] So, for example, I take it that American sailors at Pearl Harbor justly defended themselves with lethal violence even though the Japanese soldiers whom they killed were not epistemically well positioned to realize that they were initiating an unjust war. Again, American Marines were morally permitted to invade Okinawa even if large numbers of Japanese defenders were in no good epistemic position to believe anything other than that they were defending their homeland against an unjust, and indeed monstrous, aggressor.

It seems, then, that if the norm of respect requires the justification of coercion to those coerced, and if human beings are typically invincibly ignorant of the justice of the wars their communities wage, it will only very seldom, if ever, be the case that a political community may actually wage war. The killing that occurs in a just war will not be justified to those against whom military violence is justly directed. This kind of practical pacifism is unacceptable to advocates of the JWT, who therefore have excellent reason to reject the conception of justified coercion that would otherwise drive us to that dubious conclusion.

CONCLUDING REFLECTION: LESSONS FROM THE JUST WAR TRADITION REGARDING JUSTIFIED COERCION

Let me draw this critical discussion to a close by reflecting on some of the larger issues raised by my objections to the convergence view. Basic to the JWT is the claim that war must be justified, and that there must exist some appropriate rationale for a given war, but that there is no expectation, much less a requirement, that those against whom war is waged will be in a strong epistemic position to appreciate that rationale. So I take it that the conception of justified coercion implicit in the JWT is inconsistent with any and all versions of the standard view: the latter affirms, and the former denies, that the presumption against coercion can be overcome only if a given coercive measure can be justified to the coerced. It seems to me that the JWT is correct on this fundamental point: waging war is sometimes permissible in the actual world, but this is the case only if a given political community may wage war against human beings who have what they regard as no compelling reason to believe that the war that is waged against them is just, and therefore only if the constraints on justified coercion affirmed by advocates of the standard view do not apply to the use of military violence in war.

This moral fact has all manner of important implications for our understanding of the moral texture of war. For example, it shapes the way in which we think about, and treat, enemy combatants. A political community that satisfies the JWT's *ad bellum* requirements may permissibly kill enemy combatants, but it may not blame enemy combatants for resisting and it certainly should not prosecute them for using lethal violence in their own defense. Precisely because those who prosecute an unjust war typically are not in any decent epistemic position to know that the war they prosecute is unjust, blaming them, much less prosecuting them, is beyond the moral pale. Kill them we may, but blame them we must not.

I take it that the sharp distinction between justice and blameworthiness that we must employ in order to make sense of the moral status of unjust combatants can also be appropriate in domestic politics. Admittedly, whereas in war it is *typically* the case that soldiers are in no good epistemic position to evaluate the justice of the wars they fight, in domestic politics it is *sometimes* the case that citizens and public officials are in no good epistemic position to evaluate the justice of the coercive measures to which they are subject. But from this difference it follows only that whereas in war we must ordinarily decouple justice and blame, in domestic politics we must sometimes do so. Indeed, given the reasonable pluralism that characterizes a well-functioning liberal democracy, it seems to me that we should assume as a matter of course that those on whom we are morally compelled to impose some coercive measure reasonably reject that measure, and so we should refrain from blaming them for opposing us. But impose on them we will and must.

Notes

1. Included in this number are particular theorists (such as James Childress, Rowan Williams, Robert B. Miller, and C. A. J. Coady) as well as institutional agents (most

prominently, the US National Conference of Catholic Bishops). For the latter, see US National Conference of Catholic Bishops, *The Challenge of Peace: God's Promise and Our Response* (Washington, D.C.: National Conference of Catholic Bishops, 1983), 30.

2. See, generally, Nicholas Fotion, *War and Ethics: A New Just War Theory* (New York: Continuum, 2007); and Jeff McMahan, "Just Cause for War," *Ethics and International Affairs* 19, no. 3 (2005): 55–75.

3. This restriction presupposes some conception of what makes for a religious rationale. While admitting that the various competing conceptions are open to reasonable disagreement, I will simply stipulate that a rationale (or reason) R is religious just in case R has theistic content. So, for example, "God has commanded us to X" is a religious reason, as is "Zeus has commanded us to X," but "Our Dear Leader has commanded us to X" is not, precisely by virtue of the fact that the first has a monotheistic and the second a polytheistic content that the third clearly lacks.

4. Note that a religious reason can play a *decisive* role in justifying state coercion C even if that reason is not the *only* or *exclusive* rationale for C. So, for example, suppose that some secular reason S provides substantial but insufficient support for C, and further that some religious reason R provides substantial but insufficient support for C, but that those reasons jointly render C permissible. In that case, C is justified, but not in the absence of R. Of course, since the parallel point is also true of some S, it follows that, in the kind of case under consideration, *both* religious and secular reasons play a decisive role in justifying state coercion. I think that, when religious reasons do play a decisive role in justifying coercion, they will typically do so in this collaborative manner. That is, even when religious reasons play a decisive justificatory role, they will almost never do so without some secular support.

5. In due course I discuss one noteworthy exception, the convergence conception articulated by Gerald Gaus. It might seem that John Rawls provides a further exception. After all, Rawls famously asserts that his conception of "public reason . . . neither criticizes nor attacks any comprehensive doctrine, religious or secular," thus signaling his commitment to the impartial treatment of the religious and the secular (*IPRR* 132), and he explicitly refuses to equate public reason with secular reason (*IPRR* 143). So perhaps my analysis and articulation of the standard conception of justified coercion apply not to Rawls himself, but to the legions of Rawlsians (and others) who have departed from him in privileging the secular over the religious. That said, it does seem to me that Rawls's conception of public reason retains some residual discrimination between the religious and the secular. Consider in this regard his claim that "our exercise of political power is proper only when we sincerely believe that the reasons we would offer for our political actions . . . are sufficient, and we also reasonably think that other citizens might reasonably accept those reasons" (*IPRR* 137). What sorts of reasons might satisfy this conception of properly justified state power? That is, what sorts of reasons can we reasonably expect our fellow citizens reasonably to accept? Will *all* secular reasons satisfy this requirement? Rawls is clear that they will

not: those secular reasons that derive from a "secular comprehensive doctrine" will not be reasonably acceptable to all reasonable citizens (*IPRR* 148). Will *some* secular reasons satisfy this requirement? Rawls clearly indicates that they will—see the list of "political values" he specifies to give content to his conception of public reason (*IPRR* 144). These are all secular in the sense in which I use that term (see note 3 above). Will *any* of those reasons be religious in content? No, never. For no religious reason, whether a constituent of a religious comprehensive doctrine or otherwise, is reasonably acceptable to all of the reasonable citizens in a pluralistic liberal polity. Otherwise put, for Rawls, no religious claim will be included in the "overlapping consensus" between reasonable comprehensive doctrines. It therefore seems that, according to Rawls, the proper exercise of political power can be justified only by some secular reasons, whereas political power can never be decisively justified by religious reasons.

6. See Charles Larmore, *Patterns of Moral Complexity* (Cambridge: Cambridge University Press, 1987), 40–68; Larmore, *The Morals of Modernity* (Cambridge: Cambridge University Press, 1996), esp. 134ff.; and Larmore, "Respect for Persons," *Hedgehog Review* 7, no. 2 (Summer 2005): 66–76.

7. If a diversely committed population can share some premise, even when they do not actually do so, then that population has "access" to that premise. Of course, there is a large literature on the notion of an "accessible" reason, which I will largely bypass because I regard the notion of an accessible reason as so vague that unraveling its complexities would distract from my central argument.

8. Michael Blake, "Reciprocity, Stability, and Intervention: The Ethics of Disequilibrium," in *Ethics and Foreign Intervention*, ed. D. K. Chatterjee and D. Sheid (New York: Cambridge University Press, 2003), 56–57, 55.

9. Whether A, B, or C has an accessible reason is a distinct matter, complicated by the wide diversity of competing conceptions of what makes for an accessible reason. See note 7 above.

10. See, for example, Micah Schwartzman, "The Sincerity of Public Reason," *Journal of Political Philosophy* 19, no. 4 (December 2011): 375–98.

11. Corresponding points are made in defense of "reasoning from conjecture" against criticisms of manipulation, in Micah Schwartzman, "Reasoning from Conjecture: A Reply to Three Objections," chapter 6 in this volume.

12. I find plausible the understanding of proportionality developed by Thomas Hurka, "Proportionality in the Morality of War," *Philosophy and Public Affairs* 33, no. 1 (2005): 34–66.

13. For a compelling reflection on this claim, see Nigel Biggar, *In Defence of War* (Oxford: Oxford University Press, 2013), 111–48.

14. Might it be the case that secular reasons differ from religious reasons in the respect that epistemically competent and morally conscientious human beings would share the former but not the latter in relevantly idealized circumstances? My view is that, when we idealize in the relevant respects, there is no good reason to believe that

we would reach consensus on secular but not religious reasons. I have attempted to address this question in detail in Eberle, "What Does Respect Require?," in *Religion in the Liberal Polity*, ed. T. Cuneo (Notre Dame: University of Notre Dame Press, 2005), 173–94.

15. This conception has been developed in Gerald Gaus, "The Place of Religious Belief in Public Reason Liberalism," in *Multiculturalism and Moral Conflict*, ed. M. Dimovia-Cookson and P. M. R. Stirk (London: Routledge, 2009), 19–37; Gerald Gaus and Kevin Vallier, "The Roles of Religious Reason in a Publicly Justified Polity," *Philosophy and Social Criticism* 35 (January 2009): 51–76; and Kevin Vallier, "Consensus and Convergence in Public Reason," *Public Affairs Quarterly* 25, no. 4 (2011): 261–79.

16. To put it formally, in any well-functioning liberal polity, for any coercive measure M that would not be justified save for some religious reason R, there will always be at least one citizen C who is subjected to M who has what C regards as compelling reason to reject R, in which case M is not justified to C. Should C be compelled to comply with M, then C would not be treated with due respect.

17. Quoted in John Mark Mattox, *Saint Augustine and the Theory of Just War* (New York: Continuum, 2006), 15.

18. For a more detailed treatment of this figure, see Eberle, "Religion, Pacifism and the Doctrine of Restraint," *Journal of Religious Ethics* 34, no. 2 (June 2006): 203–24; and Eberle, "Basic Human Worth and Religious Restraint," *Philosophy and Social Criticism* 35, nos. 1–2 (2009): 151–81.

19. We can run this argument in many directions. I have elsewhere tried to do so with respect to the right to religious freedom. See Terence Cuneo and Christopher J. Eberle, "Religion and Political Theory," *Stanford Encyclopedia of Philosophy*, ed. Edward N. Zalta (Winter 2012), http://plato.stanford.edu/entries/religion-politics.

20. Paradoxically, the convergence conception's generous treatment of religion partly accounts for the stringency, and so the inadequacy, of its underlying conception of justified coercion. If coercive measures must be justifiable to the multitudinous and fissiparous religious believers subject to those measures, and so consistent with the theological convictions of those believers, then many more coercive measures will fail to pass moral muster than would be the case were those coercive measures exempt from this religious filter. Too many, I think.

21. I believe that the line of argument I develop here applies not only to Gaus's convergence conception, but also to many versions of the standard view.

22. Christopher J. Eberle, "God and War: Some Exploratory Questions," *Journal of Law and Religion* 28, no. 1 (2012–13): 1–46.

23. Francisco de Vitoria, "On the Law of War," in *Political Writings*, ed. A. Pagden and J. Lawrence (Cambridge: Cambridge University Press, 1991), 313. For a number of excellent essays on the normative implications of the epistemic condition of soldiers and citizens in war, see D. Rodin and H. Shue, eds., *Just and Unjust Warriors* (Oxford: Oxford University Press, 2010).

2

Religion and Liberalism

WAS RAWLS RIGHT AFTER ALL?

ROBERT B. TALISSE

The topic of this chapter is religion in liberal politics, and "liberalism" is the name of an unruly family of doctrines. So let me tighten the focus further. My concern is with the place of religious conviction in the dominant form of contemporary liberalism known as "justificatory liberalism."[1] Before explaining what justificatory liberalism is, two preliminary remarks are in order. First, my discussion is *internal* to liberalism. I am not concerned here with the question of whether liberalism is an adequate framework for political theory. The issue, rather, is whether justificatory liberalism is the *right* liberalism. Certain critics say that justificatory liberalism's view concerning religious conviction demonstrates that it is not properly liberal, and I will here defend it against this charge.[2] Second, the issue at hand is *conceptual*. Questions concerning the political behavior of religious citizens and the social benefits of religious institutions are indeed important, but beside the point; and so are constitutional concerns regarding public expressions of religiosity. The issue at hand is whether strictly religious reasons are ever sufficient to justify coercive law. The justificatory liberal says they are not, and I think that is the right view for liberals.

A lot needs to be said in order to specify what is at stake. Accordingly, the first part of the chapter is aimed at nailing down the issue. The second part sketches a critique of justificatory liberalism proposed by Christopher Eberle. The third part develops a version of justificatory liberalism that evades Eberle's criticism. Finally, in the fourth part, I compare the resulting version of justificatory liberalism with the more familiar Rawlsian version, arguing that the view I propose is, in the end, roughly equivalent to the Rawlsian position. It seems, then, that on the question of the place of religious reasons in public discourse, Rawls was right after all.) 101

LOCATING THE ISSUE

Like all liberalisms, justificatory liberalism sees the political world as (ideally) a fair system of cooperation among equals. Thus it shares with garden variety liberalism a commitment to the freedom and equality of all citizens; it recognizes the familiar schedule of basic liberties, and supports all of the usual views about distributive justice, the rule of law, and representative government. It sees political power as inherently coercive and offers an account of when coercion is permissible. Justificatory liberalism is, like all liberalisms, a view about legitimacy.

This is where the distinctive element of justificatory liberalism emerges. Justificatory liberals hold that, as John Rawls puts it, "a legitimate regime is such that its political and social institutions are justifiable to all citizens—to each and every one—by addressing their reason, theoretical and practical."[3] To get a flavor of the distinctness of the justificatory version, contrast it with a more traditional liberalism. In *On Liberty*, Mill proposes "one very simple principle"[4] for demarcating permissible from impermissible coercion. Mill's claim is that coercion is permissible only when it is necessary to prevent harm to others. A liberal regime coerces its citizens only in such cases; a state that does otherwise is despotic, illegitimate.[5]

By contrast, the justificatory liberal distinguishes permissible from impermissible coercion by appealing to a different kind of criterion: coercion is permissible only if it is *justifiable* to "every last individual."[6] Note that this justifiability requirement is not a *consensus* or *unanimity* requirement. A coercive law or policy might be justifiable to all even though it in fact enjoys little or no popular support. A justifiable policy might yet be rejected, and rejected for good reason; but when a justifiable policy is enacted, one's rejection of it is not sufficient to defeat its moral bindingness. Think of Socrates in Plato's *Crito*: the personified Laws do not convince him that he should want to be executed; they convince him that he is morally required to obey their verdict by a certain conception of justice that he himself endorses.[7] There is a difference between a law being *endorsed* by all and its being *justifiable* to all. Arguably, a law that is *endorsed* by all is not coercive, because such a law would require what everyone agrees must be done anyway. Consequently, to claim that a law is *justifiable* only if it is *endorsed* is to deny that coercion is ever permissible; and that is the philosophical anarchist's position, not the liberal's. Laws indeed *force* people to do what they otherwise would not do, and, according to the liberal, exercise of this force is, under certain conditions, morally permitted; the *justificatory* liberal claims that force is morally permitted only when it is justifiable.[8]

Hence the justificatory liberal must give an account of justifiability. On all versions of the view, the justifiability of a law is a matter of the *kind of reason* that can be proposed in its support. The justificatory liberal holds that for a coercive law to be justifiable to all, it must be recommended by a reason that is "accessible" to all. Justifiability is accessibility.

There's the rub. What does it mean for a reason to be accessible? Justificatory liberals are divided. Some say that accessible reasons are "public";[9] others say they are "common,"[10] "intelligible,"[11] or "acceptable to all qualified points of view";[12] some appeal to reasonable rejection,[13] or reasons that "can be shared";[14] and others speak of reasons that "any rational adult can endorse"[15] or reasons that "citizens can accept on the basis of their common reason."[16] Despite the significant differences between these accounts, theorists often move merrily from one formulation to the others, as if they were equivalent.[17] But I need not attempt to adjudicate this issue, because, fortunately, justificatory liberals agree that strictly religious reasons are not accessible in the relevant respect.

By *strictly* religious reasons, I mean reasons that derive *exclusively* from some particular religious perspective. The justification for a law forbidding torture that draws from considerations of human dignity need not run afoul of the justifiability requirement, because the idea that we are morally required to recognize such dignity is not *exclusive* to any particular religious perspective, but is in fact common to many perspectives, religious and secular. By contrast, laws forbidding homosexual sodomy fail to be justifiable because there is no case for forbidding homosexual sodomy that does not depend ultimately upon some sectarian religious doctrine. To put the matter differently: in order to appreciate the reasons for prohibiting homosexual sodomy—in order to *see* the proposed reasons as even relevant—one must be committed to a religious view that, in a liberal society, citizens are free to reject. Consequently, justificatory liberalism implies that accessible reasons are secular.[18]

So the justificatory liberal holds that the exercise of the coercive force of the state is improper when it cannot be justified by the right kind of reason, and strictly religious reasons are reasons of the wrong kind. Complications emerge when we consider cases in which the state offers as its reason for law L a strictly religious reason, but L also enjoys the support of reasons that are not strictly religious. Justificatory liberals disagree about whether the state's *stated* or *motivating* reason must be accessible. Some say that the state may legislate on the basis of a strictly religious reason just in case there is also an accessible reason *available* that supports the legislation;[19] others go further, adding that the accessible reason must be not only available but *sufficient* to motivate the legislation.[20] The issue is tricky, and I confess to being wary of speaking of states in this way. Fortunately, I can bracket most of this too; justificatory liberals agree that coercive laws that are supportable *only* by strictly religious reasons are illegitimate.

To feel the force of this view, consider a law forbidding the eating of pork on certain specified days of the year. It is hard to imagine a justification for such a law that is not strictly religious. And this seems to render the law illegitimate in a way that even vegetarians should recognize. But why? Notice that such a law is not a clear violation of the Establishment Clause; a law forbidding pork-eating on a few days of the year hardly *establishes* a church.[21] Arguably, the law does not harm anyone; it is not clearly a violation of anyone's rights; and probably very few people will feel coerced in any strong sense by it. Yet something is amiss. The justificatory liberal's account of the problem is intuitive: the only reasons that count in favor of the law are reasons that *do not count.*

There are distinctive advantages to a view that enables us to criticize a proposed law on the grounds that the reasons which support it are not of the right kind. We do not want the legitimacy of a law to turn on the question of which religion is correct. We want a way to object to the law's legitimacy that does not require us to argue the merits of the religious perspective that recommends it. We want to avoid having to say to our fellow citizens that their deepest religious convictions are false, yet we also want to retain the means by which we can reject the idea that everyone should live in accordance with those convictions. Justificatory liberalism fits the bill.

But the claim is not simply that coercive laws based solely on strictly religious reasons make for inconvenient or messy politics. The claim is that such laws are *objectionable.* Why? The justificatory liberal claims that such laws are *disrespectful* of those who must live under them. What drives this view of disrespect is another staple commitment of justificatory liberalism, namely, acknowledgment of what Rawls called "the fact of reasonable pluralism."[22] The claim is that deep disagreement over fundamental moral, religious, and philosophical commitments is not necessarily due to ignorance, foolishness, or wickedness; rather, responsible and intelligent persons doing their epistemic best and attending to all the relevant available considerations may nonetheless disagree deeply about fundamental matters. In short, reasonable pluralism is the inevitable result of liberal institutions.[23] A liberal polity must recognize that there are many doctrines that are consistent with responsible citizenship, despite being inconsistent with one another. Laws that can be supported only by strictly religious reasons disrespect citizens—they coerce solely on the basis of reasons that citizens are at liberty to dismiss.[24]

I take it that on almost any liberal view this much is commonplace, perhaps even unobjectionable. But things get murkier when we examine the matter from the point of view of the political activity of citizens.[25] Consider a simplified case: Abby votes for a coercive law L on the basis of her strictly religious reasons, knowing that no other kind of reason supports L. Has Abby acted wrongly?

The justificatory liberal claims that Abby has acted wrongly. To wit: in a democratic polity, citizens share political power equally—they vote, campaign, lobby, and engage in other activities designed to direct the coercive power of the state. Let's use the term "advocacy" to cover all of these varied activities. If a coercive law is illegitimate when it is not justifiable, then citizens' advocacy on the basis of strictly religious reasons is morally suspect, especially in the case of advocacy for policy that is supportable *only* by strictly religious reasons. When citizens engage in advocacy of this kind, they exercise their meager share of political power in a way that directs the state to coerce on the basis of reasons of the wrong kind. If it is wrong for the state to enact laws that are not justifiable, then it is wrong for citizens to exercise their political power such that, were the effort successful, the state would unjustly coerce. What is wrong for the state to do is wrong for the citizen to direct the state to do.[26]

Admittedly, the analogy between legislation and advocacy is imperfect. Whereas state coercion is *illegitimate* when it is not justifiable, Abby's advocacy is simply *immoral*.[27] When a state coerces for reasons of the wrong kind, it commits an *injustice*; when Abby advocates for a law that can be supported only by the wrong kind of reason, she violates a *duty of citizenship*. However, the justificatory liberal holds that both cases involve the same *kind* of wrong: just as the state disrespects its citizens when it enacts unjustifiable coercive laws, a citizen who advocates for an unjustifiable coercive law disrespects her fellow citizens.

Hence the justificatory liberal contends that citizens have a moral duty to withhold advocacy in the case of coercive laws that are supportable only by strictly religious reasons. To do otherwise is to disrespect one's fellow citizens; to use Rawls's term, it is to be "uncivil." Importantly, civility is a moral duty, not a legal one;[28] citizens who violate it are subject to blame, not sanction. Furthermore, the duty of civility constrains political *advocacy*, not speech per se. There is no duty that precludes citizens from publicly *expressing* or *discussing* the strictly religious reasons that support their favored laws. The duty of civility applies only when we exercise our powers of citizenship to direct the coercive power of the state.[29]

Civility becomes troublesome once we consider that, for many citizens, religious commitment is *constitutive*; religious citizens often see their convictions not only as *beliefs they have*, but also as *what they are*.[30] For many citizens, their religious convictions specify what justice is, what deserves toleration, and what proper citizenship consists in. Many citizens take their obligations to God to be overriding and "totalizing"; it is *part of their religious conviction* that religious obligations trump all other obligations.[31]

In requiring citizens to withhold advocacy from laws that can be supported only by their strictly religious reasons, justificatory liberalism imposes on religious citizens serious conflicts of conscience: they are required to recognize a political obligation that overrides what they take to be their religious obligations. In some cases, this seems to interfere with the free exercise of religion: some believers claim to have a *religious obligation* to engage politically in a way that manifests their faith. Thus to endorse an ethic of citizenship that would require violations of conscience seems disrespectful.[32]

Although I think that this particular line of criticism is misguided, it is easy to see why it has gained traction. Consider Macedo: "If some people . . . feel 'silenced' or 'marginalized' by the fact that some of us believe that it is wrong to seek to shape basic liberties on the basis of religious . . . claims, I can only say 'grow up!' "[33] This remark is unique in its overt intemperance; however, the potential for disrespect that lies within justificatory liberalism is often overlooked. And, as Eberle rightly observes,[34] this no doubt has to do with the fact that in the literature, the imagined religious opponent of justificatory liberalism is frequently found advocating for the legal prohibition of homosexual sex or contraception, or for some other policy that liberals have independent reasons to think odious. The badness of the desired policy *output* is projected on to the *input*.[35]

So let's consider an example borrowed from Eberle that helps to focus on the *inputs*. Betty is an *agapic pacifist*. Agapic pacifists hold, for strictly religious reasons, that "waging war is always morally prohibited," even in self-defense and even in order to save innocent lives.[36] Moreover, agapic pacifists hold that they are morally obligated to politically prevent war, and so they advocate for a Twenty-Eighth Amendment to the U.S. Constitution that would strip the federal government of the power to wage war.[37] Let us suppose that this extreme pacifism can be supported *only* by the strictly religious reasons provided by the agapic pacifist's unique brand of Christianity. Thus the issue: the justificatory liberal contends that in advocating for Amendment Twenty-Eight, Betty disrespects her fellow citizens. Is the justificatory liberal correct?

Again, this is a conceptual question. Some have suggested that it is a misguided question since there is, in fact, no real-world policy proposal that is supportable *solely* by strictly religious reasons.[38] Indeed, the familiar cases of conflict between religion and politics seem to be cases in which citizens advocate on the basis of strictly religious reasons for policies that are supportable by other reasons as well. Now, I happen to believe that a citizen who advocates solely on the basis of strictly religious reasons is morally blameworthy as a citizen, regardless of whether her favored policy also enjoys the support of accessible reasons; yet this is, again, a complicated matter that I cannot try to settle here. But one thing is clear: if Betty's advocacy is morally aboveboard, then strictly religious advocacy in the real-world cases will be too. That is, if Betty's advocacy is permissible, then it will be difficult to make the case that strictly religious reasons against such things as same-sex marriage, abortion, euthanasia, and contraception are nonjustificatory. So it is important to begin with the artificial but more clearly defined case. If it can be shown that Betty's advocacy is disrespectful, then there will still be an argument to be had concerning the real-world cases.

EBERLE'S ATTACK ON JUSTIFICATORY LIBERALISM

Eberle has launched a sophisticated two-stage attack on justificatory liberalism.[39] The first stage exposes a flaw in the structure of justificatory liberalism. The second stage presents a compelling conception of respect that can be satisfied even by citizens advocating for laws that are supportable only by strictly religious reasons. To be sure, Eberle's view is not *radically inclusive*—it declares certain kinds of religious advocacy disrespectful—but, crucially, it permits Betty's advocacy. I think that both stages of Eberle's attack fail; and that is what I shall argue below. Here, I provide a quick sketch of the core of Eberle's view.

First, the structural objection. Eberle rightly observes that the core of justificatory liberalism consists of two distinct commitments that are almost always run together. The first is what he calls the "Principle of Pursuit": "A citizen should pursue public justification for his favored coercive laws." The second is the "Doctrine of Restraint": "A citizen should not support any coercive law for which he lacks a public justification."[40] Eberle uses "public justification" here to refer to the justificatory liberal demand for reasons that are accessible, and thus justifiable, to all. His charge is that justificatory liberals treat the Doctrine of Restraint as logically equivalent to the Principle of Pursuit, often moving from the one to the other without any notice—or argument—at all. A canvass of the justificatory liberal literature confirms Eberle's observation.[41] Thus Gerald Gaus captures what seems to be the official justificatory liberal view on the matter when he writes, "the reverse side of our commitment to justify imposing our norms on others is a commitment to refrain from imposing norms that cannot be justified."[42]

Gaus's claim that the Doctrine of Restraint is the "reverse side" of the Principle of Pursuit is imprecise; it is difficult to discern what logical relation is being proposed. The Principle of Pursuit does not *entail* the Doctrine of Restraint,[43] and it is hard to formulate a plausible intervening deontic principle that would license such an immediate inference from a *duty to try* to a requirement concerning what to do if the attempt fails.[44] So the two commitments are distinct, and there is a gap between them. Again, a survey of the justificatory liberal literature reveals little by way of convincing argument that would close the gap; this has led at least one religious liberal to conclude that the gap *cannot* be closed.[45]

I will return to the gap below. Eberle's positive strategy is to show that respect requires Pursuit but not Restraint. On Eberle's view, "a citizen respects his compatriots . . . only if he accords due moral weight to the fact that they are persons, which in turn requires this fact to make a moral difference to the way he acts."[46] This requires that we regard our compatriots as "having great and equal worth."[47] From this Eberle develops a view of what respect requires of citizens when they politically advocate, what he calls the "ideal of conscientious engagement."[48] According to this ideal, a citizen must "pursue a high degree of rational justification for the moral propriety"[49] of her favored coercive laws, and "withhold support" if she cannot achieve such justification.[50] Furthermore, respect requires a citizen to "listen" to her compatriots' criticisms of her favored law "with the intention of learning from them" about the moral propriety (or lack thereof) of the law; and, finally, citizens must "sincerely and responsibly attempt to articulate reasons" for their favored laws that their compatriots "regard as sound."[51]

Eberle's contention is that Betty, our agapic pacifist, could satisfy the demands of the ideal of conscientious engagement and yet fail to discern an accessible reason for Amendment Twenty-Eight. If she has achieved a high level of rational justification for her favored law and has done her level best to find accessible reasons for it, Betty has, according to Eberle, done everything respect requires. And so with all religious believers: provided that they have achieved a high level of rational justification for their view, and have done their level best to discern accessible reasons for the laws they favor, they may advocate on the basis of strictly religious reasons, even when no other reasons are available. Eberle takes himself to have reconciled the two liberal commitments that justificatory liberals place in opposition, namely, respect for fellow citizens and freedom of conscience. The justificatory liberal's Doctrine of Restraint is not necessary from the point of view of respect, and thus is, Eberle says, "illiberal."[52]

Eberle thinks that the agapic pacifist case is especially compelling because Betty is ex hypothesi motivated by a doctrine that accords to every human life an unusually high degree of basic worth,[53] and she advocates for a policy that she rationally believes is required if we are to respect that worth.[54] Betty advocates for Amendment Twenty-Eight precisely because she holds human life in especially high regard. Consequently, Eberle finds the justificatory liberal's claim that Betty disrespects her compatriots "incredible."[55]

IN DEFENSE OF JUSTIFICATORY LIBERALISM

Although I have skipped over many details of Eberle's view, the foregoing sketch suffices for our purposes. I will press two responses on behalf of justificatory liberalism. First, the ideal of conscientious engagement itself gives rise to serious conflicts of conscience, and in fact may prove to be more burdensome than the Doctrine of Restraint. The success of this line of response of course should give no great consolation to the justificatory liberal; it is a tu quoque, and so provides no positive support for justificatory liberalism. But a second line of response sketches a conception of respect available to the justificatory liberal that requires both pursuit of public justification and restraint of nonpublic justification, that is, both of the commitments that Eberle identifies and separates. I will take these two responses up in order.

Eberle's ideal of conscientious engagement may seem plausible when we consider conflicts between religious reasons and accessible reasons, but difficulties arise when we consider conflicts between religious believers of different faiths. Consider: Stan, the local Satanist, has achieved a high level of rational justification for the moral propriety of a law calling for government-sanctioned hedonism festivals involving public orgies, blood rituals, alcohol consumption, and animal sacrifice.[56] To avoid difficulties concerning the constraint that we treat others as having "great and equal worth,"[57] let's say that the festival involves no compulsory acts of worship and no forced interpersonal contact—something more like state-sanctioned public frat parties than compulsory church attendance. Although Stan supports this law on the basis of his strictly Satanic reasons, he has done his level best to find accessible reasons and he has engaged sincerely with those who oppose him; however, no accessible reasons have surfaced. According to Eberle's view, Stan has satisfied his duty to respect his fellow citizens and may now advocate for his law.

Stan's advocacy is unlikely to succeed politically. However, Eberle's view only requires citizens to recognize the *in principle* legitimacy of a law that enjoys no other justification than a Satanic one. And this alone can create a conflict of conscience more severe than the Doctrine of Restraint. For Eberle's view requires Christian citizens to place themselves under political conditions that would morally permit coercion on the basis of reasons that they not only do not recognize the moral force of, but are religiously committed to *denying* the moral force of. By accepting the ideal of conscientious engagement as the entirety of what respect requires, religious citizens make themselves vulnerable to justified coercion on the basis of reasons they, from their religious perspectives, must deny are reasons at all.

Imagine that Stan somehow prevails. On Eberle's view, the Christian citizen has no principled objection to Stan's law; Stan has satisfied the ideal of conscientious engagement, hence there is nothing defective about the law at all. More importantly, if Stan prevails, Christian citizens would have a *moral obligation* to do what they are religiously obliged to deny they could ever have a *moral* reason to do, namely, to accept that the government sanction hedonist festivals. I must confess that this seems untenable, bordering on incoherent; at the very least, it places a far heavier burden on the religious believer than the Doctrine of Restraint would.

But the case of Stan is not ideal. One could argue, for example, that Stan's law is not really coercive, since it requires citizens merely to *allow* the festivals, or at most be *complicit* in them. Now, I think the law is coercive, but let's not get sidetracked by this issue. There is a different case which seems more clear cut. Consider the case of Marco, a Marx-inspired Christian liberation theologian. Marco believes with a high degree of rational justification that violent conflict is inevitable in the pursuit of justice, and he sees compulsory conscription into military combat forces as a necessary solidarity-building and conscience-purifying measure. Marco satisfies the ideal of conscientious engagement and finds no accessible reason for his law, but nonetheless advocates on the basis of his strictly religious reasons for universal conscription necessarily involving participation in combat forces.

Suppose that Marco prevails. Where does that leave Betty? She now must see herself as under a moral obligation to participate in combat, despite the fact that she must also regard all combat as impermissible. She could argue for an *exemption* from the law, but in making her case, she would not be able to complain that in imposing the law, the state would be *disrespecting* her. And, in my view, this is *precisely* what Betty should want to say.

It seems to me, then, that religious citizens have good reason to reject the idea that conscientious engagement is sufficient for respect. Where does that leave the justificatory liberal? Let's return to the gap Eberle identified between pursuit and restraint. Although it is true that the Principle of Pursuit does not entail the Doctrine of Restraint, it seems to me that there is a case to be made for thinking that a properly liberal conception of respect requires both.

A central liberal commitment has it that, in addition to the kind of respect persons owe to one another qua persons, there is a distinctive kind of respect that liberal citizens owe to one another qua *citizens*.[58] Call this "citizen respect." Citizen respect involves the recognition of fellow citizens *as political equals*, that is, as equal sharers in political power and responsibility. Two points are crucial. First, what it is to be a proper citizen in a liberal democracy is to recognize the moral force of certain reasons when deciding policy. For liberal citizens deliberating about some proposed law L, considerations regarding L's impact on equality, liberty, freedom, dignity, autonomy, and civil peace *must count*. Of course, citizens may disagree about how the values referenced in reasons of this kind are to be understood, and how such reasons are to be prioritized. But to deny that reasons of this kind *matter* is to call into question one's fitness for liberal citizenship. Hence we can identify a collection of reasons that citizens qua citizens must recognize as relevant when deciding policy. Appropriating a term from Bernard Williams,[59] we may say that these are reasons which must count as "internal reasons" for citizens in their role as citizens. I take it as almost definitional that, in a liberal society, strictly religious reasons cannot be internal reasons for citizens as such. To say that considerations such as "the Bible dictates that *p*" or "Saturday is the Sabbath" *must count* for citizens qua citizens is to no longer be talking about a liberal regime.

Second, all liberalisms hold that legitimate laws place *moral* obligations on citizens. When a citizen breaks a legitimate law, we hold her morally blameworthy, and not simply legally sanctionable.[60] In this way, imposing coercive laws is analogous to imposing moral obligations generally. Like moral blame in general, blame for violating a law is morally appropriate only when we can say that those who break the law had an internal reason to acknowledge the law. To take others to be morally required to acknowledge obligations that they have no internal reason to acknowledge is not to treat them as moral agents, but, in Gaus's apt term, to "browbeat" them;[61] and to browbeat fellow moral agents is to disrespect them.

Pulling these two considerations together, we can say that liberal citizens are required to recognize—for the purposes of citizenship—certain kinds of reasons as internal reasons. Additionally, citizens are in the business of placing moral obligations on one another in the form of laws. Since laws state *moral* obligations, citizens who violate the law are morally blameworthy. But assigning moral blame for violating a law is disrespectful when the violator has no internal reason for acknowledging the law. For instance, to impose on Carol a law that she qua citizen has no internal reason to acknowledge is to treat her as a mere subject of legislation, not as a citizen; and this is to disrespect her. And—here is the crucial point—liberal citizens are not required to regard strictly religious reasons as internal reasons. Therefore, to advocate a law that is supportable for strictly religious reasons is to disrespect one's fellow liberal citizens.

This kind of disrespect is precisely what is involved in the law favored by Betty. Amendment Twenty-Eight would impose on some citizens a moral obligation that they, qua citizens, have no reason to acknowledge. No matter how well-intentioned Betty is, no matter how high her regard for human life, no matter how much she respects her fellow human beings, the law she proposes fails to recognize the *political equality* of all citizens; hence it is disrespectful to her fellow citizens. If it would be disrespectful for the state to enact a given law, it is disrespectful for a citizen to direct the state to enact it. Hence advocacy for laws that are supportable only with strictly religious reasons is disrespectful.

We may say, then, that citizenship respect requires us not only to *pursue* accessible justifications for the laws we advocate, but to *succeed* at finding such justifications. To do otherwise would be to permit ourselves to impose on our fellow citizens moral requirements that they need have no internal reason to acknowledge. Again, that would be to treat our compatriots as mere subjects of legislation, not as citizens. In short, respect requires restraint.

Eberle has addressed this kind of view. Gaus runs a version of the argument above, claiming that "in order to make genuine moral demands on others . . . you must show that, somehow, their system [of beliefs] yields reasons to embrace your demand."[62] Against Gaus, Eberle denies that moral blame is appropriately assigned only when the purportedly blameworthy agent could be regarded as having a reason *of his own* for satisfying the moral obligation in question.

Eberle argues by means of two cases. First, Jeffrey is "incapable of controlling his urge to torture his fellow human beings," and thus is unable to resist violating the moral demand to not torture. Eberle claims that we should not blame Jeffrey for torturing, but we nonetheless "should impose on Jeffrey and others like him our moral demand that citizens not be tortured." Second, Jill is "incapable of forming the concept of genocide," and consequently moral obligations to not participate in genocide cannot be justified to her.[63] Eberle contends that we nonetheless ought to hold Jill to the moral obligation to not engage in genocide.[64]

Eberle takes the case of Jeffrey to show that it can be appropriate to impose a moral requirement on someone who cannot satisfy it, and the case of Jill to show that it can be morally appropriate to impose a moral requirement on another who is incapable of appreciating the reasons that support it. Eberle takes himself to have thus provided counterexamples to the view that the imposition of moral requirements is appropriate only when they are justifiable to those upon whom they are imposed.

But I do not see how these are counterexamples. Consider Jill. Eberle claims that, but for her "serious moral blind spot," she is "an ordinary moral agent."[65] It is hard to see how someone lacking the ability to form the concept of genocide could be "an ordinary moral agent"; in fact, it is hard to see what we are being asked to imagine. Does Jill have the concept of mass murder? Does she have the concept of an ethnic or cultural group? Does she have the concept of mass murder for the purpose of ridding a particular location of a particular group? It seems that someone having these further concepts would be able to form the concept of genocide. But if she does lack these concepts, it is hard to see how Jill could be "an ordinary moral agent." At the very least, Jill is not a moral person with respect to genocide. We impose the requirement to not participate in genocide, and this requirement indeed has *moral content*, but, for Jill, it cannot be a *moral* requirement; with respect to genocide, Jill is rightly regarded as a mere subject of legislation. The same goes for Jeffrey. Insofar as Jeffrey and Jill are *impaired moral agents*, they do not serve as counterexamples.[66]

Perhaps Eberle does not mean for these cases to be taken as counterexamples, but to function simply as examples of a different view of how agency and blame are related.[67] Maybe there is a viable view of these matters that permits us to impose moral requirements on those who cannot abide by them or cannot grasp the justification for them. But it is difficult to imagine how a conception of justified state coercion that adopted such a view could be a *liberal* conception.

Before moving on, it should be noted that under justificatory liberalism, just as under Eberle's liberalism of conscientious engagement, citizens like Betty are likely to suffer terrible conflicts of conscience. But liberalism does not guarantee a life of moral serenity. And justificatory liberalism permits quite a lot. For example, it allows Betty to publicly express her agapic pacifism, to publicly condemn war, and to participate in peace movements. She may organize, demonstrate, protest, and petition against war, argue for special accommodation concerning how her taxes are spent, and so on. Justificatory liberalism requires only that she refrain from advocating for Amendment Twenty-Eight or for any other policies that can be justified only on exclusively religious grounds. If Betty simply cannot abide this requirement, one wonders whether she would be able to regard any democratic law that conflicts with her agapic pacifism as morally binding.[68] Perhaps in the end Betty is incapable of responsible citizenship. Yet even in this case, if she confines her behavior to what is *legally* permitted, there is really nothing the justificatory liberal can do beyond holding her morally blameworthy. And surely from Betty's perspective *that* is not the end of the world.

WAS RAWLS RIGHT AFTER ALL?

Thus far, I have argued that Eberle's ideal of conscientious engagement would engender conflicts of conscience that are perhaps more severe than those occasioned by the Doctrine of Restraint. Moreover, I have proposed an identifiably liberal conception of respect that requires both the Principle of Pursuit and the Doctrine of Restraint. Admittedly, I have not provided arguments for such citizen respect in this chapter. But arguments are easy to anticipate: citizen respect captures core liberal thoughts about citizenship, equality, and democracy; and it also comports well with familiar Strawsonian[69] intuitions about moral responsibility, agency, and blame. Perhaps more importantly, citizen respect accommodates the liberal thought that respect is internally tied to representative and accountable government; that is, citizen respect is able to capture the core liberal commitment that there is something *intrinsically* disrespectful about, say, monarchy.[70]

There is certainly a lot more to say, and I have in the course of this chapter left many important matters hanging. But I want to conclude by taking up a different matter. Although I have avoided adopting the Rawlsian nomenclature, it should be clear that the version of justificatory liberalism I have proposed is closely allied with the mainline Rawlsian view. Consider that, in developing the idea of citizen respect, I have appealed to the idea of a kind of reason that is *intrinsic* to liberal democracy, and correspondingly to a kind of reason that citizens in their public roles must recognize as *relevant* to public decision-making; I called reasons of this kind "internal" reasons for liberal citizens. To resolutely reject the relevance of such a reason is to call into question one's fitness for liberal democratic citizenship. This view of internal reasons for liberal citizens finds its Rawlsian analogue in the terms upon which the overlapping consensus that Rawls proposed is based. As is well known, Rawls envisioned a collection of principles, norms, and values that could be recognized from within any reasonable liberal comprehensive doctrine. An individual who insists that some other kind of reason should be decisive in deciding a matter of basic justice is, according to Rawls, ipso facto unreasonable and thus not a member in good standing of a liberal society. So my distinction between internal and noninternal reasons for citizens tracks Rawls's distinction between public and nonpublic reasons.

Now, the Rawlsian view is often criticized for being too vague and loose when it comes to what look like hard cases. But it seems to me, and the position I have developed above would allow, that vagueness and looseness are *precisely* what one should want when it comes to the hard cases. Remember that the point of justificatory liberalism is to specify in broad terms how citizens should go about their public deliberations; the point is *not* to provide a framework that itself decides the hard cases or renders certain kinds of public arguments moot. That Rawlsian public reason, or my own conception of internal reasons for citizens, might leave crucial policy questions undetermined is to be expected, and should be a welcome feature of the views. In such hard cases, our popular deliberations must surely appeal to reasons that would otherwise look like reasons of the wrong kind. Justificatory liberalism requires simply that such measures be taken only when public reasons run out; we must do our best *despite* the unavailability of decisive public reasons. Thus it seems to me perfectly in keeping with justificatory liberalism to say that the following kind of consideration is itself a public reason of sorts: "We must decide a policy with respect to X, but our public reasons have run out; what other kinds of reasons can be brought to bear on the matter?"

This raises the related issue of Rawls's insistence that the requirements of public reason apply only in contexts where we must decide matters of "basic justice" and "constitutional essentials."[71] I do not here have the space to provide anything approaching a full account, but it makes sense to think about coercive acts as falling on a spectrum of severity, ranging from coercive acts that force people to do what they would not otherwise do, to coercive acts that force people to do what they do not want to do, to coercive acts that force people to do what they think they should not have to do, to coercive acts that force people to do what they think is wrong to do, and so on. We should also think of coercive acts in terms of their different degrees of irretrievability. That is, for coercive acts and policies, we should ask, "How difficult would it be to repeal this policy should it turn out to be seriously flawed?" and "How severe would the damage be to those who are wronged by it?"

With these two dimensions of evaluation in place, we can easily envision a scheme in which the requirements of public reason become increasingly more stringent as the severity and irretrievability of the proposed coercion rise. It seems likely that matters of basic justice and constitutional essentials are likely to involve severe and highly irretrievable coercion; accordingly, such matters should be decided on the basis of strictly public reasons, if possible. Other matters involving less severe forms of coercion and allowing for easier retrieval can be decided on the basis of a looser set of reasons. Perhaps there are cases in which the coercion is so mild and easily retrieved that the question of what kinds of reasons are appropriate does not really matter. The point, I take it, is simply that when liberal democratic states or communities impose on some citizens especially onerous coercion or enact coercive policies that would be difficult to retrieve should they turn out to be flawed, they should deal only in public reasons.

Once again, there is a lot more to say. But I take it that these points are much in the spirit of the original Rawlsian program, and they are easily accommodated in the version of justificatory liberalism I have sketched in this chapter. If I am correct to think that the view I have proposed is roughly equivalent to the original Rawlsian view, then it seems to me that, on the question of religion in politics, Rawls was right after all.

Notes

1. "Justificatory liberalism" was introduced by Gerald Gaus as the name of his own view. See Gaus, *Justificatory Liberalism* (New York: Oxford University Press, 1996). I follow Christopher Eberle in applying the term to cover the full range of recent liberalisms inspired by the later Rawls. See Eberle, *Religious Conviction in Liberal Politics* (Cambridge: Cambridge University Press, 2002), 339n34; and Eberle, "Basic Human Worth and Religious Restraint," *Philosophy and Social Criticism* 35 (2009), 151–81. Gaus now uses the term in this broad way. See Gerald Gaus and Kevin Vallier, "The Roles of Religious Conviction in a Publicly Justified Policy," *Philosophy and Social Criticism* 35 (2009): 51–76.

2. That my discussion is *internal* to liberalism also means that the critics I will be engaging with are *religious liberals*; I am not concerned here with the arguments of antiliberal philosophers and theologians.

3. *LHPP* 13.

4. John Stuart Mill, *On Liberty, and Other Essays* (New York: Oxford University Press, 1991), 13.

5. Mill's view is in fact much more complicated than this, given that he thinks liberty is owed only to persons who already have certain capacities. See ibid., 15. But the complications need not detain us here.

6. Jeremy Waldron, *Liberal Rights* (Cambridge: Cambridge University Press, 1993), 37.

7. See Plato, *Crito*, 50d–51c.

8. One could argue, of course, that this justificatory element is present in all liberalisms from Locke onward. And this is surely correct. The difference in the end is one of emphasis and priority.

9. *IPRR* 766.

10. Charles Larmore, *The Autonomy of Morality* (Cambridge: Cambridge University Press, 2008), 214.

11. Colin Bird, "Mutual Respect and Neutral Justification," *Ethics* 107 (1996): 62–96. Gaus and Vallier, "The Roles of Religious Conviction," 57.

12. David Estlund, *Democratic Authority* (Princeton: Princeton University Press, 2008), 43.

13. Thomas Nagel, "Moral Conflict and Political Legitimacy," *Philosophy and Public Affairs* 16 (1987): 221.

14. Stephen Macedo, "In Defense of Liberal Public Reason," in *Natural Law and Public Reason*, ed. R. P. George and C. Wolfe (Washington, D.C.: Georgetown University Press, 2000), 13.

15. Robert Audi, "Liberal Democracy and the Place of Religion in Politics," in *Religion in the Public Square*, ed. R. Audi and N. Wolterstorff (Lanham, Md.: Rowman and Littlefield, 1997), 17.

16. Paul Weithman, "Religion and the Liberalism of Reasoned Respect," in *Religion and Contemporary Liberalism*, ed. P. Weithman (Notre Dame: University of Notre Dame Press, 1997), 6. For critical discussion of these different senses of accessibility, see James Bohman and Henry Richardson, "Liberalism, Deliberative Democracy, and 'Reasons All Can Accept,'" *Journal of Political Philosophy* 17 (2009): 253–74.

17. See especially Macedo, "In Defense of Liberal Public Reason."

18. Cf. Audi, "Liberal Democracy," 17; Audi, *Religious Commitment and Secular Reason* (Cambridge: Cambridge University Press, 2002); Gaus, *Justificatory Liberalism*, 144; and Jürgen Habermas, "Religion in the Public Sphere," *European Journal of Philosophy* 14 (2006): 1–25. Larmore objects to the idea that accessible reasons should be characterized as "secular," in Larmore, *Autonomy of Morality*, 212ff.

19. See especially *IPRR* 765.

20. See especially Audi, "Liberal Democracy."

21. See Michael Perry, *Under God?* (Cambridge: Cambridge University Press, 2003), 13.

22. *PL* (exp.) 36.

23. See *PL* (exp.) 36.

24. For a clear discussion of the connection between respect and the fact of reasonable pluralism, see Stephen Macedo, "Liberal Civic Education and Religious Fundamentalism: The Case of God v. John Rawls?," *Ethics* 105 (1995): 474ff. See also Amy Gutmann and Dennis Thompson, "Moral Conflict and Political Consensus," *Ethics* 101 (1990): 64–88; and Gaus and Vallier, "The Roles of Religious Conviction," 54–55.

25. Things get murkier still when we consider the activity of public officials; I leave these complications to the side.

26. Yet Gerald Gaus disagrees. See Gaus, "The Place of Religious Belief in Public Reason Liberalism," in *Multiculturalism and Moral Conflict*, ed. M. Dimovia-Cookson and P. M. R. Stirk (London: Routledge, 2009), 19–37.

27. The difference no doubt has to do with the fact that when Abby wrongfully advocates, no one is coerced. The matter becomes more complicated when we introduce the consideration that no particular citizen's vote determines a democratic outcome.

28. *PL* (exp.) 217.

29. Complications arise once we consider that advocacy can have a significant expressive or symbolic component. Moreover, Rawls thought that the constraints of public reason apply only when "matters of basic justice" and "constitutional essentials" are at stake. *PL* (exp.) 214.

30. Hence Nicholas Wolterstorff insists that "it belongs to the religious convictions of a good many religious people in our society that they ought to base their decisions concerning fundamental issues of justice on their religious convictions." Wolterstorff, "The Role of Religion in Decision and Discussion of Political Issues," in *Religion in the Public Square*, ed. R. Audi and N. Wolterstorff (Lanham, Md.: Rowman and Littlefield,

1997), 19. Kent Greenawalt too writes that "the implicit demand that people try to compartmentalize beliefs that constitute some kind of unity in their approach to life is positively objectionable." Greenawalt, *Religious Convictions and Political Choice* (New York: Oxford University Press, 1988), 155. Ronald Dworkin claims of many Americans that "their religious convictions are political principles." Dworkin, *Is Democracy Possible Here?* (Princeton: Princeton University Press, 2006), 64.

31. Eberle, *Religious Conviction*, 145.

32. Further, in placing restrictions on what kinds of reasons are admissible, the justificatory liberal appears to have "fixed" the rules of democratic legislation in favor of certain outcomes. As many have observed, the force of the prolife case is greatly diminished when strictly religious reasons are deemed nonjustificatory. And so, to many religious believers, the restrictions imposed by justificatory liberalism seem unfair and dismissive of religious conviction. In a fateful note in *Political Liberalism*, Rawls contends that "it would go against the ideal of public reason if we voted from a comprehensive doctrine which denied" the rights specified in *Roe v. Wade*. *PL* (exp.) 244. Naturally, this has drawn fire from Thomist philosophers, like Robert George and Christopher Wolfe, who liken the task of Rawlsian public justification to "playing a game with loaded dice." George and Wolfe, *Natural Law and Public Reason*, 66. Feminist and radical democrats have joined with the Thomists on this issue; they claim that the Rawlsian constraints codify existing arrangements and thereby exclude more radical views. See Seyla Benhabib, "Towards a Deliberative Model of Democratic Legitimacy," in *Democracy and Difference*, ed. S. Benhabib (Princeton: Princeton University Press, 1996), 67–94; Nancy Frazer, "Rethinking the Public Sphere," in *Habermas and the Public Sphere*, ed. C. Calhoun (Cambridge, Mass.: MIT Press, 1992), 109–42; and Iris Marion Young, *Inclusion and Democracy* (New York: Oxford University Press, 2000), chap. 1.

33. Macedo, "In Defense of Liberal Public Reason," 35.

34. Christopher Eberle, "Basic Human Worth and Religious Restraint," *Philosophy and Social Criticism* 35 (2009): 152.

35. See Paul Weithman, *Religion and the Obligations of Citizenship* (Cambridge: Cambridge University Press, 2002), 1.

36. Eberle, "Basic Human Worth," 153.

37. Ibid., 154.

38. See, for instance, Michael Perry, "Religion as a Basis of Law-Making?" *Philosophy and Social Criticism* 35 (2009): 114.

39. See Christopher Eberle, "What Respect Requires—and What It Does Not," *Wake Forest Law Review* 36 (2001): 305–51; Eberle, Religious Conviction; "Religious Reasons in Public," *St. John's Journal of Legal Commentary* 22 (2007): 431–43; Eberle, "Basic Human Worth"; and Eberle, "Respect and War: Against the Standard View of Religion in Politics," chapter 1 in this volume. Similar arguments can be found in Micah Lott, "Restraint on Reasons and Reasons for Restraint," *Pacific Philosophical Quarterly* 87 (2006): 75–95.

40. Eberle, *Religious Conviction*, 68. Cf. Eberle, "Basic Human Worth," 167–68; and Eberle, "Religious Reasons," 437ff.

41. I will not supply the documentation here. See Eberle, *Religious Conviction*, 68ff.

42. Gaus, *Justificatory Liberalism*, 162.

43. Eberle, "Basic Human Worth," 168.

44. Cliffordian evidentialism may seem to propose something like this; but the justificatory liberal's view is stronger than evidentialism. For the justificatory liberal holds that even when a law is fully justified rationally from your own point of view, you may be required to refrain from advocating for it simply because you are not able to justify it to others. Were evidentialism this strong, it would surely be the kind of view only a skeptic could love.

45. Perry, *Under God?*, 48.

46. Eberle, *Religious Conviction*, 86. Cf. Stephen Darwall, "Two Kinds of Respect," *Ethics* 88 (1977): 36–49, on "recognition" respect.

47. Eberle, "Religious Reasons," 437.

48. Eberle, *Religious Conviction*, 104ff.

49. Rational justification is, according to Eberle, a "radically perspectival phenomenon": "whether a citizen is rationally justified in adhering to B depends, at least in part, on his point of view—on the evidence to which he has access by pursuing the appropriate procedures, on the assumptions with which he conducts his inquiry, and so on." Eberle, *Religious Conviction*, 62.

50. Eberle, "Basic Human Worth," 165. This is what makes Eberle's view not radically inclusive.

51. Ibid., 166. See Eberle, *Religious Conviction*, 104ff., for a more detailed account.

52. Eberle, "Basic Human Worth," 157.

53. Ibid., 159.

54. Ibid., 160.

55. Ibid.

56. Eberle concedes that Satanists could achieve a sufficiently high level of rational justification for their religious beliefs; he says it would be "bad faith" to deny that they could. Eberle, *Religious Conviction*, 250.

57. Eberle, "Religious Reasons," 437.

58. See James Boettcher, "Strong Inclusionist Accounts of the Role of Religion in Political Decision-Making," *Journal of Social Philosophy* 36 (2005): 497–516; Boettcher, "Respect, Recognition, and Public Reason," *Social Theory and Practice* 33 (2007): 223–49; and Martha Nussbaum, *Liberty of Conscience* (New York: Basic Books, 2008), 361ff.

59. Bernard Williams, *Moral Luck* (Cambridge: Cambridge University Press, 1981), 101–13.

60. A similar argument is found in Gaus, *Justificatory Liberalism*; and James Sterba, "Reconciling Public Reason and Religious Values," *Social Theory and Practice* 25 (1999): 1–28.

61. Gaus, *Justificatory Liberalism*, 124.

62. Ibid., 126.

63. Eberle, *Religious Conviction*, 133.

64. Ibid.

65. Ibid.

66. Moreover, if the suggestion is that Betty must see her non-agapic-pacifist compatriots as persons who are impaired as moral agents, then the proper conclusion seems to be that Betty is incapable of seeing her fellow citizens as equals.

67. Eberle claims that his understanding of the "relations between moral impositions, culpability, and justification" is "very different from Gaus's." Eberle, *Religious Conviction*, 133.

68. Gerald Gaus, "Review of Christopher Eberle, *Religious Conviction in Liberal Politics*." *Notre Dame Philosophical Reviews*, http://ndpr.nd.edu/review.cfm?id=1214.

69. P. F. Strawson, *Freedom and Resentment, and Other Essays* (New York: Routledge, 2008).

70. Note that it is easy to imagine a dictator meeting Eberle's ideal of conscientious engagement.

71. *PL* (exp.) 214.

3

Inclusivism, Stability, and Assurance

PAUL WEITHMAN

Religion is one of the most potent political forces in the contemporary world. Its power is evident in popular movements of discontent with existing institutions, including but not only terrorist and revolutionary expressions of discontent. It is evident in the ways that rulers and regimes try to demonstrate their legitimacy so as to secure the moral support of those who live under them. In many parts of the world, it is evident in the ways that the power to make political decisions is allocated among a society's constituent groups and in the content of the different legal codes to which members of the same polity are subject. In the United States, its power is evident in some of the ways that candidates appeal to voters, in some of the constituencies that are courted, and in some of the reasons for which votes are cast.

Not all of these manifestations of religion's political power touch on the subject of this chapter, which will focus on *citizenship* and religion. Whatever else citizens are, they are persons to whom those who hold political office are accountable, in a robust sense of "accountable." Their accountability to citizens is a matter not merely of prudence or good politics, but of political morality, which is worked out or discovered by philosophical reflections on political life. Citizenship, which I have just said is one of the concepts of political morality, is therefore a concept that is defined by political philosophy.

Once we see that one of the conditions of citizenship is the in principle accountability of office-holders, and once we see *why* those in office are accountable to citizens, it is clear that not all regime-types have citizens. Indeed, not even all regime-types that are decent and legitimate have citizens. Some such regime-types have subjects. But whatever may be true of other regime-types, the liberal democracies of political theory have citizens. Actual liberal democracies are largely made up of persons who should be treated as, and should behave as, citizens.

Liberal democracies, both ideal and actual, shall be my concern here. And so I shall begin by saying something about liberal democratic citizenship. This will enable me to look at arguments for norms of citizenship, including norms concerning appeals to religion in politics. Some philosophers have endorsed what might be called "exclusivist" norms, according to which citizens should not appeal to religious considerations at all in public deliberations. These philosophers generally appeal to the danger religion poses to the moral quality of public life or to political stability. Philosophers who oppose exclusivism still give considerations of civility and stability some weight. But some of them deny that this weight is sufficient to justify restrictions on public debate, and others endorse what might be called "restrictive inclusivism," according to which citizens may appeal to religious considerations in public debate, subject to restrictions that they consider sufficient to meet the concerns of exclusivists.

John Rawls developed the most influential such norms in his treatment of public reasoning and I shall pay special attention to his arguments. Rawls is sometimes read as an exclusivist. But though he was once drawn to exclusivism, he rejected that position and endorsed a sophisticated version of restrictive inclusivism instead. What makes Rawls's view especially sophisticated—and especially instructive—is that although he ostensibly shares other philosophers' concerns with mutual trust, civility, and stability, his understanding of these values and his treatment of public reasoning are ultimately motivated by a set of problems that arises from within his own theory of justice. As we shall see, Rawls's arguments connect norms of public reasoning with the need to solve an assurance problem in his ideally just society, which he calls "the well-ordered society." The assurance problem arises because the well-ordered society would enjoy not just stability, but stability of a privileged kind, which Rawls eventually referred to as "stability for the right reasons." That kind of stability requires that citizens be assured of one another's acceptance of a public conception of justice, such as Rawls's own conception of justice as fairness.

Rawls's norms of public reason are sometimes criticized for what are said to be their immediate and unwelcome implications for ongoing political discussion. Seeing the context of Rawls's discussion of public reason, we can see that these criticisms are misplaced. The recontextualization of Rawls's treatment also raises questions about what, if any, relevance that treatment has for those of us who live in societies that are not well-ordered. I shall conclude by taking up some of those questions.

LIBERAL DEMOCRATIC CITIZENSHIP AS STATUS AND ROLE

It is useful to think of citizenship as both a status and a role. Thinking of citizenship as a status conveys the fact that citizenship confers an identity that may be a source of pride, an identity in virtue of which one is entitled to press certain demands on those who administer society's governing apparatus. Under the influence of the British sociologist T. H. Marshall, the status of citizenship has sometimes been described as the status of full membership in one's society.[1] Marshall's way of thinking about citizenship in this way is suggestive and illuminating.

It is plain that people struggle for certain concomitants of citizenship, such as employment, the right to vote, or greater control over means of production, to gain greater social, political, and economic security. Thinking of citizenship as full membership adds an additional dimension to our understanding of these struggles. Full membership in an organization is distinguished from the statuses of associate membership and nonmembership, in part by the possession of certain rights and privileges. The struggle by excluded classes and groups to secure the rights and privileges of citizenship can be understood as a struggle to secure goods that are valued in part because they are indicators of full membership.[2]

Furthermore, full members participate in an organization in a way that others do not. The rights and privileges of membership are therefore enabling conditions. By likening citizenship to membership, Marshall in effect reminds us of points that have also been stressed in recent Catholic social thought. Citizens are participants in the common goods of their society.[3] Participation in those goods on a footing of equality has enabling conditions. Part of the argument for extending certain rights and privileges to members of previously excluded groups is that doing so is necessary if people are to be equal participants in the common good.

I shall simply assume that liberal democratic political morality does not allow states to tie full membership to religious convictions. That is, I shall assume that liberal democracy requires that citizens have certain rights and privileges, such as the right to hold office, the right to influence political outcomes through voting and participation, the right to publish one's opinions, and the right of access to impartial courts. And I assume that these rights and privileges should be enjoyed equally by all citizens regardless of their convictions, that citizens should be able to change their religious convictions without losing them, and that religious opinions ought not to be grounds for denying citizenship to someone who wants it. Whatever problems and puzzles religion raises for citizenship, I take these assumptions about the status of citizenship to be uncontroversial.

It is also useful to think of citizenship as a role. By that, I mean that there are certain activities that are characteristic of citizenship. Seeing what these activities are helps us to characterize citizenship or to say what it is. The role of citizenship is functional. When citizens engage—or at least when they engage well—in the activities that are characteristic of their role, they contribute to the functioning of a larger whole. That they make this contribution is what gives the characteristic activities their point. That larger whole is, of course, political society. And so the role of citizenship is a political role and its characteristic activities are political activities.

As I have already hinted, I am concerned with citizenship in a liberal democracy under modern conditions. The characteristic activities of liberal democratic citizenship are those that make for participation in democratic decision-making: discussion and voting, as well as agitating, protesting, and advocating. Not everyone who occupies the role of citizen will engage in these activities or will perform them well. But when someone in the role does engage in those activities, and does so well, she is playing or doing her part. The citizen's role is hedged in by obligations, prohibitions, and permissions. There are qualities of character that dispose incumbents to stay within the hedgerows, and to perform the characteristic activities of citizenship better. These qualities that dispose someone to perform her role well are the virtues of citizenship.

Thinking about citizenship as a role might seem to bear most directly on the subject of this chapter, for it is this way of thinking about citizenship that seems to raise many of the most interesting normative questions about the place of religion in politics. Those questions have attracted a great deal of philosophical attention. In particular, philosophers have asked what obligations citizens are under with respect to reliance on religious considerations in voting and in defending or criticizing laws and policies in public discussion. It is in this connection that the public reliance on religion is sometimes said to be forbidden because it is inherently uncivil or disruptive.

These are charges I want to examine, but first I want to point out that the first way of thinking of citizenship is of considerable interest as well. I have already noted that full membership in liberal democracies has certain enabling conditions. Should society itself bring it about that those conditions are satisfied? The answer depends upon what the enabling conditions are. The attempt to identify those conditions and to answer the question can raise questions about religion, politics, and citizenship.

Religious organizations can sometimes help to satisfy the enabling conditions by helping citizens develop some of the skills and habits of participation. But religion and religious organizations may oppose the satisfaction of other conditions that are said to be enabling. It is sometimes argued, for example, that women can be full members of liberal democracies, able to participate on a footing of equality with men, only if they can manage the demands of child-care and hence can control their fertility. This is said to require their access to legal abortions.[4] Or it may be said that wearing the burkha, even voluntarily, is incompatible with women's political equality, or that the religious teaching that women have a natural vocation for homemaking is incompatible with it. I hope I have said enough to indicate why I think the first way of thinking about citizenship raises very hard normative problems, although I shall not be able to take them up in this chapter.

THE ROLE OF CITIZENSHIP
AND ITS OBLIGATIONS

As I noted, many philosophers who have studied problems raised by the second way of thinking about citizenship, problems about the ethics of political participation by ordinary citizens, have endorsed exclusionist or restrictive inclusivist positions. The arguments for these positions are sometimes premised on the assumption that religion is disruptive or is inherently uncivil, or they rely on our intuitions about what could or does happen if citizens rely on religious conviction in political argument or act for religious reasons.[5]

There are, I think, several problems with these arguments. Consider first the argument according to which appeal to religious reasons should be excluded or restricted because reliance on such reasons in public debate is inherently uncivil, an exercise in incivility. This argument suffers from—and perhaps plays upon—an ambiguity in the word "incivility" and its cognates. In one way, to describe some behavior as an instance of incivility is to say that it is behavior that is inconsistent with or not befitting someone who is a *civis*, who occupies the role of a citizen. This charge presupposes that the norms governing behavior in that role are already in hand and so it cannot be used to ground those norms without circularity.

But in ordinary English usage, to describe behavior as exemplifying incivility can be to describe it as an instance of rudeness or impoliteness. If we assume that citizens should treat one another politely, then—if reliance on religion is indeed uncivil in this sense of the word—it would follow that citizens ought not rely on religion. But we cannot simply assume that the antecedent of the conditional is true. We need to know what relations among fellow citizens should be like, what treatment the dignity of that status merits, what civic friendship demands, and what "politely" means. In sum, we need to know a good deal about the role of citizenship and its norms *before* we can assume or grant that citizens should treat one another politely. The norms of citizenship are, however, what the argument is supposed to *deliver*. The argument gives the appearance of delivering them only by first taking "incivility" in one way, as meaning "impoliteness," and then assuming that impoliteness exemplifies the other meaning of "incivility," namely, "conduct unbecoming of someone who has the role of citizen."

Consider now the allegation that reliance on religion is somehow impolite, and so will engender mutual distrust among citizens. This accusation belongs to a family of charges according to which reliance on religion has bad consequences. Stronger members of the family hold that religion can lead to institutional instability and civil unrest. These are, of course, empirical predictions. In the large democracies of the West they do not seem especially plausible, at least without lots of qualifications regarding what positions religion is used to advocate, what religions are involved, and what the religious history of a given society is.

Because I think arguments from incivility are badly flawed, I do not think that they constitute the best defenses of the exclusivist or restrictive inclusivist position nor, indeed, are they the best way to understand what motivates the position in its most plausible form. On my reading, some kind of restrictive inclusivism is most plausibly presented as the upshot or requirement of a sophisticated Rawlsian framework. While Rawls is sometimes read as relying on the premise that public appeals to religion in political argument are inherently uncivil or destabilizing,[6] I do not think he subscribes to the argument I have just criticized.

But the claim that he relies on that argument is understandable. On my reading, Rawls both early and late was concerned to show that the terms of cooperation in an ideally just liberal democracy would enjoy a privileged form of stability. In his early work, thinking that stability would inhere in the terms of cooperation, he referred to that form of stability as "inherent stability."[7] Later, as his view developed in *Political Liberalism*, he referred to it as "stability for the right reasons."[8] Terms of cooperation will enjoy that privileged form of stability only if ordinary citizens, who do not hold political office, honor and are known to honor restrictions that Rawls made less and less demanding over a ten-year period beginning in the late 1980s.

What distinguishes the argument I impute to Rawls from the form of argument I just criticized is that the stability with which Rawls is concerned is not institutional stability, but stability of the terms of

cooperation. And so his argument, unlike the argument I just criticized, does not turn on the claim that public appeal to religion will
or may destabilize social institutions. It turns on the very different
claim that if citizens generally violate his guidelines of public reasoning, then the terms of cooperation among them may not be affirmed
for the right reasons.

The difference matters. For under nonideal conditions—indeed,
perhaps *especially* under nonideal conditions—it seems plausible that
we should refrain from behavior that will destabilize basic institutions. But under nonideal conditions, it is far less clear that we should
refrain from behavior of a type that would, were it generally engaged
in in an ideally just society, bring it about that the terms of cooperation in that society were stable for less than ideal reasons. The latter
claim is, I think, much less plausible and not one that Rawls endorses.
And it enables us to see the many complexities of questions about
appeal to religion in public political argument.

JOHN RAWLS AND
RESTRICTIVE INCLUSIVISM

I indicated above that Rawls endorses guidelines of public reasoning because he thinks that honoring those guidelines is necessary if
terms of cooperation in a well-ordered society are to be inherently stable.[9] I want to lay out Rawls's view because when we see what he was
really trying to do, we can see that his view does not have—nor was it
intended to have—the immediate implications for our own, nonideal
world that it is often taken to have. That in itself is, I hope, an interesting and important result. To see how Rawls's argument goes, it will
be useful to recall what the terms of cooperation are and how they are
arrived at.

I have stressed that citizenship is a role, defined or specified by political theory. As part of the specification of that role, citizens as such are
said to have certain interests that political society is to advance and
in the name of which public officials are accountable. Society advances
those interests justly if terms of cooperation are fair. One of Rawls's key
insights is, of course, that fair terms of cooperation are identified by
seeing what citizens would agree to as free, equal, and rational persons.

That those terms are adopted in the original position is supposed to show that when basic institutions conform to them, and when citizens take them as regulative, they live as free equals. That the terms are unanimously adopted is supposed to show that they are collectively rational. Collectively rational terms of cooperation should allow citizens to securely enjoy the conditions those terms establish so that they can make their plans accordingly. Security comes from knowing that the conditions demanded by the principles will be honored, so that certain questions—about what rights citizens enjoy and what range of inequalities are permitted—are permanently off the political agenda. Security therefore requires that the agreement reached in the original position be stable over time; an agreement on collectively rational terms would be for naught if the agreement would soon break down.

Rawls argued, very interestingly and very powerfully, that citizens who live under just institutions would develop a corresponding sense of justice, a regulative desire to accept the authority of the principles of justice and the lower-order values and principles that guide their implementation.[10] But in addition to having a sense of justice, each citizen has a conception of her own good. That each citizen has such a conception opens the possibility that she will think honoring the terms of cooperation, as well as being a just person, is not good for her. Thus terms that are collectively rational might not be individually rational. And so the rational thing for each individual to do may be to defect from terms of cooperation. And if each thinks others will defect, then each will think it rational to defect preemptively, so that society is not regulated by terms of cooperation. If this problem is to be averted, and if terms of cooperation are to be stabilized, individuals' conceptions of the good must support—or, in Rawls's terms, be "congruent" with—the principles of justice,[11] so that compliance with the terms of cooperation is individually rational. But the individual rationality of compliance is not enough. If preemptive defection is to be avoided, the fact that each citizen recognizes the individual rationality of compliance must itself be a matter of public knowledge. In sum, each must have some assurance that others accept the terms of cooperation and will not defect.

What Rawls faced, then, is the threat that terms of cooperation which are collectively rational will be destabilized by a generalized prisoner's dilemma.[12] But this was not Rawls's problem alone. The first great English-speaking political philosopher of the modern period, Thomas Hobbes, faced this threat and proposed a two-part way of averting it. Hobbes argued for an absolute sovereign who alters his subjects' payoffs by attaching severe enough punishment to defections that it is no longer in the individual's interest to defect. Public knowledge that the sovereign does this solves the assurance problem, and society is stable.[13]

The Hobbesian way of averting the threat of instability is clearly undesirable. One problem, pointed out by John Locke, is that it is not clear that an absolute sovereign solves the decision problem of the social contract. It may be that rational individuals would prefer the no-agreement point, that is, the state of nature. And even if the institution of an absolute sovereign does solve the problem, the solution is not a desirable one. For it would clearly be better if terms of cooperation were honored freely. If they are honored freely, in the appropriate sense of "free," then terms of cooperation are stable, and stable for the right reasons.

Showing how the threat of the generalized prisoner's dilemma can be averted, as well as showing how terms of cooperation arrived at in the original position can be stable for the right reasons, requires showing that there is some other way to do the two things that Hobbes's sovereign does. Specifically, it requires showing how each person's payoff tables can be made such that cooperation rather than defection is in her interest, and it requires showing how the assurance problem can be solved so that each knows others will not defect. On my reading, Rawls was deeply concerned with these two problems. In his later work, he adopted a distinctive and original answer to the first problem, in the form of an overlapping consensus. He endorsed qualified inclusivism to help answer the second. Thus if I am right, Rawls endorses qualified inclusivist norms of public reason to solve the assurance problem, avert the threat of a generalized prisoner's dilemma, and show how justice as fairness can be stable for the right reasons.

Let me now try to explain this reading. When an overlapping consensus on a political conception of justice obtains, Rawls says, "reasonable doctrines endorse the political conception, each from its own point of view."[14] So when an overlapping consensus obtains, utilitarianism provides Millian reasons for endorsing the political conception, deontology provides Kantian reasons, and Catholicism provides reasons rooted in its theological doctrine. If we assume that each citizen endorses her comprehensive doctrine and takes the reasons it provides as reasons for her, then when an overlapping consensus obtains, each citizen has reason to *affirm* the terms of cooperation from within her own comprehensive view. But are these reasons strong enough to stabilize the terms of cooperation? More precisely, do they provide each person with sufficient reason not to defect from the terms of cooperation?

To answer these questions, we need to recall what reasonable comprehensive doctrines endorse a political conception of justice, and terms of cooperation, *for*. In a well-ordered society, the public conception of justice provides a "common point of view"[15] or a "unified perspective"[16] from which the settlements of citizens' competing claims are "adjudicated."[17] Philosophical points of view are defined by rules of reasoning and information drawn on by those who occupy them. When Rawls says that the public conception of justice provides a point of view for "adjudicat[ing]" citizens' competing claims, I take it he means the conception furnishes values and principles on the basis of which questions of basic justice are to be settled and rules of reasoning for moving from those values and principles to a settlement. For citizens to "acknowledge" their "common point of view"[18] is for them to acknowledge that political outcomes are justifiable only if they can be supported by the values and principles of the political conception. Just citizens, who accept the terms of cooperation, regulate the claims they make by those values and principles. They refrain from pressing for more than they think those terms would allow them.

Adhering to the terms of cooperation thus requires that we sometimes act against our own interests or our own conception of the good. That is why justice can be costly. The costs can be especially high if no one else is adhering to terms of cooperation, or if only a small number are. The potential costs have implications for what someone's comprehensive doctrine gives him sufficient reason to do even when an overlapping consensus obtains. When there is such a consensus, each person has sufficient reason to adhere to terms of cooperation only when he has good reason to believe that others will adhere to them as well. To put the point in terms I used above, when an overlapping consensus obtains, each person's payoff table has the following structure: the payoffs are such that it is rational for a person to honor the terms of cooperation and treat the political conception of justice as authoritative only when she has the assurance that all others, or a sufficient number of others, also adhere to the terms and treat the conception as authoritative. Thus even if an overlapping consensus obtains, Rawls cannot show that terms of cooperation would be stable for the right reasons until he solves an assurance problem.

How is that problem to be solved? How can each person gain the assurance that others regard the terms of cooperation as authoritative? The game-theoretic details are surprisingly complicated and I shall skip over many of them. For now, suffice it to say that what citizens know about one another's commitment to the authority of a conception of justice depends, in part, upon what concepts and methods of reasoning they actually use when they argue about basic political questions. That, I believe, is why Rawls introduces guidelines of public reason—to provide a solution to the assurance problem. Looking at the guidelines of public reason Rawls actually endorses will help to support this conjecture.

Rawls says that he was initially drawn to what he calls the "exclusive view of public reason."[19] As the name and its affinity with my label "exclusivist" suggest, this is the view that citizens should never introduce reasons drawn from comprehensive doctrines into public debate about fundamental questions.[20] According to the exclusive view Rawls considered, the only reasons that may be brought to bear are those provided by the values and ideals of the political conception of justice. To comply with the exclusive view just would be to reason about questions exclusively from the "unified perspective" provided by that conception.

The exclusive view is highly restrictive. I believe it was attractive to Rawls because it promised an elegant solution to the assurance problem. If citizens were to use the concepts of their comprehensive doctrines to debate basic political questions, their arguments might be taken to suggest that they do not acknowledge the authority of the political conception to adjudicate those questions. On the other hand, if all the citizens of the well-ordered society were to comply with the exclusive view, then they would all adopt—and would all be seen to adopt—the "common point of view" or "unified perspective" whenever basic political questions are at issue. So long as they can be assumed sincere, the way they reason about these questions in public would then confirm their allegiance to justice as fairness and the assurance problem would disappear. The solution promised by the exclusive view depends upon the existence of an overlapping consensus, since citizens might not comply with the requirements of the view unless their comprehensive doctrines endorsed justice as fairness. But given the existence of an overlapping consensus, it seems to solve the assurance problem immediately.

Despite the attraction Rawls felt for the exclusive view, he never endorsed it. One of the reasons he did not, I think, is that he recognized that the view could not make good on its promise to eliminate the assurance problem.

Divisions about some political questions can be so deep that adherents of different comprehensive doctrines come to doubt one another's allegiance to political values. Rawls's example is the question of whether church schools should receive public funding.[21] Although he does not spell out the example in any detail, I presume what he has in mind is that even if champions of public funding publicly defend their position by appealing only to the political values of religious equality and religious liberty, their argument raises questions about whether they are also committed to church-state separation. Perhaps, it will be thought, they are using political values as a cover and do not really acknowledge the authority of those values. So the assurance problem can arise even when citizens of the well-ordered society comply with the exclusive view. "One way this doubt may be put to rest," Rawls suggests, "is for the leaders of the opposing groups to present in the public forum how their comprehensive doctrines do indeed affirm [the] values [of the public conception]."[22] This is, in effect, the suggestion that leaders of opposing groups make the existence of an overlapping consensus publicly known by explaining their religious views in public deliberation. Once the existence of an overlapping consensus is publicly known, Rawls thinks, the sincerity of each side's appeals to political values will no longer be in doubt. Mutual assurance of sincere allegiance to the political conception is therefore provided.

What is significant about Rawls's treatment of this example is that it shows that he recognizes cases in which the exclusive view fails to solve the problem it was introduced to address. To solve that problem,

Rawls *had* to allow some appeal to religion—in the example, appeal by way of explanation—in public deliberation. This and other cases led Rawls to endorse what he called the "inclusive view" of public reason. According to that view, citizens can, "in certain situations, . . . present what they regard as the basis of political values rooted in their comprehensive doctrine, provided they do this in ways that strengthen the ideal of public reason itself."[23]

But Rawls quickly came to think that even the inclusive view was too restrictive. By his last published treatment of public reason, in "The Idea of Public Reason Revisited," he famously endorsed what he called the "wide view." The wide view allows ordinary citizens to introduce their comprehensive doctrines into public political argument at any time, subject to one restriction that I shall mention below.

Some readers have thought that in moving from the exclusive to the wide view, Rawls moved from a view of public reason that was overly confining to one that is too permissive.[24] But Rawls's concern with the assurance problem explains the content and propriety of the view. The wide view allows ordinary citizens to introduce comprehensive doctrines into public political discussion—and, presumably, to vote on the basis of their comprehensive doctrines—"provided that in due course public reasons, given by a reasonable political conception, are presented sufficient to support whatever the comprehensive doctrines are introduced to support."[25] When I discussed the exclusive view to which Rawls was initially drawn, I said that to reason about political questions using exclusively public reasons is to adopt and reason from citizens' "common point of view." So the wide view allows citizens to introduce and base their votes on comprehensive doctrine, provided that in due course they adopt and reason from that common viewpoint as well.

Rawls refers to the "provided that" clause as "the proviso." The difficulty with interpreting it lies in figuring out what he means by "in due course." On my reading, Rawls allows ordinary citizens to rely on their comprehensive doctrines without adducing public reasons in support of their positions, so long as their doing so does not lead others to doubt that they acknowledge the authority of the public conception of justice. If doubts never arise, then the proviso is never triggered and they need do nothing more. Only if doubts arise, and others need assurance of their allegiance, must citizens provide assurance by actually adopting and reasoning from the "unified perspective" that the public conception of justice provides. That, I believe, is why Rawls says that "the details about how to satisfy [the] proviso must be worked out in practice and cannot feasibly be governed by a clear family of rules given in advance."[26]

Rawls does not explain what he means when he says that "the details about how to satisfy [the] proviso must be worked out in practice." He might be taken to mean that "a clear family of rules" for public deliberation—understood as a system of principles expressing citizens' duties—can only be arrived at by generalizing from observations of public deliberation as actually practiced. But my reading of Rawls, according to which the proviso is triggered by doubts that arise in the course of public deliberation, suggests a different interpretation of the passage. It suggests that what counts as an expression of doubt, or an indication that trust is wavering or is being withheld, will vary with circumstance. How doubts are best dispelled so that our interlocutors are provided with the assurance they need will also vary. Thus what triggers the proviso and how it is to be satisfied are, I suggest, highly contextual. Political wisdom consists in part in figuring out how to behave in context or, in Rawls's terms, "in practice." What we arrive at by generalizing from observation of actual practice, on this reading, is not a family of principles that express duties, but a "clear family of rules" understood as at most rules of thumb for reasoning together.[27]

Rawls's guidelines of public reason are sometimes said to show that he is deeply suspicious of comprehensive doctrines, especially religious ones, or that he thinks religious political argument is inherently destabilizing. But the wide view allows reliance on religious political argument at any time, restricted only by the proviso. The motivation for the proviso is not the conviction that religion destabilizes society or leads to civil strife. It is the fact that a person's reliance on religious argument can lead her interlocutors to doubt that she acknowledges the political authority of justice as fairness. Rawls could have required citizens to assure one another of their commitments by requiring them to comply with more restrictive guidelines of public reason than those associated with the wide view. He could, for instance, have argued that citizens must *preempt* others' doubts about their acceptance of the political conception. In that case, he might have replaced the phrase "in due course" in the proviso with the phrase "at the same time." Instead, the proviso requires citizens to adopt and deliberate in their "common point of view" only when they have good reason to think assurance is actually needed. If I am right about how the proviso is to be interpreted, then the claim that Rawls endorses guidelines of public reason because of hostility toward or fear of religion is a serious misreading. In fact, Rawls goes to some lengths to advocate what is—by construction—the weakest and least restrictive guideline of public reasoning sufficient to solve the assurance problem.

QUESTIONS AND IMPLICATIONS

We can now see why Rawls's view, although sometimes taken as exclusivist, is really a weak form of restrictive inclusivism. On his view, religious claims, and claims from other comprehensive doctrines, can be included in public discussion subject to just one restriction, that expressed by the proviso. I have tried to suggest that Rawls defends his version of restrictive inclusivism as part of his effort to spell out the details of an ideally just society. Justice as fairness will be "stable for the right reasons" only if everyone in the well-ordered society knows that everyone else is committed to living up to its values and ideals. I am inclined to think that he is right about that case. If an ideally just society is to be stable for the right reasons, then its citizens have to adhere to the demand of restrictive inclusivism. To claim that even Rawls's weak form of restrictive inclusivism is too restrictive is, in effect, to favor stability of some kind other than the one Rawls wants to show. That would, I think, be a mistake for the well-ordered society.

The more pressing question raised by this "recontextualization" is what implications Rawls's treatment has for those of us who live in societies that are not well-ordered. In his first published treatment of public reason, Rawls took up examples from such societies.[28] When Rawls introduced the proviso, he implied that it took the place of the guidelines he had drawn out of those examples, declaring peremptorily that the proviso "secures what is needed."[29] Perhaps with that phrase, he intended to signal that the proviso applies to ordinary citizens of all societies—or of all liberal democracies—both well-ordered and not.

But that intention would be thwarted by an asymmetry in the cases. Once we see Rawls's concern with stability, we can see what guidelines of public reason that apply to ordinary citizens of a well-ordered society are needed for. By contrast, it is far less clear why such guidelines are needed in societies that are not well-ordered.

There are many ways in which a society can fail to be just and hence well-ordered. An account of public reasoning that covers all of them would be extremely complicated. Rawls's principles of justice help to identify and distinguish such failures, and I shall consider just one, which I take to be of obvious relevance.

Let us consider a society—such as I take the contemporary United States to be—in which there is broad consensus on what Rawls calls "basic intuitive ideas" on which justice as fairness is based. That is, there is broad agreement on the very general propositions that citizens are to live together as politically free and equal and that society ought to be a fair scheme of social cooperation. Because of this agreement, there is general support for a constitution that institutionalizes conceptions of freedom, equality, and fairness. It protects the rights covered by Rawls's first principle of justice and establishes representative government with regular and free elections. But suppose that the conceptions of freedom, equality, and fairness that are institutionalized in this society differ from Rawls's own in significant respects. More specifically, suppose that the political liberties do not have fair value because freedom is interpreted so as to allow unlimited spending in political campaigns and that economic inequalities exceed the range allowed by Rawls's difference principle because of the way property rights are understood. Suppose too that there are some important matters to which the constitution does not extend at all, such as guaranteed health care and a guaranteed standard of living.

Such a society does not have an overlapping consensus on justice as fairness, but it does have what Kurt Baier called a "constitutional consensus."[30] A society in which there is a constitutional consensus shares some features with a well-ordered society. By affording rights and liberties constitutional protection, it removes some issues from the political agenda and so promises that citizens can be secure in their liberty. Furthermore, I shall suppose, the institutions of this society encourage something like a sense of justice: a strong attachment to the basic intuitive ideas and to the constitution, and a powerful disinclination to support extra-constitutional or unconstitutional political change.

But as in a well-ordered society so in a society with a constitutional consensus: citizens have conceptions of the good and each knows others may be tempted to defect from the consensus. One reason those temptations arise is that not all questions bearing on citizens' rights and liberties are taken off the agenda by the constitution. Some of these questions have to be decided, judicially or legislatively, in the course of society's ongoing political life. Thus a constitutional consensus, like an overlapping consensus, faces assurance problems. Citizens need to know that others accept the authority of the constitution and the basic intuitive ideas of freedom, equality, and fairness that underlie it.

The importance of ensuring that the constitution is not undermined by a generalized prisoner's dilemma and of securing the rights and liberties the constitution protects tells in favor of something like Rawls's proviso. More specifically, it tells in favor of requiring citizens whose political arguments raise doubts about their allegiance to the constitution to put those doubts to rest by showing that they accept duly enacted legislation and court decisions as legitimate, and that the measures they argue for are constitutional and can be supported by a reasonable interpretation of liberal democratic values. This is not to deny that citizens' comprehensive views, including their religious views, may contain ideas that can leaven political debate and may help to motivate ordinary citizens' efforts on behalf of reform. The requirement that I have suggested is consistent with citizens' bringing those ideas to bear and acting on those motivations. But it requires that, when necessary to assure others of their allegiance to the constitution, citizens show how the reforms they favor can be supported by liberal democratic values and are consistent with constitutional procedures, including procedures for amending the constitution, if amendment is needed.

The grounds for insisting on this requirement even in non-well-ordered societies can be understood in terms of the political autonomy with which Rawls was concerned. Citizens of a well-ordered society realize political autonomy because fundamental questions are settled on the basis of political values and principles that they would agree to as free and equal. I believe that political autonomy is best understood as an ideal that can be realized by degrees. Citizens living in a society with the constitutional consensus I have described do not realize it maximally because their society is not well-ordered by principles that would be adopted in the original position. But because fundamental political arrangements are determined by the requirements of political freedom, equality, and fairness, and because the rights and liberties covered by Rawls's first principles are honored, they realize political autonomy to some extent. If, however, a sizable number of citizens are unwilling or unable to satisfy the requirement I have suggested, then politicians and public officials may be tempted to cater to them by advocating measures that cannot be justified by democratic political values but can only be justified by, for example, religious considerations. The enactment of such measures would compromise citizens' political autonomy, or lessen the degree to which it is realized. The requirement I have suggested therefore draws further support from the importance of political autonomy.

I believe that there are two further considerations that tell in favor of this requirement. The first has to do with the history of reform that will subsequently be told and written. It is important for a people to be able to look back with pride on occasions in their past when they have made their society more just. Such pride grows out of the realization that those improvements enabled them better to live up to their collective commitment to liberal democracy. It will be easier to describe those crucial historical junctures that way if those who participated in them were willing and able to describe their own efforts in those terms. The second, and more surprising, reason is that satisfying the requirement is good for religion. For religious teachings are typically said to provide insight and guidance bearing on the most basic features of the human condition. The claim that they do is greatly strengthened if religion provides insight and guidance into the moral demands of political life. If the truth about political life is that citizens should live together as free equals, then religions that are true should help citizens of faith to live that way and to see where their societies fall short. If they can do that, then the political measures that their adherents put forward should be amenable to support by some interpretation, perhaps a prophetic interpretation, of liberal democratic values.[31]

Most discussions of religion and citizenship focus on the obligations of religious citizens. Little attention is paid to the role of their interlocutors and the obligations they have in dealing with citizens of faith. Although I have followed the lead of these discussions, I would like to conclude on a different note.

I have argued that the demands of public reason are context-dependent, and that religious citizens need a kind of sensitivity to how their arguments are received. I think those who are not inclined to rely on religious considerations are also required to show sensitivity, and to understand the position of those who are so inclined. Anglophone discussions of religion in politics, both popular and philosophical, suggest that the reasons behind the insertion of religion into democratic politics are not well understood. They need to be if those who do the inserting are to be understood. To take just one example, many religious Americans find the increasing secularization of society profoundly alienating. The response to this alienation is a retelling of the past in which religious communities emphasize their separatism. They develop a sense of themselves as, if not on pilgrimage in the world, at least at some distance from it in a world of their own. Their self-respect depends upon defining themselves in contrast to the world of secular values. Members' conception of themselves is threatened by a very attractive identity with which it seems to compete: that of shared citizenship in a secular liberal democracy. Assertions of religion in politics are assertions of political views that are thought to be true. But they are also assertions of a valued self-conception in the face of great insecurity about one's own religious identity and commitment. They need to be received as such, rather than simply as attempts to impose or control.

Notes

An earlier version of this chapter was prepared for a conference on citizenship and obligation held at the University of Valencia, April 14–16, 2010, and that version appeared in the conference proceedings as "Religion, Citizenship and Obligation," *SCIO* 6, no. 1 (2010): 103–18. I am grateful to the University of Valencia for permission to republish the essay in revised form and to an audience in Rome, and in particular to Tom Bailey, for suggestions and questions that prompted the revisions.

1. See T. H. Marshall, *Citizenship and Social Class, and Other Essays* (Cambridge: Cambridge University Press, 1950).

2. See Judith Shklar, *American Citizenship: The Quest for Inclusion* (Cambridge, Mass.: Harvard University Press, 1991).

3. See, generally, David Hollenbach, *The Common Good and Christian Ethics* (Cambridge: Cambridge University Press, 2002).

4. See Cass Sunstein, "Ginsburg's Dissent May Yet Prevail," *Los Angeles Times*, April 20, 2007.

5. A classic example is Robert Audi, "The Separation of Church and State and the Obligations of Citizenship," *Philosophy and Public Affairs* 18 (1989): esp. 296.

6. See David Hollenbach, "Contexts of the Political Role of Religion: Civil Society and Culture," *San Diego Law Review* 30 (1994): esp. 880.

7. See *TJ* (rev.) 125, 436.

8. *PL* xlii.

9. This section draws on Weithman, *Why Political Liberalism? On John Rawls's Political Turn* (Oxford: Oxford University Press, 2010), 327–35.

10. *TJ* (rev.) chap. 8.

11. *TJ* (rev.) 450–51.

12. See *TJ* (rev.) 505.

13. See Jean Hampton, *Hobbes and the Social Contract Tradition* (Cambridge: Cambridge University Press, 1986).

14. *PL* 134.

15. *TJ* (rev.) 4.

16. *TJ* (rev.) 415.

17. *TJ* (rev.) 4, 415.

18. *TJ* (rev.) 4.

19. *PL* 247n36.

20. *PL* 247.

21. *PL* 248.

22. *PL* 249.

23. *PL* 247.

24. Charles Larmore, for example, writes, "in the forum where citizens officially decide the basic principles of their political association and where the canons of public reason therefore apply, appeals to comprehensive doctrine cannot but be out of place—at least in a well-ordered society." Larmore, "Public Reason," in *The Cambridge Companion to Rawls*, ed. S. Freeman (Cambridge: Cambridge University Press, 2003), 387.

25. *PL* xlix–l.

26. *CP* 592.

27. I have tried to spell this out in more detail in Weithman, "Deliberative Character," *Journal of Political Philosophy* 13 (2005): esp. 273–75.

28. *PL* 248ff.

29. *PL* xlix.

30. Kurt Baier, "Justice and the Aims of Political Philosophy," *Ethics* 99 (1989): 771–90, passim.

31. In his "Letter from Birmingham Jail," Martin Luther King Jr. wrote, "I am in Birmingham because injustice is here. Just as the prophets of the eighth century B.C. left their villages and carried their 'thus saith the Lord' far beyond the boundaries of their home towns, and just as the Apostle Paul left his village of Tarsus and carried the gospel of Jesus Christ to the far corners of the Greco-Roman world, so am I compelled to carry the gospel of freedom beyond my own home town." King, *Why We Can't Wait* (New York: Penguin, 1964), 77.

4

Rethinking the Public Use
of Religious Reasons

ANDREW F. MARCH

THE INCLUSIVIST CHALLENGE
TO LIBERAL PUBLIC REASON

The problem of religious reasons in public justification is one of the most exhaustively treated questions in recent political philosophy, and the dispute between "exclusivist" and "inclusivist" views is well known.[1] In particular, a number of prominent political and legal theorists have recently challenged the common political liberal exclusivist view, associated most famously with John Rawls, that religious arguments are prima facie inadmissible in public deliberation over coercive laws.[2] These thinkers have tried to show that many of the arguments offered by liberal theorists in favor of a principle of religious self-restraint in reason-giving fail to justify that principle,[3] and that many positive arguments can be given in favor of welcoming religious contributions in public deliberation. These thinkers are neither theocratic perfectionists nor radical skeptics of liberal legitimacy; rather, they defend one version or another of the inclusivist idea that a "citizen is morally permitted to support (or oppose) a coercive law even if she enjoys [only] a religious rationale for that law."[4]

Although I sympathize with these inclusivist critiques, in this chapter I argue that the debate between exclusivists and inclusivists has been hampered by a tendency for advocates on both sides to treat the two central concepts at stake—"religious arguments" and "political issues"—in unitary terms.[5] Specifically, I argue that, since there is no such single entity as a "religious argument" or a "political issue," the morality of the inclusion of a religious argument in public deliberation over a political decision differs, often radically, depending on the specific properties of each, namely, the form and content of the religious argument and the subject matter of the political decision. I further argue that the morality of political reason-giving is not reducible to a single value, such as respect or consensus. Rather, I suggest, there are five especially important considerations at stake in formulating judgments about political arguments: the moral attitude toward others expressed in our public speech, the democratic legitimacy of public decisions, the justice of public decisions, social solidarity,[6] and the ability of a democratic society to respond to collective problems. Instead of focusing on the narrow question of whether an argument issued in public has a "religious" or "comprehensive" character, is immediately accessible to or shareable with others, or proceeds from and builds on an existing moral consensus, then, we can explore how religious arguments can take different forms that affect these five considerations in quite different ways, in that they involve greater or lesser degrees of appeals to revelatory or clerical authority, strictly understood, and in that the stakes for the above goods differ with different kinds of political issues. To anticipate much of what I will argue below, what often matters is the tripartite question of whether "religious arguments" are advocating for (a) interests that are generally and appropriately recognized as interests in a political community, (b) of agents or entities that are generally recognized as legitimate objects of politically enforced moral concern, (c) in ways that do not require unintelligible or unreasonable self-sacrifice of fellow citizens. Focusing on these variables will give us a clearer view of why some religious arguments violate norms of respect, civility, and fairness, while others do not.

Although this chapter is largely a response to inclusivist critics of Rawlsian public reason, I sympathize with many of their specific commitments. This should not be taken to imply that I am radically at odds with Rawls's overall project: I assume the desirability of justifying laws and policies to the widest possible group of citizens in terms that they can accept given reasonable pluralism, and much of my discussion can be seen as an explanation of why certain religious arguments are more likely than others to fit within Rawls's "wide" view of public reason or to satisfy his "proviso." But I accept many of the ways in which religious views can be beneficial to public discourse that inclusivist critics point out, while disagreeing with the conclusions that they draw. Furthermore, rather than simply reasserting or softening certain common political liberal commitments, as is commonly done in response to such inclusivist points, my endeavor here is to hold up the question of the public use of religious reasons at a slightly different angle, beginning from somewhat different questions. This leads me to diverge from Rawls's account—if not from his overall project—at some important junctures. Rawls proposes to solve the problem of religious contributions to public discourse primarily by placing moral constraints on how we argue in civil society, or in the wider public sphere. I disagree with this solution somewhat. For when we argue in civil society among persons who share our religious worldview, we are often trying to mobilize them to vote or legislate in ways that affect other fellow citizens' core interests. In such cases, the gap between the background culture and legislative politics can be slight, and we wrong those fellow citizens whose interests we try to mobilize others in the background culture to disregard. We therefore need an account of why some of that background speech seems wrong to us and some does not. Part of the answer lies in how religious arguments are constructed, and, in this regard, I will show that Rawls's categories of the "comprehensive" and the "public" do not capture the complexities of how religious traditions inform public speech. However, a larger part of the answer lies in the differences between the kinds of actions political communities legislate on, and here too I will show that Rawls's categories are inadequate: "constitutional essentials" and matters of "basic justice" fail to capture all of the nuances of how our interests as free and equal citizens are implicated in different ways by different kinds of laws. In particular, I will suggest that Rawls wrongly excludes religious considerations from social justice issues (while inclusivists include them for the wrong reasons) and that he rightly excludes them from liberty issues, but for the wrong reasons (while inclusivists wrongly include them).

In the following two sections, I introduce my typologies of religious arguments and political issues and discuss why this way of analyzing religious arguments in public justification improves on the existing models, including Rawls's own limitation of the "duty of civility" to official forums where parties holding or seeking public office debate constitutional essentials and matters of basic justice.[7] I argue that this form of analysis helps us to clarify both why the common positive examples of religious contributions to political argument are persuasive and why there remain plausible grounds for criticizing other religious interventions as violating certain norms of respect between fellow citizens. These two sections are followed by a more detailed discussion of a few paradigmatic cases of religious argument, in which I use my scheme to show why a democratic citizen can in good faith object to certain modes of using religious arguments in certain areas of political decision-making (such as those regarding sexuality and marriage) while not objecting to others (such as those regarding social justice).

WHAT IS A "RELIGIOUS REASON"?

"Religious" reasons are distinguished, on my view, less by the moral-affective disposition with which they are offered[8] and more by the *form* that religious arguments take, the claims to authority embedded in how they are structured. I suggest as a working typology four forms that religious contributions often take:

1. A command extracted from a revealed text, religious authority, or personal mystical or revelatory experience.
2. A theological or moral doctrine that is not clearly attributed to a specific claim from a revealed text, but is derived from certain theistic claims and revealed knowledge.
3. An appeal or reference to traditional religious commitments or practices.
4. An appeal to practical wisdom or moral insight found in traditions of religious thought.

This is not necessarily a final or conclusive typology and, importantly, I am not suggesting that these categories are *exclusive* vis-à-vis one another. But the distinctions do some work for us. For example, the *Evangelical Declaration Against Torture: Protecting Human Rights in an Age of Terror*, published in 2007, contains all four of these forms of religious argument, in addition to references to secular legal and moral traditions. Consider the following examples:

1. The *Declaration* first states that "we are Christians who are *commanded* by our Lord Jesus Christ to love God with all of our being and to love our neighbors as ourselves (Mt. 22:36–40)."[9]

2. The *Declaration* then invokes Genesis 1:26–27 ("And God said, 'Let us make human beings in our image, in our likeness.'") to declare that "we ground our commitment to human rights, including the rights of suspected terrorists, in the core Christian belief that human life is sacred." This basic view, which "is a moral norm that both summarizes and transcends all other particular norms in Christian moral thought," is linked to torture not through clear scriptural command but through an analogy with the torture of Jesus (after the Incarnation "the cries of the tortured are in a very real sense the cries of the Spirit") and through the claim that "human life is expressed through physicality, and the well-being of persons is tied to their physical existence."[10]

3. Later, the *Declaration* argues that a "commitment to human rights can be seen as a systematic way to look out for the interests of others, and thus as an expression of Christian love. This is now the overwhelming consensus of the Christian community."[11]

4. Finally, the *Declaration* states that "when torture is employed by a state, that act communicates to the world and to one's own people that human lives are not sacred, that they are not reflections of the Creator, that they are expendable, exploitable, and disposable, and that their intrinsic value can be overridden by utilitarian arguments that trump that value"; "a commitment to life's sacredness and to human rights is a seamless garment. It cannot be torn anywhere without compromising its integrity everywhere"; and "human rights place a shield around people, even when (especially when) our hearts cry out for vengeance."[12]

Thus there is no *single* such thing as a religious argument. Not only is "religious" too under-inclusive a category (which is why Rawls always spoke of "comprehensive" doctrines, a category that includes both religious and secular doctrines), but it is too over-inclusive a category as well. When a citizen quotes the Bible or a papal encyclical to *prove* in an authoritative and determinate manner that homosexuality or divorce ought to be forbidden, she is simply not doing the same thing morally, politically, or discursively as when she claims that human life is inherently valuable ("sacred"), that Christian just war doctrine contains enduringly wise lessons for the conduct of war, or that human sinfulness cautions us against overconfidence in the purity of our own moral intentions. It is not only that for the latter issues "in due course, we [can] give properly public reasons to support the principles and policies our comprehensive doctrine is said to support," as Rawls would have it;[13] it is that the first form of argument is an undemocratic approach to knowledge, politics, and authority, while the other, equally "comprehensive" reasons are less so from the very outset. For the moral and epistemic humility of the citizen willing to subject her arguments to evaluation and debate in public is measured less by some inscrutable interior state of affect or by her willingness to argue and engage with others than by the form and structure that her public arguments take. In particular, not all theistic contributions to public discourse are offered with an implicit authoritarian or theocratic premise, and not all *contributions* to public life are meant as general *justifications* of coercive laws, strictly construed. When Martin Luther King Jr. invoked Augustine to argue that "an unjust law is no law at all,"[14] he was not invoking him as the final word, as a literally authoritative figure to be obeyed by Americans. He was inviting others, and not only Christians, to ask whether they are really committed to a hollow form of legal positivism without regard for justice or morality.[15]

The pluralistic, fragmented nature of large societies thus forces us to interpret certain religious interventions in politics from a rhetorical standpoint, rather than assume with Rawls that all such interventions invoke a "comprehensive doctrine" of moral justification. And there is not only a lesson here for strict exclusivists.[16] There is also a familiar, more narrowly philosophical one for a certain kind of inclusivist defender of religious argument in public. For the successful demonstration that religious arguments are quite often both respectful and beneficial to public discourse need not justify any general conclusions about "religious" arguments as such: if there are certain kinds of religious arguments that are morally acceptable in public debate precisely because they are translated relatively easily into other moral languages, this might merely show that they have more in common with certain secular moral views than with certain other religious arguments.[17] Furthermore, this simply serves to isolate those religious arguments that are genuinely authoritarian in the sense of implying that clear statements from revelation (or clerical authority) can decisively settle a political question for all affected without a requirement of translation into or convergence with other doctrines. Showing that there are important counterexamples that disprove the claim "religious arguments are never permissible in public justification" does not successfully defend the counterclaim "religious arguments are always unproblematic in public justification."

This is, in fact, a necessary implication of some inclusivist views. What, after all, is the case for giving religious arguments wider latitude in debates over beginning of life issues (abortion), end of life issues (euthanasia, capital punishment, war), and livability of life issues (torture)? First, it is argued that these are unresolved questions to which freestanding public reason does not give a complete, determinate answer. At this point, there are two options. One is the "agonistic" democratic response, which holds that since such issues must be legislated on but will never be resolved by some shared public reason, we have no choice but to resolve them through open democratic competition and persuasion, in a spirit open to rupture and novelty. The other is the "wide" or "inclusivist" response, which calls for the extension of public deliberation by including deeper religious or philosophical views.

In what circumstances can certain religious arguments be offered in good (civic) faith as part of a process of conscientious mutual engagement with other citizens deliberating over questions like abortion, the welfare state, and killing through law or war?[18] If the argument is not that the indeterminacy of public reason forces us to view (and celebrate) democracy as the struggle for coalitions and majoritarian outcomes, then it must be that inclusivists think that there may be something *persuasive* in religious arguments made to fellow citizens who are not coreligionists. Presumably inclusivists do not mean wholesale conversion to the religion from which specific arguments are derived. They mean that difference in religion is not an impediment to mutual learning, to being moved in particular areas of policy by others' comprehensive religious views. One does not need to be a Catholic to appreciate and learn from Catholic writings on dignity[19] or to believe in a divine Creator to be swayed by the claim that human life as such is sacred, or at least ought to be treated *as if* it is sacred.[20]

The implication of this is that the religious authority or origin of a particular argument is unnecessary not, to be sure, to the believing citizen herself, but to the moral validity of the claim in question for *public* purposes. While the believer may very well believe that it is God, and only God, who has made human life valuable and sacred (if not always inviolable) from conception, or that the Passion of Christ teaches us that torture is an abomination, she may also believe that one need not believe in God or Christ to appreciate these claims for practical purposes, and thus that the religious premise is not what is doing the public, political work. Without denigrating the importance of the divine origin of her knowledge for *her*, what the cases of abortion, torture (of noncitizens), war, and euthanasia teach us is that religious arguments are most potent and enduring precisely in those cases where revealed religion is not a source of exclusive moral knowledge and not invoked as an authority. Where one does need to accept particular revelatory claims or the authority of certain clerical figures, as arguably in the case of religious opposition to marriage equality,[21] the religious arguments are far less compelling, troubling, and enduring.

I do not intend to trivialize religious thought by reducing all valuable and acceptable religious arguments to generic statements of universal morality or particularly effective rhetorical tools. But I do intend to suggest that there is a limited set of moral claims (as opposed to isolated premises in arguments) that are both genuinely inaccessible to outsiders and entirely dependent on their original theistic foundations, and that there are also widely accepted (if contestable) limits on the kinds of interests and the kinds of entities that are appropriate to advocate for in a pluralist, post-traditional society that takes the freedom and equality of its members seriously. I discuss this in more detail below.

What should be clear from the preceding is that public reason liberals like Rawls ought to be concerned not with "religious" arguments as such, but with a particular kind of religious argument, namely, arguments that tend to be justified by reference to a clear scriptural, revealed, or clerical command. For these are arguments given in an authoritarian manner (regardless of the overall good will of the citizen). They do not make a claim of the kind "our tradition teaches us that life is sacred or that laws ought to be moral; we think this reflects some truth which all should be able to endorse." Rather, they claim, "our revealed text has laid this down and we are not concerned about what effect this has on others or what they think about it."

These distinctions are important, but they are broadly recognized in the literature (particularly through the notion of "translation"), and I believe they still do not give us enough to understand what is at stake in the debate over religion and public reason. As I acknowledged above, religious arguments are not likely to fit clearly into one and only one of my four categories, and it might be suggested that, ultimately, all of the categories are reducible to the first. It might also be suggested that in order to make religious arguments in support of policies that I also support on nonreligious grounds (more social justice, less torture) seem less problematic, I engaged in excessive, and selective, interpretive charity. For example, the religious may be willing to say that torture is *forbidden* and charity *commanded* by a revealed scripture or religious authority that only the faithful will be able to fully appreciate. Do public reason liberals have any good way of distinguishing between a scripturalist argument that says that Catholics *must* oppose same-sex marriage and one that says Catholics *must* support universal health care? Some might insist that they do not and that any liberal attempt to argue for the difference is yet further evidence of liberal bad faith and failure to give the aspiration to neutrality the (dis)honorable dispatch that it deserves.[22] That may be the right answer. However, I think we are not there yet. Just as I have tried to unpack the concept of "religious arguments" into more basic parts, in the following section I will attempt to do the same with the idea of a "political problem" in a way that does not beg substantive questions of justice.

WHAT IS A "POLITICAL PROBLEM"?

While it may be argued that the primary salient feature of a law is that it is coercive, and thus that the main distinction is between those aspects of morality that are legitimately enforced by the state and those that are not,[23] this does not capture all the salient features of the different areas in which humans act collectively. It is even more challenging to offer a typology of political issues than to offer one of religious arguments, but the following is an attempt that does not rely on Rawls's distinction between "constitutional essentials," or matters of "basic justice," and other political issues. Religious and other moral arguments and judgments are frequently given concerning:

1. the freedom of fully self-representing citizens to act and make choices based on their understanding of their own interests;
2. the interests of those who cannot fully represent themselves within a social contract framework;
3. the interests of those who cannot represent themselves or advance claims within a social contract framework;
4. the morality of collective action and public institutions;
5. the morality of a society's overall character or direction.

The justification of these categories will require more work than my typology of religious arguments:

1. We begin with full members of the political community in good standing, namely, sane adults. The choice set of self-representing individuals is restricted by any law that we enact, from traffic regulations to taxation to public nudity ordinances. But for my first category, I have in mind restrictions on citizens' choices as to what to do with their bodies and property or with the narrow category traditionally referred to as the sphere of negative freedom. Obviously, merely to say that a law restricts one in this way is not to pronounce on its justifiability. Our individual actions, of course, often impinge on the rights and interests of others. But all of these can coherently be described in ways that identify discrete individual actions of members of a political community as objects of legislation. The scope and significance of this category will become clearer in light of the subsequent ones, particularly category 4.

2. Political communities also have partial citizens. With my second category, I primarily have in mind children, although it is not hard to recall political imaginaries in which women or racial minorities were

treated as incapable of representing themselves. Political communities do many things that directly and indirectly affect the interests of children, and it is also not hard to recall political imaginaries that deny that the state ought to provide for the education, health care, and security rights of children.[24] Political communities argue internally about what interests partial-cum-future citizens have, what interests citizens have in those future citizens, and who is entitled to enforce which interests.[25]

3. Political communities are also faced with deciding to what extent they ought to protect the most basic interests of entities and agents with no direct representation within a polity. These issues are sometimes referred to as the "who is the subject of rights?" question.[26] If all agree, *ex hypothesi*, that all fellow *citizens* are owed obligations of justice and we then seek to justify what those obligations are, we are left—by the admission of some social contract theorists—with no *decisive* answers about what we owe to others outside of the immediate social contract.[27] This is not to claim that nontheist moral thinkers have no resources derived from contractarian or constructivist methods for thinking about what obligations we have toward these various noncitizens.[28] (Many constructivists are universalists first and struggle to justify special and overriding obligations to citizens.) But there is an undeniable legal, rhetorical, and emotional deficit when it comes to persuading fellow citizens that outsiders are owed obligations of justice. Nonetheless, political communities often make laws and policies that affect in the most immediately physical and vital way the interests of noncitizens who are not directly represented within the polity in question. Importantly for my analysis, there is often no real dispute about what interests persons have, such as bare life, physical health, bodily security, and economic well-being, only about *whose* interests we have obligations to affect in certain ways.

In this third category of political problems, I place such issues as abortion, the rights of enemy combatants, stem cells, the rights of nonhuman animals, global economic and ecological justice, and the rights of future generations. On first glance these issues seem radically different from one another and my categorization seems at variance with common associations. We often speak about abortion alongside homosexuality as belonging to the concerns of religious citizens, united by a common connection to human bodies and sexual choices.[29] However, from a contractarian standpoint these issues all have something more philosophically compelling in common, namely, that they pertain to the domain of legislating on the bare life, physical integrity, or minimal welfare of noncitizens.

In religious moral systems, obligations to entities beyond the political community often include nonhuman and nonnatural entities. God, "the Church," the honor of this or that prophet or messiah figure, human souls, holy texts, sacred places and buildings, and even "the sacred" as such are often claimed to be objects of moral concern. In rights-based religious moralities, this form of thought is perhaps best included in this third category. Islamic law, for example, speaks of the "the rights of God" and the rights of the Prophet Muhammad, entities who make claims on but cannot directly represent themselves within the social contract. While I would also place these entities in my third category, it is clear why religious arguments in support of protections for the most basic and uncontroversial interests of certain kinds of noncitizens, such as foreigners or the climate, are a very different political act from similarly structured arguments on behalf of other kinds of noncitizens, such as deceased prophets.

4. My fourth category of collective political action can be difficult to distinguish decisively from the previous ones, since all coercive laws have a public, collective character. But there are certain acts, policies, and institutions that are predominantly, if not always irreducibly, collective. To give two relatively clear examples, a political community has nuclear weapons or a state religion only as a collective act. All resolutions of collective action problems—from traffic laws to the exploitation of natural resources—are also a form of political action larger than the sum of the individual acts restricted or regulated. This category also includes a community's basic political institutions, including its electoral laws and its system of distributing wealth.

What a society does with its public money thus falls into this category—and, notably, is also involved in enforcing all of the laws discussed above, as restricting the freedom of particular, discrete agents. There is something in the collective nature of the welfare state that exceeds the mere coercive element and the rights-claims involved. A mandate to send your child to any school, to purchase health care, or to subscribe to a protection agency at your own expense is a somewhat different public act than financing these projects out of public funds. Moreover, many religious and secular arguments stress this collective dimension. Political argument is often about more than the claim that specific rights are involved or that certain policies would be more optimal than others; it is often about what we are willing to accept "in our name."[30]

5. With my fifth category, I have in mind reflections on the moral quality of a society's present historical consciousness and practices of valuing and judging that see that quality as transcending any of its individual moral acts or judgments. Consider religious interventions that take the form of prophetic witnessing. Prophetic witnessing is very often tied to the specific things a society is doing—practicing slavery, tolerating homosexuality, permitting blasphemy or heresy, cultivating feminism or gender equality, abandoning the poor—but the critique goes beyond the call to rectify this or that policy. The idea is that society itself is somehow lost, ungodly, or fallen. Rectifying specific policies or acts is only a first step, a condition for an overall repentance or return to a different state of character that would never have permitted these impieties in the first place.[31]

Declinist narratives about modernity often involve a similar scope. For instance, Alasdair MacIntyre's critique of modern morality goes beyond a concern with specific policies or practices; he is reflecting on the loss of a common moral vocabulary about the good and our failure to replace it with anything equally stable and valuable.[32] MacIntyre's Thomism is representative of a wider school of (particularly Catholic) thought that laments the theological turn in late medieval Europe toward a nominalist metaphysics and voluntarist God.[33] For thinkers in this tradition, we are now incapable of seeing ourselves as wholly rational and connected to the divine through our participation in unchanging reason.

RELIGION AND PUBLIC REASON: RESTATING THE QUESTION

I do not imagine the previous sketch to be perfectly conclusive or stable. However, even more than with the distinction of different modes of religious argument, I think it allows us to hold up the question of religious argument in public debate at a different angle. Recalling the most compelling political issues about which inclusivists have defended religious contributions—slavery, abortion, global justice, domestic social justice, torture, punishment, nuclear weapons, war, and imperialism—we see not only that religious argument takes many different forms besides the paradigmatic one of scriptural command, but also that the kinds of religious arguments we are discussing are interventions into radically different areas of democratic political action.

What do we think is either threatened or enhanced by the use of "religious" arguments in public debate? As noted in my introduction, in answering this question I regard the following as the most important considerations: the fundamental moral attitude toward others expressed in our public speech, the democratic legitimacy of public decisions, the justice of public decisions, social solidarity, and the ability of a democratic society to respond to collective problems. Whether an argument issued in public has a "religious" or "comprehensive" character is insufficient for evaluating its impact on these important political goods. The various forms that religious arguments take affect the above considerations in quite different ways, and the stakes for the above considerations differ with different kinds of political issues.

An ideal of public reason is obviously most challenged by religious arguments of my first form, those that appeal directly to scriptural or ecclesiastical authority (in the most strict sense of the term) in order to justify a law or a position within practical ethics. However, even that form of argument plays morally distinct roles in different areas of collective political life. Invoking a literal reading of the revealed scripture of one's own religion is a very different act vis-à-vis fellow citizens when it is done (a) to restrict the personal freedoms of others to make decisions about their bodies and property based on a paternalistic understanding of their interests, (b) to exhort fellow citizens to protect the rights of other fellow citizens, or (c) to persuade fellow citizens to protect the relatively uncontroversial interests of noncitizens. (Note that any, or none, of these three kinds of political advocacy may relate to what Rawls calls "constitutional essentials." My categories cut across Rawls's way of distinguishing between types of political problems.) I will try to demonstrate this with a few select examples.

RELIGIOUS ARGUMENTS ON SEXUALITY
AND SOCIAL JUSTICE: A PRINCIPLED DISTINCTION?

To return to a question I asked above: do (public reason) liberals have any good way of distinguishing between the public use of an argument from scripture or authority that says that Christians *must* oppose same-sex marriage and one that says Christians *must* support universal health care? I noted that a tempting answer is to say that they do not and that any liberal attempt to argue for the difference is an insincere attempt to claim false neutrality for their own rules of engagement. On this view, liberals who concede that Christians ought to be encouraged to promote social justice through religious arguments would simply have to live with Christian arguments about sexual morality. But is the fact that liberals tend to agree with Catholics on social justice and disagree with them on sexuality and marriage the only variable in these two positions? According to the analysis I have developed in this chapter, we should also ask broader questions about the area of human activity being legislated on in these two areas.

Before we get to the question of same-sex marriage, consider the question of tolerance for homosexuality per se, understood as the decriminalization of homosexual acts between consenting adults.[34] Such an issue clearly belongs to my first category, since it involves bringing the law to bear on what humans do with their bodies and property. This is the category of legislation regarding which political liberalism is most concerned about the authoritarian and paternalistic influence of religious and other comprehensive, perfectionist arguments. Moreover, of all forms of religious arguments, those of the first kind—scripturalist, authoritative, divine command arguments—are the most authoritarian and theocratic.

It is not hard to justify this. Human negative freedom is the most obvious standard that we use to judge the extent to which some human beings hold the most obvious form of authority over others. Furthermore, the use of our own bodies for pleasure and self-expression is the clearest case of a sphere of human activity where a direct justification to the person being coerced is required if we endorse any conception of freedom and equality between citizens. To coercively restrain and punish such activity for no other reason than that God, as my reading of scripture or nature has it, has declared it vile and sinful is the clearest possible example of regarding other human beings as subject to one's own extrapolitical epistemic and moral authority. If any area ought to be regulated in a democratic society by a strict application of the harm principle, this is it. And this is not a statement only about *religious* authority. Liberal opposition to European bans on wearing the Muslim face-veil in public has exactly this logic. The sense on the part of some that an adult voluntarily wearing a face-veil is incompatible per se with her *own* dignity or freedom is regarded by most liberals as an insufficient justificatory reason for enacting a coercive law.[35]

However, while contemporary liberalism is right to discourage religious and other perfectionist arguments in the sphere of individual negative freedom where they are unavoidably and unacceptably paternalistic,[36] the lessons from this sphere would need to be argued for independently in other areas of collective political life. Same-sex marriage is an issue that overlaps a number of my categories of political action and is highly dependent on how we describe it. Regulating marriage is not something that a state needs to be in the business of. It is highly likely that a modern state will want to keep track of new citizens, tax property, defend some interests of children, and arbitrate civil litigation. But it is far from clear that the state needs to concern itself with who can form civil partnerships with whom. On this view of "marriage," the question of same-sex marriage is as much a negative liberty question as that of protection for homosexual conduct, insofar as we have a presumptive right to form partnerships and legal contracts and the state's interference in our private decisions is what requires special justification. On this description, it is hard to imagine a nonauthoritarian, nondominating use of any kind of religious reason to prevent same-sex legal partnerships.

But, on another interpretation, marriage is a quasi-public institution, something we establish as a community collectively, like nuclear weapons or a national church, and it thus belongs to my fourth category of political decisions. Of course, the very decision to characterize domestic partnerships in one way or the other is a political act. Of what kind, though? In this case, we can observe that the attempt to characterize marriage as a public institution is an attempt to remove it from the realm of debate about what kinds of personal choices are permissible in their own right or how people should live their own lives. For many—myself included—this is precisely what is objectionable about this form of opposition to same-sex marriage. Rights-claims are suppressed by changing the subject; the core interests of some citizens are weighed at near to zero in order to protect a symbolic institution from a marginal harm.

My scheme also provides resources to say much more about a religious, even scripturalist argument against same-sex marriage. First, we can distinguish between religious arguments that object to same-sex marriage because homosexuality itself is a sin—an affront to God or a harm to the self—and those arguments that say that "marriage" is a public institution that ought to be treated in a different way than the criminal law. The least that can be said is that the latter way of framing the question does not subject the personal realm of choice, freedom, and expression to a *complete* (theo)democratic veto. Furthermore, the religious framing of the political issue of "marriage" as one about a collective, public institution is compatible with permitting same-sex civil unions that extend to homosexuals the same substantive legal rights and protections.

We also see the precise grounds for objecting to religious arguments from revelation or authority against permitting same-sex marriage, beyond the mere point that "religious arguments" should be kept out of "politics." Marriage is not merely a symbolic institution like a flag, a powerless monarch, or a national flower. It is one that regulates access to crucial social goods, at least in many contemporary societies (although it is far from clear that a democratic society ought to distribute benefits and rights through a formal legal status like marriage). It would be arbitrary to suppose that the interests of religious citizens in preserving their monopoly over how the state defines this institution for symbolic and affective purposes outweigh the interests of free and equal citizens to the substantive goods and rights distributed through this institution. Because the costs of this exclusion from certain publicly distributed goods are specifically targeted at a particular class of free and equal fellow citizens, justifications are owed directly to those particular persons.

My scheme permits us to draw still further distinctions. Suppose the religious response to the demand for same-sex marriage is to propose a "leveling down" to a universal civil union status for *all* citizens, reserving "marriage"—like baptism—for the realm of religious associations. Suppose this religious move, even if it uses scripturalist forms of religious argument, is not to deny civic and moral goods to homosexual fellow citizens, but to remove the state from the marriage business entirely, to save the symbolic and sacred associations by removing "marriage" from state power. This is not only politically reasonable, but something that many liberal, feminist, and queer theorists might equally endorse because of their own reservations about "marriage" as a symbolic institution with which they, or the state, can identify.[37]

This does not mean there are no grounds for objecting to certain religious arguments in this case. For example, do these hypothetical scripturalist arguments for privatizing marriage (a policy that we are assuming here to be at least reasonable) imply that such scripturalist reasoning binds the state as such, that a state representing all of its citizens is bound to enact that marriage law preferred by the most convincing interpretation of scripture? Or rather do we interpret such statements as arguments only directed to fellow believers, justifying to them why they should accept same-sex civil unions? The former obviously is subject to certain objections. The scheme I have proposed in this chapter thus allows us to make finer distinctions between the roles that even the same kind of religious arguments play in different political contexts.

Now consider my second example, the case of Christian arguments for social justice from scripture or authority. According to my scheme, the realm of political decision at stake is my fourth category, that of collective action pertaining to how much a state should tax its citizens and what it should do with this money. Religious arguments are obviously controversial in this area, precisely because of the public, coercive, and collective nature of such political action. We object to the state endorsing and sponsoring one religion, or religion as such, because it sends the message that the public sphere belongs to one moral community more than to others. Scripturalist arguments for redistributive taxation run the risk of asserting that a sectarian interpretation of revealed truth can serve for everyone as a good justificatory reason regarding the kinds of things a state can do with public money, money collected coercively from citizens. Arguments for universal health care, say, could easily become arguments for subsidies to religious organizations for sectarian religious goals.

Why, then, are Christian public interventions in support of social justice not as authoritarian, theocratic, or disrespectful as equally scripturalist arguments about personal sexual decisions and individual citizens' access to important publicly distributed goods? I think there are three readily perceptible considerations. First, the political demand at stake is *other-regarding*. It speaks to what we owe one another within the political community, not what we owe God or other entities that we reasonably might not recognize as objects of moral concern. Obviously, the deeper arguments for what we owe one another might be based on obligations to God, to Jesus, or to ourselves in a natural law sense. But the demand is to treat other persons in a particular way that benefits them.

Second, the way we are being asked to benefit others is *not demeaning or humiliating to us*. Unlike demands to accept that our sexual life is inferior to that of others such that we should accept material, emotional, and moral deprivations, we are not being asked in this case to accept our own inferiority by being singled out for exclusion or disadvantage. We are not asked to render goods or duties to others in a servile or self-negating way, or to regard our own material welfare as insignificant or spiritually tainted. We are only being asked to see a gap between our possessions and our selves, to accept that property is acquired through social relationships. Such arguments about obligations to others are thus inherently different from, for example, religious arguments exhorting women to obey men or homosexuals to deny the value of their self-expression. The most intimate sphere of our own negative liberty is not being encroached on when we legislate about obligations to fellow citizens realized through proportionate financial contributions to public institutions.

Third, the way we are being asked to benefit others is *not problematically paternalistic to the beneficiaries*. The goods and interests that we are being asked to provide for others are relatively uncontroversial *as* goods and interests. We are not asked to provide goods or interests that are themselves sectarian in the sense of only being valued as goods or interests from within a particular moral doctrine—we are not asked to contribute Bibles or instruction in sacred tantric sex to the poor, say. Rather, we are being asked to contribute goods that (almost) everyone recognizes as goods—food, housing, employment, health care, money.

I do not claim neutrality for my view or for the demands of social justice. Deep religious views have been essential to progress (as well as reaction) in the areas of racial and social justice precisely when no prior consensus existed, and I have merely tried here to defend the public *use* of religious arguments for social justice, not to proclaim them self-evident or victorious. But I believe that I have shown that there are still some principled grounds for democratic citizens to distinguish between religious arguments on the question of sexual equality and religious arguments on the question of social justice and, thus, that the acceptability of advancing religious arguments in public does not apply in the same way for all subject matters of political action. It does not come down to whether the policies being advanced are themselves just or unjust—perhaps other citizens reasonably reject the social justice policies advocated for in religious terms. Rather, it is that the very advocacy of coercive action in different dimensions of political life makes different levels of demands on fellow citizens because of the kinds of interests involved, and that the use of equally "religious" arguments in public can thus express quite distinct moral attitudes toward others as free and equal fellow citizens. It seems to me that, however inclusive they are, blanket treatments of religious arguments like Rawls's fail to grasp these important differences.

EXPANDING THE SPHERE OF JUSTICE: RELIGIOUS ARGUMENTS ON BEHALF OF OTHERS

To recall: on my scheme, questions of abortion, the torture of enemy combatants, the global environment, and global justice, for all their differences, share an important feature, namely, a concern with the basic, relatively uncontroversial interests of persons (including future persons) outside of the immediate political community.[38] Religious intervention in such cases is often about expanding the sphere of our most basic moral concern for others. As far as the relationship between free and equal citizens is concerned, saying on the basis of religious arguments that our collective power and resources should be deployed or constrained to protect the bare life of some noncitizen is quite different from saying that our collective power should be deployed to ensure that said noncitizen be saved through Jesus Christ. No moral doctrine (with the possible exception of Stoicism)[39] disputes that bare life, physical integrity, or bodily health are goods. Thus, one way of viewing religious argumentation in the above cases is that believers are not advancing a controversial account of the good or of justice for public enforcement, but are rather merely expanding the sphere of justice, by defending those persons whose vital interests are adversely affected by policy decisions we make, and yet who do not speak for themselves within a particular body politic.

There are powerful reasons why those attracted to the ideal of public justification should not regard religious interventions in disputes about what we owe those outside the social contract as a priori uncivil. First, the terms of public reason are best suited to routine, non-exceptional problems of collective self-governance in already well-ordered societies. In societies with strong commitments to civil and human rights, including rights to personal expression and privacy, those capable of representing themselves within the social contract will likely not have to establish themselves as subjects of rights. Religious and other metaphysical arguments, or appeals to affect, meant to extend considerations of justice to them will thus be superfluous, and religious attempts to export sectarian ethical standards into the common system of rights will be unwelcome.

However, political communities never expand their sphere of moral concern without a struggle. Even domestically, contrary to Rawls's view that the constraints of public reason apply only, or with particular force, when communities seek to justify constitutional essentials and the basic principles of justice, it seems that it is precisely at these moments of founding and refounding within a polity, when obligations of justice are extended to previously excluded groups, that religious, philosophical, and extra-rational modes of persuasion are most urgently needed. In such situations, the challenge of extending moral concern to outsiders, who are not only excluded from official political institutions, but unable even to engage in extra-constitutional political struggles within the public sphere of the polity in question, is that much greater. As a kind of political particularism, nationalism has a morally constraining quality. Outsiders are easily seen as enemies, competitors, or strangers and their interests are easily dismissed or disdained. And yet it is hard to deny that we have moral obligations to those outside the state, that the global community is always itself a form of political community insofar as the global political structure distributes benefits, advantages, costs, and suffering.

How to bridge this gap between the fact of moral obligation to others and the morally cramping powers of nationalism? Our moral concern, understood as an uncoerced willingness to sacrifice any of our own interests for the interests of others, is contracted and expanded in a variety of ways, most of them nonrational. Religious argument and persuasion include both rational and nonrational processes of moral growth. Religious efforts of various forms to persuade us that we have moral obligations to those who are not protected and represented within the social contract—enemy combatants, the distant poor, fetuses, and other future persons—cannot be dismissed by political liberals for two core and mutually defining reasons: first, the terms of political and social cooperation do not claim to have settled the rights of such entities, and thus religious interventions do not challenge some existing political achievement (here even political liberals should be able to join in the politics of rupture and risk celebrated by agonists); and second, most political liberals are uneasy about the nation-state as an exhaustive context for moral and political obligation, at least in the world as it is, and are open to domestic laws that protect the interests of certain entities outside the social contract. While some such entities may be presumptively inappropriate as objects of political protection (the Qur'an, Jesus Christ, the sun god Ra), I do not believe that the entities we have focused on here—enemy combatants, the distant poor, and future persons—are inappropriate in this way. Liberals may welcome or solicit this help in areas of global poverty and torture more than regarding abortion, but if my scheme is persuasive, then liberals ought to at least regard religious interventions about abortion as belonging to the same sphere of political activity.[40]

If the preceding is convincing, there is also a greater lesson for inclusivists. Religious advocacy for the protection of the basic, uncontroversial interests of entities and agents beyond the social contract ought to be tolerated, respected, and welcomed by secular political actors under three very concrete limiting conditions: first, we accept that such entities have interests that ought to be protected; second, there is no real dispute over what interests those entities have; and, third, we recognize that the interests of such entities are often terribly hard to advocate for in national political contexts—we need all the help we can get and in a partially religious society some such help ought to be religious. But there is no implication that advocating for the protection of entities one might reasonably deny the existence of (spirits, saints, sun gods) or for the imposition of interests one might reasonably reject as interests (to be saved in Jesus Christ, to be liberated from sinful desires) is equally acceptable.

This is not to suggest that religious exhortations to protect the basic entities of persons outside the political community are trivial and make no controversial demands on fellow citizens. In the case of the exhortation to not torture a suspected terrorist, for example, a protorture citizen might claim that the religious citizen is asking her to accept the risk of losing her life if the captive is not compelled to divulge the information he supposedly possesses. Indeed, in this she would be right, although she may be wildly wrong about the actual size of the risk. But if the religious argument is derived from the value of the human life of the terrorist, rather than, say, from the idea that our own death is insignificant since we will be given an afterlife by God, then that particular "religious" argument is no *more* controversial, demanding, or paternalistic than identical "secular" arguments that it is better to live with the risk of violent death than to live in a world where torture is acceptable.[41] Whether demanding that I expose myself to mortal danger on the basis of revelation or theology is uncivil and disrespectful thus seems to depend as much on the reasonableness of the demand deriving from the theistic premises as on the mere use of those premises. I may reasonably reject both faith-based attempts to persuade me, but there is (quite literally) a world of difference between the moral attitude expressed toward me when I am told that the life of another human matters and the one expressed when I am told that my own death does not.

Most inclusivist positions do not go as far as admitting any religious justification, but rather endorse religious contributions that are largely justifiable as attempts to expand the sphere of moral concern by protecting the generally recognized interests of entities that are generally recognized as worthy of moral concern in ways that do not require unintelligible or unreasonable self-sacrifice. I have employed my scheme to argue that such inclusivists are right. But it also shows precisely why this cannot be leveraged into a defense of religious arguments in those areas where they would be paternalistic, inaccessible, or authoritarian vis-à-vis free and equal fellow citizens.

CONCLUSION

My primary conclusion is that the enduring appeal of religious reasoning in democratic life has less to do with the general incompleteness of public reason as such, or with concerns about fairness to religious citizens who want to act on their conscientious commitments, than with the limitations of public reason in a certain select set of areas, particularly those regarding how to conclusively justify basic obligations to those outside the bounded political community and how to remedy failures to secure basic justice within it. But it worth noting that even here the scope for religious contributions seems limited. In the case of expanding the sphere of moral obligation, we are almost always discussing policies where the human interests at stake—life, physical integrity, primary goods—are relatively uncontroversial and religious contributions are less a matter of justifying moral knowledge than of providing moral motivation. In areas such as torture, global poverty, the rights of future persons, or the ill effects of greed, religious arguments do not quite complete the terms of public reason so that the latter has a device or language for definitively resolving political disputes. Rather, they prick the consciences or enlarge the moral imaginations of those who are predisposed to experiencing religiously based exhortations as moving in areas that are neither matters of applying existing norms of justice nor merely matters of making policy beneath the radar of justice. Thus, the appeal of religious arguments or forms of persuasion is primarily related to the dilemmas faced by bounded political communities in conditions of universal morality.

There remain harder cases that I do not claim to be able to address with such a brief treatment. Public problems such as the interests of children, a society's use of natural resources, modes of relating to nonhuman life, the cultivation of political virtues (such as charity and sacrifice) among citizens, the protection of entities of nonin-strumental value, the use of public space, or the quality of social rela-tionships are not easily reduced to determinations of core interests held by identifiable agents that others ought to observe or protect—that is, rights. Deep and controversial moral reasoning over these topics is not exactly excluded by or in tension with public reason, but they exceed the realm within which Rawlsian forms of public delibera-tion excel at giving complete and determinate answers. Thus, we often do not know what public discourse about such issues will look like; indeed, we often do not know what the issues themselves will be and whether public coercive power is an appropriate tool for addressing them. For democratic citizens, "religious," or even "comprehensive," should not be the primary category by which public contributions on such emergent, novel, and startling problems are morally evaluated.

But inclusivist advocates of religious reasoning should also be mod-est in their extrapolations from this. What is doing the work in mak-ing room for certain kinds of religious arguments here are certain spe-cific features of these problems of collective action, rather than some general failure of political liberalism to justify the discouragement of any kinds of religious reasons. It is possible for moral exhortation in such areas of political life to be nontrivial and morally controversial (which religious arguments often are), yet not involve paternalistic or authoritarian attempts to discipline, exclude, or disadvantage individ-ual lives. For example, to say that torture not only violates the rights of the tortured but also corrupts and makes wicked the soul of the nation that enacts torture as a policy[42] does not import religious ethi-cal standards for individual behavior in the same way that religious arguments against homosexuality, gender equality, birth control, or the HPV vaccine do. Of course, public money and energies are often directed to projects that many citizens would not have chosen or actively object to. But having one's own share of the collective dispos-able income diverted to something we would not have chosen is not the same kind of assault on our dignity and autonomy as having the criminal law brought to bear on our personal choices or being excluded for arbitrary reasons from public goods or institutions. Many collec-tive acts reflect a conception of the good or of virtue, yet not necessar-ily in an unjust way. Creating national parks and other public spaces, public service obligations, public mourning and memory, exhortations to love and sacrifice, and other similar political practices are not best discussed through the language of rights, and yet the priority of justice as the first virtue of a political community does not exclude public consideration of non-justice-impinging public acts. As with basic obligations to noncitizens, public reason leaves a gap that must be filled.

Nonetheless, while there are good reasons to welcome many kinds of religious contributions to public life, this does not leave us devoid of any resources for a nonhypocritical, good-faith rejection of the use of specific kinds of religious premises in debates over specific problems of political life. Public reason liberals can save the most important parts of the doctrine of religious self-restraint—the freedom of individuals from arbitrary external domination and fairness in the distribution of the costs and benefits of association—without requiring that all religious arguments be considered suspect in public life.

Notes

This chapter is a revised extract of Andrew March, "Rethinking Religious Reasons in Public Justification," *American Political Science Review* 107, no. 3 (August 2013): 523–39.

1. See, for example, the following collections: J. C. Clanton, ed., *The Ethics of Citizenship: Liberal Democracy and Religious Convictions* (Waco, Tex.: Baylor University Press, 2009); N. L. Rosenblum, ed., *Obligations of Citizenship and Demands of Faith: Religious Accommodation in Pluralist Democracies* (Princeton: Princeton University Press, 2000); S. Macedo, ed., *Deliberative Politics: Essays on Democracy and Disagreement* (New York: Oxford University Press, 1999); and P. J. Weithman, ed., *Religion and Contemporary Liberalism* (Notre Dame: University of Notre Dame Press, 1997).

2. The standard public reason argument proceeds from a characterization of the moral requirements of democratic deliberation (such as respect, recognition of moral pluralism, or a commitment to democratic legitimacy) to the conclusion that arguments derived solely from a particular religious doctrine are prima facie uncivil and inappropriate. Besides *PL*, see Martha Nussbaum, "Perfectionist Liberalism and Political Liberalism," *Philosophy and Public Affairs* 39, no. 1 (2011): 3–45; Jürgen Habermas, "Religion in the Public Sphere," *European Journal of Philosophy* 14, no. 1 (2006): 1–25; Robert Audi, *Religious Commitment and Secular Reason* (Cambridge: Cambridge University Press, 2000); Charles Larmore, "The Moral Basis of Political Liberalism," *Journal of Philosophy* 96, no. 12 (1999): 599–625; Larmore, "Political Liberalism," *Political Theory* 18, no. 3 (1990): 339–60; Stephen Macedo, "In Defense of Liberal Public Reason: Are Slavery and Abortion Hard Cases?," *American Journal of Jurisprudence* 42 (1997): 1–29; Amy Gutmann and Robert Thompson, *Democracy and Disagreement* (Cambridge,

Mass.: Harvard University Press, 1996); Gutmann and Thompson, "Moral Conflict and Political Consensus," *Ethics* 101, no. 1 (1990): 64–88; Kent Greenawalt, *Private Consciences and Public Reasons* (New York: Oxford University Press, 1995); Greenawalt, *Religious Convictions and Political Choice* (New York: Oxford University Press, 1988); Richard Rorty, "Religion as a Conversation-Stopper," in *Philosophy and Social Hope* (New York: Penguin, 1999), 168–74; Seyla Benhabib, "Deliberative Rationality and Models of Democratic Legitimacy," *Constellations* 1, no. 1 (1994): 26–52; Donald J. Moon, *Constructing Community: Moral Pluralism and Tragic Conflicts* (Princeton: Princeton University Press, 1993); Lawrence Solum, "Constructing an Ideal of Public Reason," *San Diego Law Review* 30 (1993): 729–62; and Joshua Cohen, "Deliberation and Democratic Legitimacy," in *The Good Polity*, ed. A. Hamlin and P. Pettit (Oxford: Blackwell, 1989), 17–34.

3. Inclusivists devote most of their energies to demonstrating the defects of exclusivism in its own terms. Common criticisms are that public reason is incomplete and that the liberal terms of public reason are arbitrary, such that demands of self-restraint in a society with many religious citizens both are unfair to believers and unduly diminish political life. Given these charges, inclusivists usually argue, directly or by implication, for a different understanding of democracy, a less deliberative, consensus-seeking one and a more competitive or agonistic one. For the incompleteness criticism, see John Horton, "Rawls, Public Reason and the Limits of Liberal Justification," *Contemporary Political Theory* 2, no. 1 (2003): 5–23; David A. Reidy, "Rawls's Wide View of Public Reason: Not Wide Enough," *Res Publica* 6, no. 1 (2000): 49–72; and, in response, Micah Schwartzman, "The Completeness of Public Reason," *Politics, Philosophy, and Economics* 3, no. 2 (2004): 191–220; and Andrew Williams, "The Alleged Incompleteness of Public Reason," *Res Publica* 6, no. 2 (2000): 199–211. For the arbitrariness criticism, see Romand Coles, *Beyond Gated Politics: Reflections for the Possibility of Democracy* (Minneapolis: University of Minnesota Press, 2005); Michael McConnell, "Five Reasons to Reject the Claim That Religious Arguments Should Be Excluded from Democratic Deliberation," *Utah Law Review* 3 (1999): 639–57; Stanley Fish, "Mission Impossible: Settling the Just Bounds Between Church and State," *Columbia Law Review* 97, no. 8 (1997): 2255–333; Philip L. Quinn, "Political Liberalisms and Their Exclusions of the Religious," in *Religion and Contemporary Liberalism*, ed. P. Weithman (Notre Dame: University of Notre Dame Press, 1997), 138–61; and Paul. F. Campos, "Secular Fundamentalism," *Columbia Law Review* 94, no. 6 (1994): 1814–27. For comprehensive lists of objections to liberal ideals of public reason, see Kevin Vallier and Fred D'Agostino, "Public Justification," *Stanford Encyclopedia of Philosophy*, ed. E. N. Zalta (Spring 2014), http://plato.stanford.edu/entries/justification-public; and Jonathan Quong, *Liberalism Without Perfection* (New York: Oxford University Press, 2011), 259–60. For inclusivist responses, see Linda M. G. Zerilli, "Value Pluralism and the Problem of Judgment: Farewell to Public Reason," *Political Theory* 40, no. 1 (2012): 6–31; Bonnie Honig, *Emergency Politics: Paradox, Law, Democracy* (Princeton: Princeton

University Press, 2009); Honig, *Political Theory and the Displacement of Politics* (Ithaca: Cornell University Press, 1993); Veit Bader, "Secularism, Public Reason or Moderately Agonistic Democracy?," in *Secularism, Religion and Multicultural Citizenship*, ed. G. B. Levey and T. Modood (Cambridge: Cambridge University Press, 2008), 110–35; Romand Coles, *Beyond Gated Politics*; Chantal Mouffe, "Deliberative Democracy or Agonistic Pluralism?," *Social Research* 66, no. 3 (1999): 745–58; William E. Connolly, *Why I Am Not a Secularist* (Minneapolis: University of Minnesota Press, 1999); and David Dyzenhaus, "Liberalism After the Fall: Schmitt, Rawls and the Problem of Justification," *Philosophy and Social Criticism* 22, no. 3 (1996): 9–37.

4. Christopher Eberle, *Religious Conviction in Liberal Politics* (Cambridge: Cambridge University Press, 2002), 10. Such inclusivist critiques often proceed by presenting a religious argument that even public-reason, left liberals are likely to appreciate—for example, the role of religious citizens in opposing slavery, torture, or cuts to social services—or by warning about the dangers of excluding religious energies from politics, and thus conclude that religious arguments are prima facie acceptable or even desirable in political argument. There are also many hybrid or qualified positions, according to which the morality of using religion in political argument depends on the political *roles* or *offices* that citizens occupy, the different *arenas* or *sites* of political argument, or the various moral-affective *dispositions* citizens cultivate toward reasoning and disagreeing with other citizens. Inclusivists include Jeremy Waldron, "Two-Way Translation: The Ethics of Engaging with Religious Contributions in Public Deliberation," *Mercer Law Review* 63, no. 3 (2012): 845–68; Kevin Vallier, "Liberalism, Religion and Integrity," *Australasian Journal of Philosophy* 90, no. 1 (2012): 149–65; Simone Chambers, "Secularism Minus Exclusion: Developing a Religious-Friendly Idea of Public Reason," *Good Society* 19, no. 2 (2010): 16–21; Gerald Gaus and Kevin Vallier, "The Roles of Religious Conviction in a Publicly Justified Polity: The Implications of Convergence, Asymmetry and Political Institutions," *Philosophy and Social Criticism* 35, nos. 1–2 (2009): 51–76; McConnell, "Five Reasons to Reject"; McConnell, "Secular Reason and the Misguided Attempt to Exclude Religious Argument from Democratic Deliberation," *Journal of Law, Philosophy and Culture* 1, no. 1 (2007): 159–74; Jeffrey Stout, *Democracy and Tradition* (Princeton: Princeton University Press, 2004); Michael Perry, *Under God? Religious Faith and Liberal Democracy* (Cambridge: Cambridge University Press, 2003); Perry, "Why Political Reliance on Religious Grounded Morality Is Not Illegitimate in a Liberal Democracy," *Wake Forest Law Review* 36, no. 2 (2001): 217–49; Perry, "Religious Arguments in Public Political Debate," *Loyola of Los Angeles Law Review* 29 (1996): 1421–58; Perry, "A Critique of the 'Liberal' Political-Philosophical Project," *William and Mary Law Review* 28, no. 2 (1987): 205–33; James Bohman, "Deliberative Toleration," *Political Theory* 31, no. 6 (2003): 757–79; Paul Weithman, *Religion and the Obligations of Citizenship* (Cambridge: Cambridge University Press, 2002); Steven Shiffrin, "Religion and Democracy," *Notre Dame Law Review* 74, no. 5 (1999): 1631–56; Philip Quinn,

"Political Liberalisms"; Nicholas Wolterstorff, "The Role of Religion in Decision and Discussion of Political Issues," in *Religion in the Public Square: The Place of Religious Convictions in Political Debate*, ed. R. Audi and N. Wolterstorff (Lanham, Md.: Rowman and Littlefield, 1997), 67–120; and Wolterstorff, "Why We Should Reject What Liberalism Tells Us About Speaking and Acting in Public for Religious Reasons," in *Religion and Contemporary Liberalism*, ed. P. J. Weithman (Notre Dame: University of Notre Dame Press, 1997), 162–81. Among inclusivists, appeal is made to the religious opposition to slavery in Zerilli, "Value Pluralism," to torture in Waldron, "Two-Way Translation," and to cuts in social services in Wolterstorff, "Why We Should Reject." For inclusivists' warnings about the dangers of excluding religious energies from politics, see Connolly, *Why I Am Not a Secularist*; Coles, *Beyond Gated Politics*; Jeremy Waldron, "Secularism and the Limits of Community," in *Globalization Challenged: Conviction, Conflict, Community*, ed. G. Rupp (New York: Columbia University Press, 2006), 52–67; and Michael Walzer, "Drawing the Line: Religion and Politics," *Utah Law Review* 3 (1999): 619–38.

5. Obviously, no one regards all religious arguments and all political decisions as identical, and most theorists have qualified in some way their arguments for the inclusion or exclusion of religious reasons. However, I will show that there is a *tendency* to treat religious arguments and political life in a unitary manner and that moving the debate in a pluralizing direction can advance it substantially. For example, while Waldron devotes considerable attention to breaking down the various modes of using religion in political argument, he does so in support of the conclusion that "so long as there is due recognition of the multi-faith and secular aspects of our society and due recognition of the constitutional structure that responds to that, there is no particular reason for church people to refrain from participation *in public life* on the basis of their values." Waldron, "Two-Way Translation," 849, emphasis added. Just as there is a world of difference between a religious argument taking the form of "a crude prescription from God, backed up with a threat of hellfire, derived from general or particular revelation" (Waldron, *God, Locke, and Equality: Christian Foundations in Locke's Political Thought* [Cambridge: Cambridge University Press, 2002], 20) and one taking the form of an appeal to the absolute value of the human person, so are there crucial differences between torture, welfare rights, abortion, racial justice, parental leave, homosexuality, birth control, and the HPV vaccine as subject matters and areas of collective political action. Similarly, while Eberle argues convincingly that respect need not require a principle of self-restraint from offering "religious" arguments, I argue that his requirement of conscientious engagement (after the fulfilling of which one is free to give religious arguments) fails to distinguish between different ways of deriving religious arguments and presenting them in public debate, on the one hand, and different areas of political action, on the other. My aim in this chapter is to show how so distinguishing can give us a better account of the morality of using religious arguments in public.

6. I do not explore the idea of solidarity in depth in this chapter, except to note here that both including and excluding religious arguments in public can be said to adversely affect feelings of solidarity among citizens. The ideal of public reason is partially motivated by a concern about the impact on social solidarity of citizens' failure (to feel obligated) to justify laws to fellow citizens affected by them. As Rawls puts it, "the role of the criterion of reciprocity in public reason . . . is to specify the nature of the political relation in a constitutional democratic regime as one of civic friendship" (*PL* [pbk.] li). However, insofar as religious citizens feel alienated from the public sphere or inhibited from sharing views derived from religious traditions, this can also be said to inhibit bonds of civic solidarity. And whether a concern for solidarity as one political good among many calls for more or less religious argumentation in public depends on a nuanced contextual analysis of the kind of religious reasons in question and the subject matter of political argument about which they are given. A concern for solidarity does not militate unambiguously for or against either view.

7. See *PL* (pbk.) l, 213–16; and, in response, Jonathan Quong, "The Scope of Public Reason," *Political Studies* 52 (2004): 233–50.

8. Just as Rawls qualifies the acceptability of arguing from religious reasons by requiring that nonreligious, public reasons be given in due course, inclusivists often argue that the primary requirement on religious citizens is to cultivate a certain attitude of goodwill for citizens of other moral persuasions (see Robert P. George, "Law, Democracy, and Moral Disagreement," *Harvard Law Review* 110, no. 7 [1997]: 1388–406), to make some initial conscientious attempt to search for shared reasons (Eberle, *Religious Conviction in Liberal Politics*), or to be willing to subject one's own religious arguments to critical scrutiny and possible defeat (see J. Caleb Clanton, "Democratic Deliberation *After* Religious Gag Rules," in Clanton, *The Ethics of Citizenship*, 365–92).

9. National Association of Evangelicals, *An Evangelical Declaration Against Torture: Protecting Human Rights in an Age of Terror*, 2007, www.nae.net/government-relations/endorsed-documents/409-an-evangelical-declaration-against-torture-protecting-human-rights-in-an-age-of-terror.

10. Ibid.

11. Ibid.

12. Ibid.

13. *IPRR* 144.

14. Martin Luther King Jr., *A Testament of Hope: The Essential Writings and Speeches of Martin Luther King, Jr.*, ed. J. M. Washington (New York: Harper, 1991), 293.

15. Similarly, the *Evangelical Declaration Against Torture* is presented as a way of inviting fellow citizens into an imaginative space through the dramatic use of religious imagery: "However remote to us may be the victim of torture, abuse, or mistreatment, Christians must seek to develop the moral imagination to enter into the suffering of all who are victimized."

16. In this regard, see Audi, *Religious Commitment and Secular Reason*; and Macedo, "In Defense of Liberal Public Reason."

17. Here I have in mind Habermas, "Religion in the Public Sphere."

18. I do not take a strong position here on the conflict between agonistic and deliberative conceptions of democracy. My goal is to present an analysis that speaks to partisans of both. I merely note that a number of important advocates of religious arguments in political debate see inclusivism as compatible with justificatory and deliberative aspirations. Gaus and Vallier have tried to elaborate an alternative position that allows for the use of religious reasons, provided that the law advocated for does not preclude a *convergence* of distinct reasons. My position shares with theirs a focus on the moral content of the proposed political outcome, namely, whether the law or policy is reasonably demanded of all affected by it.

19. See Michael Rosen, *Dignity: Its History and Meaning* (Cambridge, Mass.: Harvard University Press, 2012).

20. See Ronald Dworkin, *Life's Dominion: An Argument About Abortion, Euthanasia, and Individual Freedom* (New York: Knopf, 1993), 71–84.

21. *Pace* Sherif Girgis, Ryan T. Anderson, and Robert P. George, *What Is Marriage? Man and Woman: A Defense* (New York: Encounter Books, 2012).

22. See Zerilli, "Value Pluralism."

23. See, in this regard, *PL* (pbk.) 12; Vallier and D'Agostino, "Public Justification"; Quong, *Liberalism Without Perfection*, 233–50; Charles Larmore, *The Autonomy of Morality* (New York: Cambridge University Press, 2008), 86; and Solum, "Constructing an Ideal of Public Reason," 738–39.

24. Some of the political agenda of the religious Right in the United States focuses on a restoration of more robust parental rights over children, including through a proposed Parental Rights Amendment to the U.S. Constitution. See Linda L. Lane, "The Parental Rights Movement," *University of Colorado Law Review* 69 (1998): 825–50.

25. There may be subjects of political power that fall in between these first two categories at times. There are persons who are neither foreigners nor children yet who are often spoken of in paternalistic terms. Debates over punishment, prostitution, exploited workers, the elderly, the mentally infirm, women in patriarchal religious communities, the poor, and resident noncitizens are often conducted in a way that does not quite reflect a desire to enforce a single controversial conception of the good or of virtue on all persons, but yet involves the assumption that certain persons must be spoken for and defended by others. Here I merely want to note and bring attention to this hybrid category of persons who are often the object of political debate in this way. Laws and policies that we oppose or defend on moral grounds (including religious ones) are often not about the rights of sane adults capable of representing themselves or about children or others outside the social contract, but about certain classes of persons who would normally belong in the first category but for some contingent politically, economically, or culturally disenabling condition.

26. See, for example, Seyla Benhabib, *Dignity in Adversity: Human Rights in Troubled Times* (Cambridge: Polity, 2011); and Benhabib, *The Rights of Others: Aliens, Residents, and Citizens* (Cambridge: Cambridge University Press, 2004).

27. See Joshua Cohen and Charles Sabel, "Extra Rempublicam Nulla Justitia?," *Philosophy and Public Affairs* 34, no. 2 (2006): 147–75; and Thomas Nagel, "The Problem of Global Justice," *Philosophy and Public Affairs* 33, no. 2 (2005): 113–47.

28. See, for instance, Rainer Forst, *The Right to Justification: Elements of a Constructivist Theory of Justice* (New York: Columbia University Press, 2012); Martha Nussbaum, *Frontiers of Justice: Disability, Nationality, Species Membership* (Cambridge, Mass.: Harvard University Press, 2006); and Thomas Pogge, *World Poverty and Human Rights: Cosmopolitan Responsibilities and Reforms* (Cambridge: Polity, 2002).

29. See, for instance, Robert P. George, "Public Reason and Political Conflict: Abortion and Homosexuality," *Yale Law Journal* 106, no. 8 (1997): 2475–504.

30. Consider, again, a passage from the *Evangelical Declaration Against Torture*: "We live in a free society, a representative democracy, and while only a few may be direct perpetrators of human rights violations or even torture, we all share the responsibility because we are the citizens on whose behalf interrogators and military personnel are working. Whether we commit an offense against humanity, or simply sin by refusing to speak up for someone who is being victimized, as individuals and a society we are accountable for the indignities that are authorized and carried out by our nation." See also Eric Beerbohm, *In Our Name: The Ethics of Democracy* (Princeton: Princeton University Press, 2012).

31. On this, see Benjamin Hertzberg, "Both Citizen and Saint: Religious Integrity and Liberal Democracy" (PhD diss., Duke University, 2011).

32. Alasdair MacIntyre, *After Virtue: A Study in Moral Theory* (Notre Dame: University of Notre Dame Press, 1981).

33. See, for instance, Brad S. Gregory, *The Unintended Reformation: How a Religious Reformation Secularized Society* (Cambridge, Mass.: Harvard University Press, 2012); and Jean Bethke Elshtain, *Sovereignty: God, State, and Self* (New York: Basic Books, 2008).

34. A number of U.S. states still had criminal sodomy laws before *Lawrence v. Texas* (2003), a decision from which three justices dissented.

35. See, for instance, Martha Nussbaum, "Veiled Threats," *New York Times Opinionator*, July 11, 2010, http://opinionator.blogs.nytimes.com/2010/07/11/veiled-threats. For a paternalistic use of "dignity" in European human rights jurisprudence on the issue of dwarf-tossing, see Rosen, *Dignity*, 63–77.

36. This is not to claim that paternalistic policies, including over the actions of self-representing adults, can never be justified. But it is to presume a prima facie right to justification and to articulate and act on a conception of one's own interests. I also mean to posit certain limits on the sources of knowledge about others' interests that can be used to justify paternalistic coercion. For recent discussion, see Cass Sunstein,

"It's For Your Own Good!" *New York Review of Books* 60, no. 7 (2013): 53–54; and Sarah Conly, *Against Autonomy: Justifying Coercive Paternalism* (Cambridge: Cambridge University Press, 2012). Conly, for example, is primarily interested in faulty human reasoning in advancing our interests and choosing effective means to our ends, rather than in identifying our true interests and ends.

37. See, for instance, Clare Chambers, "The Marriage-Free State," *Proceedings of the Aristotelian Society* 113, no. 2 (2013): 123–43; March, "Is There a Right to Polygamy? Marriage, Equality and Subsidizing Families in Liberal Public Justification," *Journal of Moral Philosophy* 8, no. 2 (2011): 244–70; March, "What Lies Beyond Same-Sex Marriage? Marriage, Reproductive Freedom and Future Persons in Liberal Public Justification," *Journal of Applied Philosophy* 27, no. 1 (2010): 39–58; Tamara Metz, *Untying the Knot: Marriage, the State and the Case for Their Divorce* (Princeton: Princeton University Press, 2010); Cass Sunstein and Richard Thaler, "Privatizing Marriage," *Monist* 91, no. 3–4 (2008): 377–87; Nancy D. Polikoff, *Beyond (Straight and Gay) Marriage: Valuing All Families Under the Law* (Boston: Beacon, 2008); Judith Butler, "Is Kinship Always Already Heterosexual?," *differences: A Journal of Feminist Cultural Studies* 13, no. 1 (2002): 14–44; Nancy Cott, *Public Vows: A History of Marriage and the Nation* (Cambridge, Mass.: Harvard University Press, 2000); and Michael Warner, *The Trouble with Normal: Sex, Politics, and the Ethics of Queer Life* (Cambridge, Mass.: Harvard University Press, 1999).

38. I say this without endorsing any particular policy prescription on any of them, particularly abortion, which obviously involves also the bodily and moral interests of self-representing citizens (women) in ways the other issues do not.

39. Moral doctrines dispute only the weight and importance of these goods relative to other ones, and even the Stoic objection is as much semantic as categorical. See Cicero, *On Moral Ends*, ed. J. Annas (Cambridge: Cambridge University Press, 2001), 67–89.

40. Obligations to the nonhuman natural world, including animals, are a harder case, which I do not address here, and which perhaps does not admit of determinate answers.

41. See David Sussman, "What's Wrong with Torture?," *Philosophy and Public Affairs* 33, no. 1 (2005): 1–33; and Henry Shue, "Torture," *Philosophy and Public Affairs* 7, no. 2 (1978): 124–43.

42. Again from the *Evangelical Declaration Against Torture*: "Torture is but one of many violations of human rights. . . . All these and the like are criminal: they poison civilization; and they debase the perpetrators more than the victims and militate against the honor of the creator."

PART II

ACCOMMODATING
RELIGIONS
WITH RAWLS

5

The Liberal State
and the Religious Citizen

JUSTIFICATORY PERSPECTIVES
IN POLITICAL LIBERALISM

PATRICK NEAL

Does Rawls's conception of political liberalism ask too much of religious citizens? Many discussions of this question focus on what the demands of Rawls's political theory are, and how they relate to the point of view of the conscientious religious citizen. But this cannot be the whole of the story. Whether Rawls's theory asks "too much" depends not only on what it demands, but also on how these demands compare with some alternative set proposed as candidates for governing the public sphere of a pluralistic democracy. When assessed by that standard, my claim is that Rawls's political liberalism is attractive from the point of view of many—although certainly not all—religious citizens, *despite* the fact that it does indeed make considerable demands upon the religious citizen. However, in my view, it does not follow from this that the citizen should, all things considered, accede to those demands. That is a question that rests upon the conscientious judgment of particular citizens in light of both their comprehensive moral or religious views and their understanding of the good of political life. And, perhaps surprisingly, I maintain that this was Rawls's view as well. That is, contrary to many readings, I maintain that Rawls does not hold that the demands of political liberalism must take priority over one's most fundamental religious or moral commitments, let alone require that they—and thus, by implication, one's personal integrity—be sacrificed to the demands of political liberalism. In light of these claims, I maintain that Rawls's concept of political liberalism is far more accommodating, and indeed inviting, to conscientious religious commitment than is ordinarily thought to be the case.

In developing this argument, I place considerable emphasis upon the different justificatory perspectives that are involved in Rawls's theory of political liberalism. Distinguishing these perspectives is, I claim, essential to a clear and fair understanding of the way that he conceives the relation between religion and political liberalism. The dominant perspective is that of a liberal democratic state trying to articulate, explain, and justify to its citizens the political conception of justice underlying the basic constitutional principles that comprise the state or constitute citizens as a polity. This "official" perspective is decidedly not the perspective of an individual person trying to assess his or her duties as both a religious and a political agent, although of course it bears upon this second perspective. Rawls rarely assumes this second perspective in presenting his theory of political liberalism. In particular, he does not discuss his own comprehensive moral or religious views, and so he does not specify how they lead to an affirmation of political liberalism. Although this might lead one to think that he considers the perspective of the conscientious individual to be unimportant for his theory, I will show below that this is not the case. I will also show that a third perspective is involved in Rawls's theory, namely, that of a detached observer considering the possible tensions between the other two perspectives, those of the liberal democratic state and the individual. In organizing the following analysis around these three perspectives, I aim both to clarify aspects of Rawls's theory of political liberalism and to show that it is far more "religion-friendly" than is often thought. I count the latter claim as a virtue. Some supporters of political liberalism may not, for the idea that political liberalism is hostile to religious commitment and integrity is a view held not only by many religious critics of the theory, but also by many secular liberal supporters of it. What follows is intended to show that both are mistaken.

In the first part of the chapter, I briefly discuss two important preliminary matters, one being the nature of Rawls's own understanding of political liberalism's relation to religion and the other concerning the meaning of the controversial concept of "reasonableness." I then employ the notion of Rawls's three justificatory perspectives to discuss two fundamental issues regarding the relation between religion and political liberalism. Thus, in the second part of the chapter, I consider whether political liberalism requires the religious citizen to subordinate her religious commitments to the demands of political liberalism, and in the third and final part I consider Rawls's moral grounds for presenting political liberalism as the right kind of political conception for us, and how alternative political conceptions might compare.

Before proceeding, it is important to state two constraints within which my analysis is carried out. First, I do not attempt to provide a foundational defense of political liberalism as the right way to understand the political relation in a democratic society. I am concerned rather with the issue of how political liberalism relates to religious conscience and commitment, and so I assume for the sake of argument that political liberalism is at least a plausible candidate from the point of view of a foundational defense. Second, I am concerned with what might be called the "core structure" of political liberalism as an account of the political relationship, rather than with the particular components of that structure. I will not, for example, consider the details of the particular demands of public reason as they relate to religious citizens. Rather, I will focus upon the core issue of whether and in what sense political liberalism involves the subordination of religious commitment.

PRELIMINARIES: RAWLS'S AIMS
AND THE CONCEPT OF "REASONABLENESS"

An important resource for understanding Rawls's thinking about the relationship between political liberalism and religion is a fascinating interview he gave to Bernard Prusak for *Commonweal* magazine in 1998, one of his last public presentations before his death in 2002. Admittedly, an interview is not an essay, article, or book containing the considered views that an author knowingly commits to the forum of scholarly debate. But I will not appeal to this interview to try to show something novel and arresting, like an important change Rawls made in his ideas or some inconsistency between his "official" ideas and the ideas expressed in the interview. Indeed, there is nothing fundamentally new or inconsistent with his previous published work in the *Commonweal* interview. Rather, the interview is important because it brings out so vividly and clearly the meaning of some of Rawls's earlier work from his own point of view, and especially some aspects that had been ambiguous.

The single idea that animates Rawls most throughout the interview is the thought that political liberalism might be hostile to religion. Rawls does not simply deny this; he denies it passionately and repeatedly and he strains to make clear to Prusak and his audience that political liberalism is misunderstood if taken to embody such a hostile attitude. At one point Prusak puts to Rawls the fact that many take him to be making a "veiled argument for secularism" through his defense of the idea of public reason. Rawls responds, "I emphatically deny it." He explains that he is attempting to articulate the terms of common political ground between adherents of both religious and secular comprehensive views, although he acknowledges the difficulty of the task, given that "those of religious faith will say I give a veiled argument for secularism, and the latter [that is, secularists] will say I give a veiled argument for religion."[1] Later, Prusak puts to Rawls the common criticism that insofar as public reason requires religious citizens to make political arguments in nonreligious terms, it threatens the integrity of the believer. Prusak says, "Take the argument for the sacredness of life. A believer might say this has been revealed. But by having to make arguments in terms everybody recognizes, I'm being asked to renounce the truth as I know it." Rawls interrupts Prusak at this point and exclaims, "No, you're not being asked to renounce it! Of course not."[2] He then develops his response as follows:

See, what I should do is turn around and say, what's the better suggestion, what's your solution to it? And I can't see any other solution. This solution has been followed in the United States since the First Amendment. . . . People can make arguments from the Bible if they want to. But I want them to see that they should also give arguments that all reasonable citizens might agree to. Again, what's the alternative? How are you going to get along in a constitutional regime with all these other comprehensive doctrines?[3]

Admittedly, the fact that Rawls himself thought that his critics had misunderstood his theory does not necessarily mean that he was correct in so thinking. Doubtless all of us are more fond of our own views than we should be. Still, Rawls's comments here counsel us to try to understand his theory of political liberalism on the interpretive assumption that it is intended to treat religious citizens with respect. We may decide on reflection that it fails in that endeavor, but I think that it is clear that this was Rawls's endeavor. Moreover, many aspects of his theory take on a different hue than is commonly given them when it is examined from this angle.

Let us turn now to the other preliminary matter, namely, the notorious concept of the "reasonable" in political liberalism. A person who rejects the basic tenets of political liberalism is, in the terms of political liberalism, "unreasonable." In my view, this term was a particularly unfortunate one for Rawls to use. It could not but be understood in a wider and more pejorative sense than it really has in his theory, and thus give rise to the view that, for Rawls, if you are not a political liberal in his sense, you are not a reasonable person in a general sense. But he is clear enough in stating that he uses "reasonableness" as a moral, rather than an epistemic, category, and, on my understanding of it, all that it means is "one who refuses to affirm the principles of political liberalism as terms of political order," or, more specifically, "one who rejects Rawls's understanding of the principle of political reciprocity."[4] Some such persons (like some persons who affirm political liberalism) are "unreasonable" in many other senses, some of them highly pejorative, just as some such persons (again, like some persons who affirm political liberalism) are highly reasonable in many other senses, some of them highly laudatory. I will use the category of unreasonableness in the limited, nonpejorative, and essentially circular sense I have defined above, since it is awkward to "translate" it each time it occurs into versions of "not committed to the principles of political liberalism," but I implore the reader to recall that, in my view, it means nothing more than that. A crucial implication of this is that knowing whether a person is "reasonable" in Rawls's sense cannot tell us whether political liberalism is worth affirming or rejecting, because it is already defined in terms of affirming it.

COMPREHENSIVE COMMITMENTS AND POLITICAL VALUES

These preliminaries taken care of, consider now the question of what it means for religion to be "subordinated" to the demands of public reason and political liberalism. I take it as obvious that there is a sense in which political liberalism does entail the subordination of religious reasons in the practice of public justification, and that this subordination is the primary stumbling block for any attempt to demonstrate that there is greater room for agreement between political liberalism and religious views than is often thought to be the case. On the face of things, there does not seem to be much room for agreement here: religious demands are often, and normally, understood to be fundamental and overriding by conscientious religious believers, and so the apparent demand that they be subordinated to some other standard of behavior seems like a simple nonstarter. Many of the most strident criticisms of Rawls from the point of view of religious concerns proceed from just this point.

Let us distinguish, though, between two models of how this subordination might be understood to work, which I will label "direct" and "indirect." Direct subordination is the view that the terms of political order are fundamental and basic in the order of demands made upon persons, and that any and all alternative sources of self-understood obligation—be they religious, ethnic, familial, or of any other kind—must therefore be limited and defined by the sovereign terms of political order, whatever they are. This would itself constitute a "comprehensive" view in Rawls's sense, and so would necessarily conflict with the conscientious moral or religious commitments of those who rejected it. I grant that if Rawls's theory invokes this model of direct subordination, it fails as an account of the political relation.

Indirect subordination is different. Here, the terms of political order are understood as placing themselves before the tribunal of the individual citizen's judgment, a judgment to be made in full light of his or her religious (or moral or philosophical comprehensive) views. The

Rawlsian terms of political order, considered in this way, will ask of the conscientious religious citizen that she affirm the terms of order, and the consequent demands of public reason, in full light of her religious duties and understandings. At this "moment," the demands of political order are "subordinate" to the conscientious demands of the citizen's comprehensive view, whether this is religious or not. Now the citizen either will or will not make this affirmation. In essence, what she will be deciding is whether the politically liberal terms of order are, considered in relation to the available alternative terms of political order, the best way to understand and practice her life as a citizen in light of her more fundamental conscientious duties, religious or otherwise. If she does judge that it is best to affirm the politically liberal principles of order in light of these considerations, then the practice of those terms of order will, it is true, "subordinate" her use of religious reasons in the practice of public political justification. However, this subordination is "indirect" in the sense that it is the consequence of her own conscientious decision to impose the subordination upon herself as a civic actor, made with full understanding of her own religious commitments and how they relate to political life, and therefore made at least partly because of, not in spite of, her religious views. For example, in a given setting a Christian citizen might come to judge political liberalism as a means of expressing religious duties of charity and humility, and so affirm it as an act of political friendship toward one's equals, whether they be Christian or not.

Let us now consider Rawls's own view of what I am calling indirect subordination. Without going so far as to claim that indirect subordination entirely overcomes the tension between political liberalism and the religious citizen, I take it that it is at least not as objectionable as direct subordination from the point of view of religious conscience. And I think that Rawls intended political liberalism to be understood as enacting the process of indirect subordination, rather than as an expression of a political ethic of direct subordination, even though it is often described and vilified as the latter.

Certain key passages are particularly telling in this respect. They show not only that Rawls conceived the relationship of political liberalism to religion on the model of indirect subordination, but also how this involves the three justificatory perspectives that I introduced at the beginning.

One of the most interesting passages in Rawls's writings on political liberalism is in his essay "The Priority of Right and Ideas of the Good." There, in the context of explaining how political liberalism can achieve stability by generating its own support, Rawls writes, "Of course, there can be no guarantee of stability. Political good, no matter how important, can never in general outweigh the transcendent values—certain religious, philosophical, and moral values—that may possibly come into conflict with it. That idea is not being suggested."[5] This is one of Rawls's clearest indications of his awareness of the possibility that citizen's "comprehensive views" may leave them in a position where they cannot in good conscience affirm the principles of political liberalism. Moreover, this possibility is not criticized, but rather recognized as an existential possibility that cannot be avoided. The stance taken by Rawls in this passage therefore sits uneasily with the "direct subordination" understanding of the principles of political liberalism, and the attendant requirements of public reason, as intended to always take rightful priority over the conscientious demands of one's comprehensive view or conception of the good.[6]

Considering this passage in terms of the perspectives of the liberal state, the citizen, and the observer also helps to illuminate Rawls's understanding of political liberalism. The principles of political liberalism present themselves as terms of political order that can enable adherents of different comprehensive views to live together politically in a manner that embodies and respects their status as free and equal persons. The principles present themselves as an interpretation of what a constitutional democracy is—that is, not of any particular constitutional democracy, but of the type. Thus, from the perspective of the principles themselves—that is, from the specifically public perspective of the regime embodying them—their "priority" over individual conscience is simply a matter of course. They have "priority" over citizens' various conceptions of the good for the mundane reason that that is precisely what they are designed to do. They are, or they are presented to citizens by the state seeking citizens' assent as, principles for authoritatively governing the political relations among citizens. For an analogy, consider the sense in which constitutional principles have "priority" over ordinary legislation; having priority in this sense is just part of what it means to be constitutional and not ordinary.

But the regime's perspective is not the only one in play here. There is also the perspective of the citizen, who is (or at least may be) also a person with a comprehensive view. Each citizen must examine and assess the relationship between her comprehensive view and the political principles presenting themselves for her assent. The political principles request assent, but the assent must be given by the citizen in light of her comprehensive view. This is, loosely, the state's attempt to elicit an "overlapping consensus" of support for the political principles. From this perspective, the "priority" of the political conception is not assumed at all, but is rather being evaluated as a possible commitment to be made by the individual in light of, rather than in spite of, her comprehensive moral or religious views.

Moreover, in the passage of "The Priority of Right and Ideas of the Good" quoted above Rawls adopts a third perspective on this activity, namely, that of an observer of it. It is from this perspective that he remarks that "there can be no guarantee" of such an overlapping consensus developing.

Confusion can arise because Rawls does not commonly adopt the latter two perspectives in his accounts of political liberalism. The most common perspective he takes is that of the state, of the public view of the principles of political order, as he develops, articulates, and explains the fundamental terms of "political liberalism." When adopting that perspective, I think of Rawls the writer as, in a sense, occupying a kind of hypothetical public office. The "type" of constitutional democracy needs to announce and explain its constituent parts, its duties and purposes, to its audience of potential consenters. Rawls writes, as it were, as the public official charged with the duty of doing this, and so much of his account of "political liberalism" can be understood as him articulating this public perspective. By contrast, Rawls the writer almost never inhabits or speaks from the perspective of the citizen with a comprehensive moral or religious conception looking at the political principles and judging whether to affirm them or not. So, for example, he does not speak to us about his own comprehensive conception, nor does he assess the principles of political liberalism from that particular perspective. That is not to say that he as a person did not ever take such a perspective. Of course he did. But it is largely absent, at least overtly, from his writings about political liberalism.

The third perspective, what I have here called that of the "observer" of all this, also appears in his writing, and I suggest that it is especially evident in the passage quoted above. Rawls the public official of political liberalism certainly hopes that political liberalism will attract and also reproduce a broad and deep base of support by winning the consent of most comprehensive views likely to grow and flourish in a constitutional regime. And we may reasonably assume that Rawls the individual person shared this hope because he was able to affirm those political principles on the basis of the comprehensive view with which he identified. But Rawls the observer of all this takes a perspective different from those two perspectives. From that observer's view, it is an interesting and open question as to whether political liberalism can or will succeed at generating an overlapping consensus of comprehensive views in support of itself. The question is open precisely because that support must be *won*. It must be won because it is taken as normal and appropriate that our comprehensive view is going to be ultimately decisive for us as we wrestle with conscientious decisions about political allegiance.

It is important to note also that in this passage in "The Priority of Right and Ideas of the Good," Rawls the observer is not simply acknowledging the empirical fact that some people might reject the principles of political liberalism. That fact is obviously true, but it would not follow from it that such a rejection is normatively defensible. From the state perspective of political liberalism itself, such a rejection is normatively wrong. Citizens who reject the terms of political liberalism are, by definition, wrong to do so—in Rawls's language, they are "unreasonable." This is the perspective informing the well-known and controversial passage where Rawls speaks of a society containing "unreasonable and irrational and even mad, comprehensive doctrines. In their case the problem is to contain them so that they do not undermine the unity and justice of society."[7] But in the passage under consideration here, Rawls is not speaking from this perspective, and he is not assuming that the rejection of political liberalism is normatively wrong. Rather, he takes the observer perspective. The "of course" clause of the passage overtly recognizes that "political good" is subordinate to the transcendent values embodied in our comprehensive views, and that this subordination is not itself normatively wrong.

Consider, in line with what I have just said, other comments that Rawls makes in the course of his "Reply to Habermas." The context is his explanation of how the public justification of the political conception itself can be carried out. It might seem at first that this could not be done, because the terms of the political conception are already presupposed when they are applied as the ground rules of political debate on constitutional questions. This is the way the matter appears from the state perspective of the principles composing the political conception. Again, however, this is not the whole story. For Rawls acknowledges that each citizen must also engage in the process of judging whether the political conception itself is to be affirmed, in light of his or her comprehensive moral or religious view. He writes:

> Full justification is carried out by an individual citizen as a member of civil society. (We assume that each citizen affirms both a political conception and a comprehensive doctrine.) In this case, the citizen accepts a political conception and fills out its justification by embedding it in some way into the citizen's comprehensive doctrine as either true or reasonable, depending on what the doctrine allows. . . . Thus it is left to each citizen, individually or in association with others, to say how the claims of political justice are to be ordered, or weighed, against nonpolitical values. *The political conception gives no guidance in such questions.*[8]

So again we see that Rawls clearly recognizes that the political conception is itself dependent for its support and affirmation upon the judgment of citizens, and that these judgments proceed directly from their comprehensive moral or religious views. The "priority" of the political conception becomes operative only when it is authorized to do so by the judgment of the citizen him- or herself, reasoning about the matter with full awareness of his or her own comprehensive view. The "overlapping consensus" of support for the political conception (or, as Rawls later says, the family of political conceptions) is constituted by these multiple affirmations from various comprehensive points of view. As Rawls puts it later in his "Reply to Habermas," "we hope that citizens will judge (by their comprehensive view) that political values either outweigh or are normally (though not always) ordered prior to whatever nonpolitical values may conflict with them."[9] I do not take

Rawls to be speaking here as the official voice of the political conception, because from that perspective the "outweighing" referred to here would simply be required, and so would not need to be "hoped" for. Rather, the "we" who "hope" for this outweighing would be those citizens who have reached the judgment that political liberalism is worthy of affirmation as a political conception by evaluating it in light of our comprehensive views, whatever they are. Such citizens would naturally "hope" that others would join the overlapping consensus of support for political liberalism so that the regime they affirm might be strong and stable. But they have to "hope" this precisely because it is not taken for granted. Again, this is not merely an empirical matter. Political liberalism can descriptively distinguish between those who affirm it (the "reasonable") and those who do not (the "unreasonable"), but it cannot therefore say that the unreasonable have invoked comprehensive views that are wrong or false. Ultimately, the political conception itself simply distinguishes as a matter of fact between those who affirm it and those who do not, in exactly the same sense in which we might say in ordinary political discourse that some people accept and abide by the principles of the constitution and others do not.

Rawls is so concerned not to be misunderstood on this point that he makes an interesting comment in a note attached to his remark about his "hope." He writes:

> If one fails to note the background condition of a reasonable overlapping consensus, the assertion in the text taken alone appears to express a comprehensive moral point of view that ranks the duties owed to just basic institutions ahead of all other human commitments. . . . A troubling assertion, however, occurs only when one forgets that a reasonable overlapping consensus is assumed to obtain and that the text is commenting on the public justification of the political conception carried out by members of society.[10]

Again, then, Rawls's claim is that statements regarding the superiority of political values are to be understood as presupposing that citizens have *already* decided, for their own different conscientious reasons, to proceed with the use of political values in public justification. He does not offer a general argument to the effect that, all things considered, political values ought always to take priority over comprehensive moral or religious values. That judgment is to be made by citizens themselves, and Rawls the "observing" expositor of political liberalism accepts the rightness, the normative appropriateness, of that state of affairs.

Rawls makes an even more striking affirmation of the priority of the individual's conscientious (religious or moral) judgment in relation to the principles of political liberalism in a later passage of his "Reply to Habermas." There he writes:

> These statements [that a sovereign democratic people may legitimately, though not justly, pass laws that violate the moral rights of citizens] simply express the risk for justice of all government, democratic or otherwise; for there is no human institution—political or social, judicial or ecclesiastical—that can guarantee that legitimate (or just) laws are always enacted and just rights always respected. To this add: *certainly, and never to be questioned*, a single person may stand alone and be right in saying that law and government are wrong and unjust.[11]

The fact that the lone dissenting individual can be right is another way of saying that the political conception itself cannot ultimately be the measure of moral or religious truth. Affirming and following the political conception is a judgment we make on the basis of our own understanding of moral or religious truth. Whether we are right or wrong in our understanding of that truth is not something that the political conception can tell us, and while being a part of a widespread overlapping consensus in support of a political conception is proof of our "reasonableness," it is not proof of our moral or religious rightness.

This crucial point is reiterated in the remarks that Rawls makes about the idea of overlapping consensus in *Justice as Fairness: A Restatement*. There he writes, "political liberalism does not say that the values articulated by a political conception of justice, though of basic significance, outweigh the transcendent values (as people may interpret them)—religious, philosophical, or moral—with which the political conception may possibly conflict. To say that would go beyond the political."[12] Given the point being made in the passage, it might have been better not to refer here to the political values as "basic." In other places, Rawls refers instead to the "very great value" of the political values, which of course leaves open the issue of whether others might not be of even greater value.[13] Nevertheless, the meaning is clear: political liberalism does not mandate the direct subordination of the religious to the political, from the perspective of an individual citizen's conscientious judgment.

Consideration of these various passages shows, I think, that Rawls's theory of political liberalism is best understood as embodying the indirect model of the subordination of religious to political claims. It is thus decidedly less hostile to the claims of religious conscience than is supposed by those who take political liberalism to embody the direct subordination model. Of course, the road to hell may be paved with reasonable intentions, and some will count this as a mark against political liberalism, which after all cannot and does not attempt to deny it. But those with less confidence in their own, or other human beings', ability to chart the geography of ultimate things will not count it as a fault of political liberalism that it eschews the attempt.

THE PROBLEM OF ALTERNATIVE
POLITICAL CONCEPTIONS

In the passage quoted from the *Commonweal* interview, Rawls twice stresses, with a note of exasperation, that if political liberalism is rejected, we still need an account of the political relation for a pluralistic constitutional democracy. He says, "See, what I should do is turn around and say, what's the better suggestion, what's your solution to it?"; and, then, "Again, what's the alternative? How are you going to get along in a constitutional regime with all these other comprehensive doctrines?" One reading of these passages is that Rawls is simply displaying the elitist liberal's incredulity that others do not see the evident validity of liberalism as he does. A more charitable view is that he is pointing out that the perspective of the liberal democratic state and the perspective of the individual are not the same, and that the question to which the political conception is proposed as an answer is a question about the terms of the political relation between citizens, and not a question about the conscience of the individual citizen. To put it more bluntly, any citizen who rejects the political conception on grounds of conscience may have answered an important question to herself as an individual, but she has not thereby answered the question posed from the political perspective, namely, "What's the alternative? What alternative account of the political relation is superior to the one given by political liberalism?" Some such account is needed because the normal plurality of conscientious moral and religious consciences means that, although one's conscience is determinative for oneself as an individual, it alone cannot provide an adequate account of the political relation. Thus Rawls is asking the individual to assume the hypothetical public office that he has assumed and, from *that* perspective, to offer an account of the political relation.

This point may seem rather obvious, but I think that its implications for assessing the relation between political liberalism and religion are often not appreciated. It is easy to think that if one demonstrates a sense in which political liberalism conflicts with the view of a particular comprehensive view, religious or otherwise, then one has demonstrated a flaw in political liberalism as an account of the political relation. However, it takes an account of the political relation to beat an account of the political relation. And *any* such account will conflict with the comprehensive views of some, if we take the plurality of reasonable comprehensive views as given. So before we reject political liberalism as an account of the political relation, we need an alternative with which to compare it. For example, it is often said that Rawls's view of political liberalism is objectionable because while it can accommodate religious comprehensive views that are themselves somewhat modern, self-critical, and liberal, it cannot accommodate religious comprehensive views that are committed to the idea of having access to divine truths that are directly politically relevant. This is true. However, I disagree with those defenders of Rawls who respond to this criticism by first acknowledging that such believers cannot be accommodated within the terms of political liberalism and then arguing that such an "exclusion" is justified because those religious views fail some independent standard of judgment, such as "reasonableness" is often taken to be. On my reading of Rawls, there is no such independent standard to be appealed to as a "neutral" justification for exclusion. Rather, I think that the political liberal should respond by acknowledging the nonneutral moral judgment that underwrites the criteria of political liberalism—that is, what Rawls labels the "principle of reciprocity"—and then asking of the excluded religious believer exactly the question that Rawls asked in his interview, namely, "what's the alternative?"[14]

Now, I do not deny that an answer may be, and sometimes is, forthcoming from critics of Rawls. Rawls is not the only one answering the question. Rather, my claim is that, in the absence of an alternative political proposal to compare it with, the fact that political liberalism pinches the conscience of some citizens is not enough to tell us anything significant about it. The exclusions and limits of political liberalism have to be measured not against the utopian standard of an account of the political relation that "includes" each and every conscientious comprehensive view and commitment, but against the standard of other political accounts that will also inevitably limit and exclude some claims of conscience.

Considered in this way, I think that political liberalism would do well in terms of the support it could attract from various religious comprehensive views.[15] The reason is simple. Since the evaluation of various accounts of the political relation cannot be carried out by judging whether or not they exclude religious and other comprehensive doctrines, we will have to look at which they exclude and, most fundamentally, why. That means that we will have to compare political liberalism with alternative accounts in light of the substantive value positions that define our own comprehensive views. Rawls articulates an account of the political relation that tries to work itself up from a view about what it means to live with others politically in a way that respects them as free and equal to oneself. That foundation is fortunately of fairly wide appeal to citizens in modern, pluralistic constitutional democracies. Admittedly, there are other ways of working it up into a political conception than that followed by Rawls. Still, there are lots of ways of developing an account of the political relation that will fare poorly when compared to political liberalism. In particular, I have in mind accounts that might be developed out of comprehensive views that cannot join the overlapping consensus in support of political liberalism. So, for example, the non-"modern" religious believer described above might argue that the political relation should instantiate the divine truth of which she claims to have knowledge, and that the freedom and political status of all should be defined in terms of this truth, a truth that might or might not allow freedom of religious conscience to individuals. Or, someone might argue that the political relation should aim at the instantiation of the true good for human beings, and that the freedom and political status of all should be defined in terms of that good, a good that might or might not involve treating individuals as free and equal. Adherents of these views will, of course, prefer them to political liberalism, and consequently may refuse to join the overlapping consensus of support for it. But I think of Rawls as designing political liberalism to appeal not so much to those dissenters—who, after all, disagree with him at a fundamental level—but rather to those who we might call the "undecideds," that is, those who affirm a comprehensive conception as true and right, but who nevertheless think that the fact that others do not affirm that conception does not at all impugn their standing as civic peers deserving of equal treatment and their freedom to follow their own consciences in affirming whatever comprehensive views they endorse. Political liberalism is an account of the political relation that amounts to treating a plurality of comprehensive views as perfectly acceptable choices of individuals. To affirm political liberalism is just this: to see civic equals who disagree about the question of the good as persons who have reached different, but respectable, judgments about fundamental matters, and to see these differences as never constituting a reason for unequal civic treatment.

There is no question that this is a "demanding" point of view. It is an exaggeration to say that it involves relativizing one's religious commitments to the point of treating them as a preference—or "hobby," as Stephen Carter once put it.[16] But it does entail that one grapple with the difficulty of living faithfully in service to a religious view while nevertheless treating the different views of others as being every bit as normatively warranted as one's own from a political point of view. The degree to which one accepts that tension as one to be lived with and negotiated, rather than resisted and avoided, will depend greatly upon the guidance that one receives in such matters from the substance of one's comprehensive view, religious or moral. That is, religious citizens' willingness to affirm political liberalism as an account of the political relation will depend upon the theology that informs their religious views.

Rawls did not attempt to write such a theology. Had he done so, he would have followed the estimable example of John Locke, who wrote not only a "political" defense of toleration, but also a Christian theology to accompany it, asserting, "I esteem that toleration to be the chief characteristic mark of the true Church."[17] Occasionally, however,

Rawls does hint at the religious sensibility that might yield such a theology. Speaking of how various comprehensive views might affirm political liberalism in *Justice as Fairness*, he remarks that "in endorsing a constitutional democratic regime, a religious doctrine may say that such are the limits God sets to our liberty; a nonreligious doctrine will express itself otherwise."[18] I take Rawls here to be imagining a theology that need not endorse political liberalism in any direct way, but that does teach individuals that God has set limits on their ability to know the truth about fundamental things, limits that require them to respect the consciences of their fellows who are, after all, subject to the same limits. Political liberalism could thus be an account of the political relation that works itself out plausibly from this theological sensibility. Of course, this is not a sensibility that all religious believers will endorse, but it is one that many have endorsed, with Locke and Immanuel Kant perhaps being its primary modern voices. Some view that tradition cynically, as the betrayal of "real" Christian religion in the name of a pseudo religion artfully constructed by modern political liberals to "tame" Christian religion and make it serviceable for modern politics. Perhaps. But I take it to be one—and certainly not the only—genuine expression of a religious instantiation of the principle of the equal dignity of all human beings.

What of those religious citizens who reject political liberalism? We will want to know what terms of political order they propose in its stead, and we will want to know how those terms bear upon our liberty of conscience. Rejecters may claim that their interest is in defending the right of everyone to speak and politically pursue the truth as they see it, in defiance of the limits upon this activity that political liberalism proposes with the idea of public reason. They may say that they are concerned with defending the integrity of conscientious citizens, and not with laying down the rules of political order that threaten it. But someone has to establish rules of political order, and all such rules threaten the integrity of conscience. This is why the issue of perspective is so important in understanding Rawls's position on religion and political liberalism. The standards of political liberalism are proposals for fulfilling this necessary public task, and they are offered from that particular and limited perspective. They are an attempt to give an account of the political relation that places liberty of individual conscience at the heart of political order, while insisting that no individual's conscience is more important than another's and that every individual ought to recognize in all others a conscientious agent like himself. Those values of freedom and equality are certainly not universally shared. But those who affirm them, including those millions who affirm them for religious reasons, will think that any political account must be measured by its fidelity to the purpose of upholding them, and they will recognize political liberalism as an attempt to do just that.

Notes

1. *CP* 619.

2. *CP* 620.

3. Ibid.

4. See the interesting discussion in Stephen Mulhall and Adam Swift, "Rawls and Communitarianism," in *The Cambridge Companion to Rawls*, ed. S. Freeman (Cambridge: Cambridge University Press, 2003), 460–87.

5. *CP* 471.

6. See, for example, Stuart Hampshire, "Liberalism: The New Twist," *New York Review of Books* 40, no. 14 (1993): 43–47.

7. *PL* (pbk.) xviii–xix.

8. *CP* 386, emphasis added.

9. *CP* 392.

10. *PL* (pbk.) 392n29.

11. *CP* 416, emphasis added.

12. *JF* 37.

13. *PL* (pbk.) 138–39.

14. For example, see Charles Larmore, "The Moral Basis of Political Liberalism," *Journal of Philosophy* 96, no. 12 (1999): 599–625.

15. For examples of defenses of political liberalism from religious perspectives, see Leslie C. Griffin, "Good Catholics Should Be Rawlsian Liberals," *Southern California Interdisciplinary Law Journal* 5, no. 3 (1997): 297–371; and Christopher J. Insole, *The Politics of Human Frailty: A Theological Defense of Political Liberalism* (Notre Dame: University of Notre Dame Press, 2005).

16. Stephen Carter, "Evolutionism, Creationism, and Treating Religion as a Hobby," *Duke Law Journal* 6 (1987): 977–96.

17. John Locke, *Two Treatises of Government, and a Letter Concerning Toleration*, ed. Ian Shapiro (New Haven: Yale University Press, 2004), 211.

18. *JF* 151; see also *JF* 173.

6

Reasoning from Conjecture

A REPLY TO THREE OBJECTIONS

MICAH SCHWARTZMAN

An important objection to political liberalism is that it has no way to adjudicate conflicts between public and nonpublic reasons.[1] It cannot explain why citizens should adhere to the constraints of public reason when these are at odds with their comprehensive ethical or religious perspectives. In such circumstances, citizens may wonder why they must conform to public reason rather than giving priority to conflicting nonpublic values.

Consider the following schematic example: Suppose citizen C agrees with the broad outlines of the ideal of public reason; she attaches great value to a political system in which citizens justify the exercise of their collective power in terms that everyone can reasonably accept. Suppose further that C is faced with a choice between two mutually exclusive public policies, α and β. After thinking carefully about the issues, she concludes that only β can be supported by a reasonable balance of political values. Thus, she has a *pro tanto*, or political, justification for β. This means that, so far as public reason is concerned, β is politically justifiable.[2] Now, under normal circumstances, C might be satisfied with this outcome. She accords significant weight to the value of giving others public reasons, and the fact that public reasoning reaches a conclusive determination is usually sufficient to settle the matter for her. In this case, however, C worries that her comprehensive view conflicts with her *pro tanto* justification for β. She believes that she has weighty nonpublic reasons to favor α, and these reasons conflict with the *pro tanto* political justification of β. To arrive at a *full*, or all-things-considered, justification of α or β, she must balance two competing sets of values. On one side is the set of political values that justifies β, as well as the political values that support the general practice of giving public reasons; on the other is the set of nonpublic values drawn from C's comprehensive view. The question is: why should she give priority to the values of public reason?

Critics argue that even if the ideal of public reason is supported by weighty values such as fair social cooperation, mutual respect, and political autonomy, there are significant costs attached to "bracketing" or setting aside the values of one's comprehensive doctrine.[3] An adequate defense of public reason would have to evaluate such costs and show that they are insufficient to undermine the duty of civility, which requires citizens to give public reasons for their political decisions. Unfortunately, the objection continues, political liberalism cannot provide such a defense because it is constrained by its own agnosticism about the nature and truth of comprehensive doctrines. The only way to establish the priority of public reason is to weigh conflicting public and nonpublic values, and this political liberalism is either unwilling or unable to do.

It is worth exploring the possibility of using a form of *non*public reason to help answer this objection. The basic strategy is to argue that C should respect the limits of public reason by demonstrating that the *pro tanto* justification of β is indeed fully justified according to her comprehensive view. The *full* justification of β is based, at least in part, on a nonpublic justification, according to which C is committed to supporting β because her comprehensive view, when properly understood, is compatible with and perhaps even justifies the practice of providing others with public reasons. John Rawls refers to this type of argument as "reasoning from conjecture." As he describes it, "we reason from what we believe, or conjecture, may be other people's basic doctrines, religious or philosophical, and seek to show them that, despite what they might think, they can still endorse a reasonable political conception of justice."[4]

My purpose here is to elucidate and defend the idea of reasoning in this way. In particular, I hope to show that engagement with comprehensive ethical and religious views can play a limited but potentially significant role in defending a commitment to public reason. I do not argue that reasoning from conjecture provides a complete response to objections concerning the priority of public reason, only that such reasoning may open up a domain of nonpublic justification for promoting the ideal of public reason. Nor is my aim to do the first-order work of engaging in reasoning from conjecture.[5] My broader purpose is to describe the structure of this form of reasoning (the first part of the chapter) and to show that, at least in principle, it can be defended against objections based on concerns about insincere argumentation (the second part), threats to cultural sovereignty (the third part), and challenges to the epistemic authority of those who reason from within comprehensive views other than their own (the fourth part). After responding to these three objections, in the fifth part of the chapter I discuss some limits to reasoning from conjecture, and then conclude.

REASONING FROM CONJECTURE

In "The Idea of Public Reason Revisited," Rawls introduces the idea of reasoning from conjecture as a way of responding to those who believe that their comprehensive doctrines conflict with the demands of public reason.[6] Rawls writes:

> We argue from what we believe, or conjecture, are other people's basic doctrines, religious or secular, and try to show them that, despite what they might think, they can still endorse a reasonable political conception that can provide a basis for public reasons. The ideal of public reason is thereby strengthened. However, it is important that conjecture be sincere and not manipulative. We must openly explain our intentions and state that we do not assert the premises from which we argue, but that we proceed as we do to clear up what we take to be a misunderstanding on others' part, and perhaps equally on ours.[7]

Three aspects of reasoning from conjecture (or conjecture, for short) are worth noting here. First, as its name suggests, reasoning from conjecture is a form of *reasoning*.[8] It is not simply an attempt at rhetorical persuasion. The idea is to present others with arguments that give them good reasons, as evaluated from within their own comprehensive views, for supporting a reasonable political conception as the basis for public reasoning. Thus, reasoning from conjecture is a form of nonpublic justification. Its purpose is to generate rational agreement on a shared or public basis for political decision-making.

Another way of describing the aim of conjecture is in terms of Rawls's distinction between *pro tanto* and *full* justification. As mentioned above, C has a *pro tanto*, or political, justification for policy β when that policy is supported by a reasonable balance of political values.[9] But she does not yet have a *full*, or all-things-considered, justification for supporting β. If her comprehensive view contains nonpublic values that conflict with the *pro tanto* justification for β, then she may decide to give priority to those values. In that case, C has a *pro tanto* justification for β, but not a *full* justification for it. The aim of conjecture is to bridge the gap between *pro tanto* and *full* justification by showing that C's comprehensive view supports, is consistent with, or at least is not in conflict with β.[10]

In general, political liberalism leaves it up to individual citizens to determine how *pro tanto* political justifications fit within their comprehensive doctrines.[11] But when citizens fail in this regard, or when they appear to be unable to reconcile the demands of a reasonable political conception with their comprehensive views, it may be possible to continue deliberating on the basis of conjectural arguments. If it can be shown that a comprehensive view is at least consistent with a reasonable political conception, and not in conflict with all such conceptions, then perhaps the weighty values that support providing others with public reasons—such as mutual respect, reciprocity, and political autonomy[12]—will be sufficient to establish a *full* justification for a reasonable political conception as the basis for making political decisions.

If it is asked why a *full* justification is required, or why it is not sufficient for political liberalism to provide a *pro tanto* justification for a political conception, the answer is that, without a full justification,

citizens may believe they have nonpublic reasons to act in violation of principles acceptable under a reasonable political conception. Because it is undesirable, and perhaps unjust, for citizens to
act in this way, reasoning from conjecture is justified as a means of
showing that citizens may have nonpublic grounds for respecting the
demands of public reason. In other words, conjecture aims at providing a nonpublic justification for being reasonable.[13] Since political liberalism avoids specifying a complete account of why people
ought to be reasonable, conjecture may facilitate the development of
such accounts for particular comprehensive views, if and when they
are needed.[14]

Second, those who engage in conjecture—call them "conjecturers,"
for lack of a better term—offer arguments based on premises they do
not accept. They argue from within comprehensive doctrines *other
than their own*,[15] for the purpose of justifying a reasonable political
conception. For example, if A conjectures that C should endorse justice as fairness, what she says to C is, "You should agree with Rawls's
principles of justice because your comprehensive doctrine commits
you to endorsing them. I don't happen to agree with your comprehensive doctrine. As I see it, I am committed to justice as fairness
for different reasons. But given what you believe, I think you should
be committed to the same conception of justice." Those who reason
from conjecture must make clear that, as Rawls says, "we do not
assert the premises from which we argue." This is, in part, to reas-
sure others of our sincerity. In making this clarification, however, we
are also asking others to take our arguments seriously on the ground
that these arguments are based on premises to which we believe they
are committed.

Third, despite what its name might suggest, reasoning from conjecture need not be based on arguments that are merely tentative or
suggestive. To some extent, Rawls trades on the uncertainty implied
by the word "conjecture." But this is not essential to the basic idea.
Conjecturers may be quite certain that their claims are conclusively
justified on the basis of particular comprehensive doctrines. The
central feature of conjecture is not a matter of epistemic credibility, or a lack thereof. It is rather that those who advance conjectural
arguments do not share a belief in their premises. Of course, in
defense of Rawls's terminology, it might be said that, in most cases,

conjectural arguments really are conjectures, in the ordinary sense of the word.[16] Unless conjecturers know a great deal about specific comprehensive views, their arguments will often be speculative and inconclusive. For that matter, even when they are deeply familiar with particular doctrines, their arguments may still be relatively uncertain. This may be simply the natural result of differences in judgment. How much of a problem this poses for reasoning from conjecture is a serious question, addressed below. For now, however, the important point is that conjecture is (or should be) defined by the kind of reasoning involved, and not by the degree of confidence expressed by that reasoning.

With these three points about reasoning from conjecture in place, I now want to consider three corresponding objections. The first is that conjecture is not a form of justification but rather an insincere mode of argument designed to manipulate people into accepting liberal political principles. The second objection is that, even if conjecture is sincere and nonmanipulative, it is an attempt to impose alien interpretations on particular comprehensive doctrines. According to this objection, internal criticism of a doctrine is legitimate only when it comes from people committed to that doctrine. The third objection is that conjecture lacks epistemic credibility. It presumes that conjecturers have a better understanding of comprehensive doctrines than those who affirm them. Since this is a dubious assumption, conjecture is unlikely to achieve the goal of generating rational agreement on a reasonable political conception. I shall argue that none of these objections is decisive, although the third presents a challenge that citizens and public officials must take seriously if they are to engage in this form of nonpublic reasoning.

INSINCERITY, MANIPULATION, AND DISRESPECT

Does reasoning from conjecture permit, or perhaps even require, engaging in insincere, manipulative, or disrespectful forms of argument? According to Rawls, conjecturers should be open about their intentions. They should state for the record, so to speak, that their aim is to justify a political conception on the basis of beliefs and values that they do not accept as valid from within their own comprehensive doctrines. If sincerity is defined, minimally, as believing what you say, then conjecturers are sincere only if they disclose the fact that they do not assert the premises from which they argue. Call this the *principle of disclosure*. Meeting it is a necessary condition of sincere conjecture. The question is whether it is sufficient.

Consider a case in which A conjectures that C should vote for β because C is committed to a nonpublic belief, N, that justifies voting for policies supported by public reason. She offers C the justification "N → β." As required by the principle of disclosure, A explains to C that she does not believe N. What she says, and what she believes, is that, if you believe N, then you are committed to voting for β. Now suppose A knows that C holds belief N on grounds that are mistaken *even from within C's comprehensive view*. Suppose, further, that A has some piece of evidence that would undermine C's belief in N. If A tells C about the existence of this piece of evidence, C will recognize her mistake and change her mind. We can suppose that, given this revision in her set of beliefs, C would then decide to vote against β. As it is, A says nothing about this piece of evidence. All she says to C is, "You believe that N, and on that basis you should vote for β. From my perspective, N is false. I believe that my commitment to voting for β is supported by different reasons. All the same, we should both vote for β."

In this case, reasoning from conjecture is both insincere and manipulative. A argues that C should adopt a political position on the basis of a belief that is invalid even from within C's perspective. She knows that C is not personally justified in accepting that N → β. So when A says that C should vote for β because C has good reason from her perspective to do so, she is being insincere. A is simply playing on beliefs that she knows C would have reason to reject from within her own comprehensive view. As Gerald Gaus rightly says about such a case, "This may do its pragmatic job, but it hardly counts as a justification. Justification gives way to mere rhetoric (and perhaps cynicism) when one 'justifies' a belief to another by citing reasons that one thinks are inadequate even from the perspective of the person to whom they are presented."[17]

If we accept that justification is about giving others *good* reasons, even when the "goodness" of the reason is judged from within their perspectives, then the principle of disclosure is insufficient to guarantee the sincerity of conjecture. Since conjecture is a form of justification, and thus a matter of giving good reasons, conjecturers must do more than disclose that they do not believe the premises from which they argue. They must also disclose whether they believe their arguments are justifiable from within the comprehensive views of those with whom they are reasoning. We can call this the *principle of full disclosure*. It says that reasoning from conjecture is sincere and non-manipulative if, and only if, conjecturers (a) disclose that they do not believe the premises from which they argue, and (b) disclose whether they believe their arguments are justifiable from within the comprehensive views of their intended audience. Provided that conjecturers are open about their intentions, and about the conditional status of their arguments, it is difficult to see why their claims should give rise to accusations of insincerity and manipulation.

Here one might respond that conjectural arguments manipulate people simply because they appeal to premises that conjecturers themselves do not accept. Notice that, while this objection is framed in terms of reasoning from conjecture, it has much broader reach. The basic argument is that whenever we offer others reasons we do not believe, we are, in some sense, attempting to manipulate them. As Robert Audi asks, "Does it not smack of manipulation to give reasons that do not move me, in order to get others to do what I want? I use the reasons as psychological levers to produce belief on a basis that does not carry my own conviction."[18] Audi calls this "leveraging by reasons," which he defines as the attempt "to move an audience to a view by noting one or more reasons there are for it from the audience's point of view."[19]

Importantly, however, Audi accepts that "leveraging" loses its manipulative force when those engaged in it openly explain that they do not believe the arguments they are presenting. Conceding that leveraging by reasons is not necessarily manipulative,[20] Audi presents a further argument to defend his underlying intuition about the wrongness of giving others reasons we do not believe. This argument, which does not rest on claims about insincerity or deceit, is that offering others such reasons demonstrates a lack of respect for them. Audi offers this argument in the context of defending his principle of secular motivation. His claim is that it is illegitimate to give others non-motivational secular reasons—defined as secular reasons that do not move one—to justify coercive public policies. Audi writes that "there is a sense of 'respect' in which, if we manipulate others, we thereby show a lack of respect for them. But I also suggested that there is a lack of respect in offering, as adequate secular reasons, considerations that are not persuasive to oneself. Why should others be moved if I am not? Do they have lower standards?"[21]

Although Audi is concerned here with the special case of religious believers offering secular reasons they do not believe, a similar point might seem to apply in the case of conjecture. If we do not accept the reasons we offer to others, why should we expect them to accept those reasons? This objection might be carried even further by contrasting conjecture with the demands of public reason. Assuming that any plausible conception of public reason requires that political justifications be based on reasons we sincerely believe,[22] why is it acceptable in nonpublic reasoning to offer justifications based on reasons we do not believe? Why is it that, in some situations, we demand that others give us reasons we share, but in other situations we do not?

The answer to these questions appeals to the fact of reasonable pluralism. This fact suggests that people may reasonably disagree about doctrines that address matters of fundamental importance, such as the meaning and value of human life. To recognize this fact is to see that people will often have different reasons for coming to similar moral and political conclusions. Thus, it is appropriate in nonpublic reasoning to assume that others may be motivated by reasons that are different from our own. By contrast, from the point of view of public reason, justification for state action based on nonpublic reasoning is a remedial or second-best solution, adopted only under special circumstances. To the extent possible, we ought to justify our collective decisions by appealing to public values that we share with others in virtue of our common citizenship.[23] But if some people hold comprehensive doctrines that seem to them to reject such values, even if only in particular cases, arguments that appeal to public values will not provide them with justifications they can accept from their own perspectives. Under these circumstances, we may[24] appeal to values drawn from their comprehensive doctrines to try to show them that they are mistaken. For political liberals, this is the only remaining form of justification available, short of appealing to considerations of prudence. Provided we are clear about our intentions, then, I see no reason to think that engaging in conjecture is insincere, manipulative, or otherwise disrespectful.

CULTURAL IMPERIALISM

A second objection to reasoning from conjecture is that it manifests a form of cultural imperialism. This type of objection has been suggested by Abdullahi An-Naʻim, a Muslim legal scholar who has argued for a progressive account of Islamic reformation,[25] which Rawls mentions as a "perfect example of overlapping consensus."[26] In developing his views, however, An-Naʻim argues from within a tradition to which he is committed and indeed warns that Islamic arguments for liberal principles must be developed by Muslims and not by those who are outside the tradition.

For example, in a discussion of Islamic law and women's rights, An-Naʻim argues that only Muslims may participate in deliberations about Islamic reformation.[27] He writes, "this is an internal debate for the Muslims to conduct and settle among themselves."[28] An-Naʻim offers two main arguments for this view. The first is that criticisms made by outsiders are often perceived, and rejected, as forms of cultural imperialism. As he says, "to avoid even the appearance of dictation by outsiders, which is likely only to be counterproductive, the classification of certain cultural (legal or religious) norms, as archaic and oppressive, must be done by the members of the cultural or religious group themselves."[29]

Of course, resistance to external sources of criticism may give rise to practical reasons for refraining from conjecture. Engaging in it may be pointless or counterproductive. But that some might perceive conjecture as a form of alien imposition is not, in itself, a principled argument against presenting criticisms based on sources internal to their cultural or religious traditions. It may be the case that, when dealing with illiberal cultural or religious groups, conjecturers find that the only way to gain an audience is through cautious cooperation with internal social critics. And even this may be overly optimistic. Those who resist reform often attempt to suppress criticism from within.[30] Under these circumstances, however, conjecture might be used to voice criticisms that would otherwise have been made by social critics. Whether this is possible or desirable is a question that can only be answered by looking at specific examples. The important point here is that resistance to conjecture by groups that stifle criticism, whether it originates internally or externally, does not represent a moral, or otherwise principled, objection to justifying, or at least attempting to justify, liberal principles on the basis of beliefs and values to which such groups are committed.

An-Na'im's second argument is a stronger claim for cultural or religious sovereignty. He suggests that every cultural or religious tradition should have the opportunity to determine its own understandings of, and justifications for, basic human rights, without "allowing any tradition to dictate to the others."[31] Yet this claim is not necessarily inconsistent with reasoning from conjecture. Insofar as conjecture is based on appeal to internal sources, it does not impose alien standards on cultural or religious traditions. Indeed, the very possibility of conjecture is premised on the idea that various traditions will have different ways of justifying moral and political principles, including those that call for the protection of human rights. Note, further, that the purpose of conjecture is, in part, to address cultural or religious groups that adhere to "archaic and oppressive" norms. As An-Na'im himself recognizes, such groups "cannot be left to themselves completely."[32] They must be open to criticism, even on their own terms, unless they develop beliefs and practices consistent with respect for basic human rights and liberties.

EPISTEMIC AUTHORITY

Perhaps the strongest objection to reasoning from conjecture is that conjecturers cannot defend their claim to argue validly from what others believe. A conjecturer must be able to explain why her interpretation of a particular comprehensive doctrine is the *right* interpretation of that doctrine. To see the need for such an explanation, consider a standoff between two people who disagree about how to interpret a particular comprehensive view. A says that C's comprehensive doctrine commits C to Rawls's principles of justice. C rejects this claim in favor of an alternative conception. Why should C accept A's interpretation of her own comprehensive view? To answer this question, A needs to explain why she knows better. That is, she has to give a justification for her epistemic authority.[33] If A cannot give a justification, then presumably C has good reason to trust her own interpretation of the beliefs and values to which she is committed.

It has to be admitted that a conclusive reply to this objection may not be available. Comprehensive doctrines may be so complex or esoteric that few people can claim to interpret them authoritatively. Some religions seem to fit this description. Believers might point out that nonbelievers have not been trained to read texts correctly, to draw on relevant analogies and metaphors, to reference apposite commentaries and interpretations, or, more generally, to frame moral arguments in terms acceptable within their religious traditions. One can imagine a Talmudist or an Islamic jurist (*faqih*) saying such things. Furthermore, some religious communities delegate the responsibility of answering ethical and political questions to specific authorities. The average member of the community may not be qualified to assert an opinion on such important matters. If ordinary members of a commu- nity cannot interpret with authority, how can outsiders, of all people, expect anyone to take them seriously?

Conjecturers can give one of at least three answers to questions about their epistemic authority. The first would be simply to concede the point by admitting that they are not qualified to make authoritative statements about how to interpret a comprehensive doctrine other than their own. As noted above, the word "conjecture" implies speculation, a proposition that has not been proved, or an educated guess. In the end, maybe Rawls is right to frame the matter in these terms. Perhaps tentative suggestions are all that conjecturers can hope to provide.

Those who are unsatisfied with this response, especially those committed to justifying a liberal political conception on the basis of a particular comprehensive doctrine, can undertake the task—and it may be an enormously difficult one—of becoming authorities on a particular doctrine. Obviously, they will not be authorities in the eyes of those who accord authority only to the leaders of their own communities. But if conjecturers are, or become, educated enough to argue intelligently from sources recognized by the leaders of such communities, perhaps they can make a plausible case for having their arguments taken seriously.[34] The second answer, then, is that conjecturers who become students of particular comprehensive doctrines can say that they have learned what they can about those doctrines, that they have listened carefully to the moral and political claims made on the basis of them, and that they are committed to a process of sincere argumentation based on what they have learned. This reply may not always be convincing, but it is the most that can reasonably be expected of anyone not already committed to a particular comprehensive doctrine.

The third answer challenges the reasonableness of excluding an outsider, or a nonbeliever, solely on the basis of epistemic considerations. Recall that the purpose of conjecture is to try to reconcile conflicts between nonpublic and public values. If a person, or a community, asserts that nonpublic values should take priority in cases of conflict, then it is reasonable to ask for a justification for that view. Perhaps a justification can be given that will at least be intelligible, if not defensible, to outsiders. But if the proffered justification is not even intelligible, if an outsider cannot even hope to understand the beliefs or values on which that justification is based, then there are strong grounds for questioning whether it is an appropriate basis for justifying the exercise of political power.

THE LIMITS OF CONJECTURE

As with all forms of moral justification, reasoning from conjecture must acknowledge certain limits. I shall focus here on two in particular, one dealing with comprehensive doctrines that continue to reject the priority of political values and the other with doctrines so fundamentally unreasonable that reasonable citizens should not attempt to argue from within them.

First, even if conjecturers can support their claims to arguing validly from what others believe—for example, by demonstrating expert knowledge of particular comprehensive doctrines—and even if the supporters of those doctrines accept their authority, nothing guarantees that those doctrines will contain the resources necessary to reconcile conflicts between public and nonpublic values. Thus, the main practical limitation to conjecture is that some doctrines may simply be opposed to certain political values or the manner in which they are applied. If no authoritative interpretation of a particular doctrine yields a commitment to the values of public reason, then conjecture has not resolved the conflict at hand. Furthermore, if reasoning from conjecture is to be sincere, those who engage in it must be prepared to admit this possibility. The principle of full disclosure requires that conjecturers disclose whether they believe their arguments can be justified from within a particular doctrine. If they do not believe this is possible, they should not pretend otherwise. To do so would be to muddle the aim of rational justification with that of mere, and perhaps even deceitful or manipulative, rhetorical persuasion. If conjecture is not to be mistaken for a form of propaganda, conjecturers should not sacrifice their claim to sincerity in moments of justificatory defeat. Better to acknowledge that some doctrines cannot justify the values of public reason than to cast aspersion on the larger project of justifying a commitment to liberal principles.

Second, some comprehensive doctrines may be based on beliefs or values that reasonable citizens cannot, in good conscience, take as starting points for justifying the values of public reason. For example, some doctrines are defined in essentially racist terms. It is, therefore, no surprise to find that those who espouse them typically reject the values of public reason.[35] Yet, even if it were possible to offer conjectural arguments on the basis of morally bankrupt views,[36] it may seem perverse to engage in such reasoning. Indeed, insofar as reasoning from conjecture might confer some level of social or political legitimacy, there may be good reason to refrain from engaging with such views, except perhaps to discredit them. Rather than attempting to tailor moral arguments to doctrines that are completely unreasonable, it may be preferable to contain them as much as possible, and by whatever means are legally permissible according to a reasonable political conception of justice.[37]

One might object that if we do not engage racist doctrines, or doctrines otherwise bent on domination, there is no purpose in reasoning from conjecture. After all, the need for conjecture arises because some citizens believe that they are justified in coercing others to act according to values that cannot be publicly justified. What else can this be but an attempt to dominate others through the illegitimate imposition of a particular comprehensive doctrine? We may decide not to engage such doctrines, but then what is there to conjecture about? To answer this question, it may help to draw a distinction between doctrines that are completely or fundamentally unreasonable and doctrines that contain unreasonable elements. Examples of the former include ideologies that define their politics in terms of racial, ethnic, or religious supremacy. The central beliefs and values of these doctrines may be so warped or morally corrupted that they are irredeemable from the point of view of public reason. By contrast, some doctrines may contain elements that conflict with the values of public reason. As a whole, these doctrines may be worthy of respect, even if they fail to recognize certain limitations imposed by reasonable conceptions of justice. Again, some religious doctrines may fall into this category. Although they are prima facie unreasonable, at least on some moral and political issues, internal criticism may reveal the potential for such doctrines to endorse views compatible with the demands of public reason. This possibility is, at any rate, what motivates the idea of reasoning from conjecture.

When nonpublic and public values conflict, the idea of public reason requires that citizens give priority to the latter. Yet, as critics have often pointed out, this priority cannot be justified according to political values alone. A *pro tanto* justification of a reasonable political conception must be confirmed by a *full* justification that draws on the beliefs and values of a particular comprehensive doctrine. In other words, political values must be endorsed by, or at least held to be compatible or congruent with, a broader ethical, philosophical, or religious perspective. Although political liberalism provides reasons for thinking that reasonable comprehensive doctrines will affirm a liberal political conception, it does not provide a conclusive argument for this view. Rather, it defends the possibility of an overlapping consensus as an article of liberal faith. Thus, when faced with a comprehensive doctrine that conflicts with the political values of a liberal political conception, or the values of public reason, political liberalism may seem to run out of answers. I have argued that reasoning from conjecture is a way of continuing the process of rational justification beyond the limits of public reason. It may be possible, in some cases, to appeal to beliefs and values within particular comprehensive doctrines for the purpose of showing that they can, indeed, affirm political decisions based on public reasons. Moreover, by adhering to certain precautions, this form of nonpublic reasoning can be conducted in a manner that is sincere and respectful, not culturally imperialist, and as epistemologically authoritative as anyone could reasonably expect. Conjecture may not ultimately succeed in demonstrating that particular doctrines should endorse a commitment to public reason. But that conclusion need not be assumed in advance of efforts to engage citizens on their own terms.

Notes

This chapter is a substantially revised version of Micah Schwartzman, "The Ethics of Reasoning from Conjecture," *Journal of Moral Philosophy* 9 (2012): 521–44. Copyright © 2012 by Koninklijke Brill NV, Leiden.

1. Here I assume familiarity with political liberalism and the idea of public reason, as presented in *PL* and *IPRR*.

2. I follow Rawls in equating *pro tanto* justification with justification based on a reasonable balance of political values. For this reason, I use the phrases "*pro tanto* justification" and "political justification" interchangeably. See *PL* (pbk.) 386.

3. For this objection, see, for example, Michael Sandel, *Liberalism and the Limits of Justice*, 2nd ed. (Cambridge: Cambridge University Press, 1998), 196–202, 215–17; Stephen Mulhall and Adam Swift, *Liberals and Communitarians*, 2nd ed. (Cambridge: Blackwell, 1996), 228–31; and Christopher Eberle, "Basic Human Worth and Religious Restraint," *Philosophy and Social Criticism* 35 (2009): 151–81.

4. *IPRR* 152.

5. For some recent examples of reasoning from conjecture, see Andrew March, *Islam and Liberal Citizenship: The Search for Overlapping Consensus* (Oxford: Oxford University Press, 2009); Lucas Swaine, "Demanding Deliberation: Political Liberalism and the Inclusion of Islam," *Journal of Islamic Law and Culture* 11 (2009): 92–110; and Joshua Cohen, "Minimalism About Human Rights: The Most We Can Hope For?" *Journal of Political Philosophy* 12 (2004): 190–213.

6. *IPRR* 155–56.

7. Ibid.

8. Rawls writes, "we *reason* from what we believe, or conjecture, may be other people's basic doctrines" (*IPRR* 152, emphasis added).

9. *PL* (pbk.) 386.

10. Although Rawls describes conjecture as an attempt to show others they can *endorse* a reasonable political conception, in some cases conjecture might have more modest goals. It might be used to show that a comprehensive view is *consistent with*, or perhaps *not in conflict with*, a reasonable political conception (or with political claims derived from such a conception). In what follows, I shall not distinguish between these various forms of reconciling nonpublic and public reason. If conjecture can achieve any of them, it will have served an important purpose. I thank Tom Bailey for clarification on this point.

11. *PL* (pbk.) 386.

12. See *IPRR* 136–37.

13. Within political liberalism, citizens are "reasonable" only if they accept (1) that political society is a fair system of social cooperation between free and equal people, and (2) that any liberal society will be marked by the fact of reasonable pluralism that results from the burdens of judgment. Accepting these two ideas, reasonable citizens recognize that the exercise of political power cannot be justified to others on the basis of any particular comprehensive doctrine. This recognition leads, in turn, to the demand for political justifications based on public reason. For discussion of these points, see Jonathan Quong, *Liberalism Without Perfection* (Oxford: Oxford University Press, 2011), 37–39, 166–67.

14. Again I thank Tom Bailey for raising the question addressed in this paragraph.

15. This condition might be arbitrary to some extent, and it could be relaxed. If comprehensive doctrines are broadly construed as traditions of thought, then chances are good that people can argue on the basis of premises they do not accept, even though these premises in some sense belong to or are associated with their own comprehensive doctrines. Nevertheless, I shall keep this restriction in place for now, if only because it simplifies matters and tends to bring out objections that might not be raised against those who argue from within their own ethical or religious traditions.

16. The *Oxford English Dictionary* defines "conjecture" as "To conclude, infer, or judge, from appearances or probabilities"; "To form an opinion or supposition as to facts on grounds admittedly insufficient; to guess, surmise."

17. Gerald Gaus, *Justificatory Liberalism* (Oxford: Oxford University Press, 1996), 139. My example above borrows from Gaus's discussion. Cf. ibid., 138–40.

18. Robert Audi, "The Separation of Church and State and the Obligations of Citizenship," *Philosophy and Public Affairs* 18 (1989): 282.

19. Robert Audi, *Religious Convictions and Secular Reason* (Cambridge: Cambridge University Press, 2000), 110.

20. See Robert Audi, "Religious Commitment and Secular Reason: A Reply to Professor Weithman," *Philosophy and Public Affairs* 20 (1991): 73.

21. Ibid., 74.

22. See Micah Schwartzman, "The Sincerity of Public Reason," *Journal of Political Philosophy* 19 (2011): 375–98.

23. For the view that public reasons must be shared, see Quong, *Liberalism Without Perfection*, chap. 9.

24. I use "may" here advisedly, since political liberals are not necessarily obligated to engage in conjecture. Some comprehensive doctrines may be so unreasonable that it would be pointless or even degrading to argue from within them. I discuss this limitation further below.

25. See Abdullahi An-Na'im, *Toward an Islamic Reformation: Civil Liberties, Human Rights, and International Law* (Syracuse: Syracuse University Press, 1990); and

An-Na'im, "Islamic Politics and the Neutral State: A Friendly Amendment to Rawls?," chapter 10 in this volume.

26. *IPRR* 151n46.

27. Abdullahi An-Na'im, "The Rights of Women and International Law in the Muslim Context," *Whittier Law Review* 9 (1987): 501.

28. Ibid., 514.

29. Ibid., 515.

30. See Abduallahi An-Na'im, "Islam and Human Rights: Beyond the Universality Debate," *American Society of International·Law Proceedings* 94 (2000): 100.

31. An-Na'im, "The Rights of Women," 515.

32. Ibid.

33. Here I follow Alan Gibbard, *Wise Choices, Apt Feelings* (Oxford: Oxford University Press, 1990), 192–93.

34. See, for example, March, *Islam and Liberal Citizenship*.

35. For the possibility that people who hold some racist views can still be reasonable citizens, see Erin Kelly and Lionel McPherson, "On Tolerating the Unreasonable," *Journal of Political Philosophy* 9 (2001): 38–55; but cf. Jonathan Quong, "The Rights of Unreasonable Citizens," *Journal of Political Philosophy* 12 (2004): 314–35.

36. I do not know what such arguments would look like. Perhaps they are an impossibility, in which case the point is moot.

37. See *PL* (pbk.) 64n19.

7

The Religious Hermeneutics of Public Reasoning

FROM PAUL TO RAWLS

JOHANNES A. VAN DER VEN

John Rawls poses a fundamental question to religions when he asks, "How is it possible for those affirming a religious doctrine that is based on religious authority, for example, the Church or the Bible, also to hold a reasonable political conception that supports a just democratic regime?"[1] The standard Catholic answer to this question appeals to natural law, and Rawls himself cites John Courtney Murray in this regard.[2] But this answer may be considered too Catholic, insofar as it is unacceptable to other religious and nonreligious worldviews, or not Catholic enough, insofar as it limits a believer's terms of political reasoning to those of natural law. It is also far from clear that natural law can provide believers with a functional framework for dealing with political questions.[3]

In this chapter, I will attempt to provide a theological answer to Rawls's question by taking an alternative, hermeneutic approach. Hermeneutics interprets the meaning of statements in their contexts, rather than simply considering their truth claims, and creative hermeneutics attempts to translate traditional statements diachronically from their past contexts into terms that fit in contemporary contexts, and synchronically in the diversity of contemporary contexts. I take it that religions in general, and Christianity in particular, always adopt hermeneutic methods in translating their concerns into terms appropriate to the context in which they find themselves. Thus there is no interpretation-free essence of any religion, but only a history of varying interpretative paradigms and reconstructive interpretations. As an especially fruitful example of this, I will take as my focus one of the main passages in the New Testament, Luke's narrative of Paul's speech to the Athenians in the Acts of the Apostles (hereafter, "Acts"), chapter 17, verses 16–34. This narrative is permeated by a Jewish-Hellenistic paradigm that resonates with the Jewish-Hellenistic religiosity of Paul's context in Asia Minor. After first pointing out some crucial features of the narrative itself, I will consider its possible lessons for Christian citizens in societies that lack a predominant religious worldview of the kind to which Paul's speech was addressed. Despite this crucial difference between Paul's society and our own, I will argue that contemporary Christian citizens ought to make a hermeneutic turn analogous to that made by the Lukan Paul by using a paradigm to interpret religious notions in ways that are at least reasonably acceptable to other citizens. My claim will be that Rawls's political theory offers precisely such a paradigm.

LUKE'S NARRATIVE OF PAUL'S SPEECH TO THE ATHENIANS

Acts was probably written at the end of the first or the beginning of the second century A.D., about two generations after Paul's second missionary journey to Athens. It constitutes Luke's contribution to the literary genre of stories about the great deeds of nations, cities, and civil and religious leaders.[4] It begins by recounting the stir caused by Paul's arrival in Athens: perturbed by the many temples and statues of gods on display, he argued with those he met and was eventually taken to the Areopagus, the building on the hill of Ares (*Areios pagos*) that housed the city's council for educational, judicial, cultural, moral, and religious affairs.[5] This stir was understandable, given the close relations between religion, society, and politics that characterized the Athenian state. Faced with the Areopagus, the Lukan Paul launched into his speech, focusing on the fact that, besides the altars to all the gods known in Athens, there was one bearing the inscription "To an unknown god."[6] For Paul, this unknown God is the God who created everything, from the life and breath of his listeners to the seasons and inhabitable zones, but who neither dwells nor needs to be served in temples. This God's intention is rather that people seek and, gradually, find him, which, Paul claims, is not difficult, since "he is not far from each one of us" and "in him we live and move and have our being." Paul also remarks that, "as even some of your own poets have said, we too are his offspring."[7] In concluding, he informs his listeners that God calls them to start a new, Christian life and he refers to "a man" appointed by God to judge mankind, a man God raised from the dead.

This narrative has been called the most Hellenistic text of the most Hellenistic book in the New Testament.[8] This is significant, since Luke portrays Paul in differentiated ways, using the languages and cultures of the relevant context: as a Jew to the Jews, a Greek to the Greeks, and, in the sequel to the speech to the Areopagus, a Roman to the Romans.[9] Why, then, does Luke present Paul as a Hellenistic Greek in the Areopagus speech? Part of the answer can be traced to the Jewish-Hellenistic diaspora in the Middle East, where Jews engaged in their religion in terms of beliefs and practices adopted from the surrounding Hellenistic world. Judaism was consequently influenced by Hellenism, and, conversely, Hellenism, and especially later Stoicism, was subject to Semitic influence via Jewish propaganda—indeed, there are often strong similarities between Hellenistic and Jewish texts.[10] It is therefore not surprising that Luke's version of Paul's speech too contains a substratum of ideas, or common ground, shared with his Athenian audience, the Stoics and the Epicureans.[11]

But this common ground is not sufficient to explain the function of the speech, which is not historical, dogmatic, or missiological—that is, the speech is not a report, a doctrinal summary, or a model for converting Athenians.[12] It is rather an exercise in deliberative rhetoric intended to convince the Athenians of Christianity's value as a *paideia*, or guideline for education, morals, and culture, that could compete with Hellenistic *paideiai*.[13] To emphasize this, Luke sets the narrative not in an obscure town, but in the illustrious city of

Athens, which at that time was not comparable in size to Antioch or Alexandria, but still had an age-old philosophical and cultural reputation. Nor does it occur just anywhere in Athens: Luke stages it at the Areopagus, Athens's educational, moral, cultural, and political center. He also stages it as a debate not with ordinary citizens, but with Stoic and Epicurean intellectuals. Indeed, one might even say that he imbues Paul with Socrates's "aura," as if he were a kind of second Socrates:[14] like Socrates, the Lukan Paul defends novel religious ideas and practices against the accusation of undermining Athens's dominant *paideia*, and he does so by using deliberative rhetoric to convince, rather than emotionally persuade, his audience.[15] Their stories end very differently, of course: Socrates's with his condemnation to death by hemlock and Paul's with his exoneration, a remarkable achievement considering that the introduction of new gods was a grave offence.[16]

What is particularly significant about Paul's speech, then, is how it employs deliberative rhetoric to show the Athenians that they need not consider Christianity foreign to their own religiosity, for it shares common grounds with the religious thinking of the Athenian elite. In commenting in more detail on the speech, I will try to bring out this hermeneutic strategy for bridging the divide between the Christian and Hellenistic religious cultures, and how Judaism operates as the bridge between them. The speech begins as follows:

[v22] Then Paul stood in front of the Areopagus and said: "Athenians, I see how extremely religious you are in every way. [v23] For as I went through the city and looked carefully at the objects of your worship, I found among them an altar with the inscription, 'To an unknown god.' What therefore you worship as unknown, this I proclaim to you. [v24] The God who made the world and everything in it, he who is Lord of heaven and earth, does not live in shrines made by human hands, [v25] nor is he served by human hands, as though he needed anything, since he himself gives to all mortals life and breath and all things."[17]

This pericope does not start with a strategic *captatio benevolentiae*, but by emphasizing the common ground between Christian and Hellenistic beliefs (v22) and by connecting the Hellenistic "unknown god" with the Christian God (v23). Paul's main claim is that, unlike idols, this God is not made by human hands (v24) and does not need offerings, for he is not a human creation, but the very source of creation (v25). Fabricated gods are thus distinguished from the living God, visible gods from the invisible God. Crucially, this criticism of idolatry rests on grounds common to the Bible and Hellenistic philosophy.[18] Rejection of idolatry can be found throughout the Jewish Bible[19] and in the works of numerous Greek and Hellenistic authors as well, especially among the Stoics,[20] although neither the Stoics nor the Epicureans abstained from worship, at any rate in public.[21] God's lack of needs also has sources in both the Jewish Bible[22] and Hellenism, again especially among the Stoics,[23] but also in the Epicureans' belief in the gods' perfect happiness.[24]

The speech continues as follows:

> "[v26] From one ancestor he made all nations to inhabit the whole earth, and he allotted the times of their existence and the boundaries of the places where they would live, [v27] so that they would search for God and perhaps grope for him and find him—though indeed he is not far from each one of us. [v28] For 'in him we live and move and have our being'; as even some of your own poets have said, 'For we too are his offspring.' [v29] Since we are God's offspring, we ought not to think that the deity is like gold, or silver, or stone, an image formed by the art and imagination of mortals."

The reference to the myth of Adam here, albeit without mentioning his name (v26), serves to indicate that the Christian *paideia* is destined for all by postulating not so much a shared origin of all human beings as the unity of all humanity (cf. v29), a unity that was also affirmed by the Stoics.[25] The Lukan Paul then reflects on God's gentleness: his intention is that humans should go in search of him, however gropingly, almost like a blind person (v27). This remark alludes to both the Jewish Bible (Wisdom 13:6) and Stoicism.[26] The optative mode used in "perhaps find him [*euroien*]" indicates that finding God may well be beyond human reach,[27] an idea to which there are again Hellenistic parallels.[28] But Paul also insists that it is perfectly possible to find God, for he is "not far from each one of us." This echoes both the psalms (Psalms 139:7) and Hellenistic literature—for instance, the Stoic

Seneca's claim that "God is close to you, with you, in you" (*Epistula* 41:1) and the Epicurean claim that we should not fear the gods since they cherish friendship and love with human beings.[29]

The intimate relationship between God and humans is further elaborated upon in the following verse. The first words, "in him [*en autooi*]," of the phrase "in him we live and move and have our being" (v28) already indicate intimacy, a reciprocal inherence of God and humans in each other.[30] And, notably, while it is now part of one of the Catholic Eucharistic prayers, the triad of "living," "moving," and "being" is not found in the Bible, but constitutes the core of Hellenistic thought. For instance, Epimenides's *Cretica* has Minos pray to the Greeks' supreme god, Zeus, by saying, "You live and stay for ever, for in you we live, move, and have our being."[31] And Plato,[32] Seneca, and Cicero[33] all similarly combine two of the three concepts, "living", "moving," and "being," in their conceptions of the divine, not as Parmenides's immovable God, but as a "moving" God, the source and process of becoming.[34] Paul himself attributes to the Greeks' own poets the quotation, "For we too are his offspring," which is the only nonbiblical poetic quotation in the New Testament.[35] One of these poets may be Aratos,[36] and another possible source is Cleanthes's hymn to Zeus.[37] This again indicates the universality of the Christian message by emphasizing the unity of humanity, an idea common to both the Bible and Hellenistic thought, as in Seneca[38] and in the Sophists' and Cynics' ideas of the brotherhood of all people.[39] Luke employs it to indicate that the Christian message was intended not only for Jews, as the Christian community in Jerusalem thought it was, but for all people, and in particular for those who stemmed from the Hellenistic legacy of Alexander the Great. In his address the Lukan Paul completes that legacy by embracing the inhabited world (*oikoumenē gē*) in a religious whole.[40] The criticism of idolatry is then repeated again in the last verse, with its rejection of any "image" of God in "gold, or silver, or stone."

Paul concludes his speech with the following verses:

"[v30] While God has overlooked the times of human ignorance, now he commands all people everywhere to repent [v31] because he has fixed a day on which he will have the world judged in righteousness by a man whom he has appointed, and of this he has given assurance to all by raising him from the dead."

In contrast with the letter to the Romans, here Luke's Paul refrains from criticizing his audience for their "heathen" rituals—he simply rejects them. Nor does he command his listeners to do penance—he merely tells them that God does not dwell on their past, but calls them to embark on a new life (*metanoeĩn*) (v30). And, in the last verse, he emphasizes judgment over resurrection,[41] since resurrection simply legitimizes the judgment of the man appointed by God for that purpose.[42] Jesus is not mentioned by name, an anonymity that Luke perhaps meant to convey that, despite what the Athenians had first thought of Paul's claims, Jesus is not a foreign god and his resurrection (*anastasis*) is not a foreign goddess.[43]

THE IMPLICATIONS OF PAUL'S SPEECH
FOR MODERN POLITICS

As a classical text, one that has withstood the test of time, it is worth considering the meaning of Paul's speech for our own time. What would Paul have said had he lived in our context? What would have been his *paideia* for our age? In exploring such a hypothetical *irrealis potentialis*, one is in good company, for Luke's own account is an interpretative reconstruction of what Paul had said some two generations earlier. And any telling of stories involves deciphering their different meanings in different contexts, in a never-ending hermeneutic reconstruction,[44] if we are not to lapse into what Schleiermacher calls "lax" exegesis.[45]

The cardinal difference between Paul's Athenian context and the North-Western European and North American context of today is what sociologists call the "functional differentiation" of modern society.[46] If in premodern times all individual and institutional actions were regulated, integrated, and legitimatized, directly or indirectly, by religion, in modern times that heavenly hierarchy has imploded. This is due to the differentiation of society into functional systems guided not by God's will, but each by their own, relatively autonomous codes, rules, programs, and institutions. Religion has thus lost its overarching role—it is now just one of many systems, alongside economic, political, legal, social, and cultural ones, and it is relevant to society only insofar as it is relevant to these other systems.[47] Secularization is a consequence of this: in many European countries today, and particularly in North-Western Europe, believers constitute a (cognitive) minority, and the chief division is no longer between Catholics and Protestants or between Christians and adherents of other religions, but between religious and nonreligious people.[48]

It is in this context that I think the Lukan Paul's hermeneutic strategy can illuminate and legitimate Rawls's answer to the question of religion's place in political deliberation. For while Paul pursued a common ground between Christians' and Athenians' religious beliefs, Rawls recognizes that today there is no such religious common ground. I agree: Catholics should not entrust their politics to the philosophy of natural law,[49] since what "nature" is is contested not only by developments in the natural sciences and the cultural sciences, but even within the Catholic tradition, which has always championed natural law.[50] Furthermore, Rawls recognizes that there is no philosophical common ground either. In view of the multiplicity of philosophies in our age, no such basic philosophical structure is available: there simply is no homogeneous philosophy.[51] Indeed, Rawls denies that there is any rational common ground to which political deliberation could appeal—in his words, there is no "form of argument that will always prove convincing against all other arguments."[52]

If neither a religious nor a philosophical common ground of the kind Paul appealed to can be found, where else can common ground be found? I believe that Rawls's political theory provides an answer. The political framework that he proposes offers citizens adhering to all-encompassing religious and nonreligious worldviews, or "comprehensive doctrines," reasonably adequate scope to participate in public debate. This framework may be said to offer a political common ground in the absence of a religious common one.

This political common ground has three characteristics. The first concerns the acceptance of democracy for the right reasons. Rawls consistently stresses that religious and nonreligious participants in public debate must accept the basic principles of constitutional democracy for their intrinsic value. These principles are freedom and equality as reflected in civil liberties and rights, plus opportunities to realize these; the rule of law; and the majority principle.[53] Their acceptance, Rawls insists, must not be just a matter of accepting these principles as a modus vivendi for opportunistic reasons—for instance, because they are part of present-day conventions, or because they yield temporary gains and therefore may be abandoned as soon as they are no longer profitable.

The second characteristic is the acceptance of a plurality of religious and nonreligious worldviews, especially when these worldviews do not merely differ from one another, but also conflict with one another, even irreconcilably. This is based on Rawls's epistemological notion of the "burdens of judgment,"[54] according to which, since truth is inexhaustible, no religious or nonreligious worldview can comprehend all of it—each is only an approximation, and therefore contains merely some facets of truth. It follows that all citizens may raise their worldviews for discussion in the public forum, including their metaphysical and religious aspects, because otherwise potentially important insights may be lost. This right of citizens, including religious ones, to employ their worldviews in public debate is therefore not based merely on their individual freedom (particularly their freedom of expression) or simply on the social value of worldviews, requiring a "free market" for the exchange of views. It is also, and primarily, based on the epistemological notion that truth is perspectival, which is an inevitable consequence of the spatiotemporal finitude of human life, rooted in its contingency.

The third characteristic concerns Rawls's accompanying "proviso," according to which religious and nonreligious worldviews introduced into public debate must "in due course" be translated into the language of public reason, the language that refers to the three democratic principles mentioned. As examples of this bilingual play between religious and political language games, Rawls refers to the prophets in the narratives of the Jewish Bible, the parable of the good Samaritan in the New Testament, the rhetoric of religious leaders in the struggle for the abolition of slavery, and the ministry of the Reverend Martin Luther King in the civil rights movement.[55] Rawls might also have referred to the Anglican archbishop Desmond Tutu's and the Reverend Beyers Naudé's struggles against the South African apartheid system, or even to President Barack Obama's eloquent expression of the same idea in his *The Audacity of Hope*:

Surely, secularists are wrong when they ask believers to leave their religion at the door before entering the public square. . . . What our deliberative, pluralistic democracy does demand is that the religiously motivated translate their concerns into universal, rather than religious-specific values. . . . If I want others to listen to me, then I have to explain why abortion violates some principle that is accessible to people of all faiths, including those with no faith at all.[56]

Admittedly, Rawls leaves open some crucial questions about his "in due course" requirement, such as those regarding when the translation should be made, who should make it, whether the translation needs only to be available or should actually be offered, and which criteria it should satisfy. This has led to accusations of decisional poverty,[57] but Rawls insists that what is "due" can only be decided in practice.[58]

It is here that I think hermeneutic strategies are significant. For the translation of worldviews into the language of public reason does not involve simply (as it were, blindly) applying such principles as civil liberties and rights without regard to the conflictual plurality of their past and present meanings. To make worldviews understandable and reasonably acceptable, they must be made hermeneutically accessible,[59] that is, "outsiders" must be able to understand and reasonably accept them without actually appropriating them themselves. This marks the fundamental difference between Rawls's theory, on the one hand, and secular and religious political theories, on the other. For while both secular and religious theories run the risk of excluding opposing worldviews from politics and of imposing a worldview on citizens who do not share it, Rawls's theory admits both religious and nonreligious worldviews, requiring only that they be translatable and acceptable to citizens who do not share them.

Rawls's proviso may be seen as a logical consequence of the principle of the separation of church and state. He interprets this principle in terms of the equality of religious and nonreligious worldviews before the law, on the grounds that in the United States "the various religions have been protected by the First Amendment from the state, and none has been able to dominate and suppress the other religions by the capture and use of state power."[60] However, this principle of religious pluralism, and for that matter the pluralism of religious and nonreligious worldviews, does not always belong to its adherents' most inner attitudes. Consider, for instance, the debates on euthanasia and abortion currently taking place in various parts of the world, and politicians' difficulties in responding to them. Here pluralism has two aspects. The first is that the citizens which politicians represent hold a diversity of beliefs about euthanasia and abortion, from vehement rejection to unqualified assent. The second regards the separation of church and state itself, that is, the requirement that, as members of legislative bodies, politicians transcend not only their own personal beliefs on euthanasia and abortion, but also the beliefs of the communities they belong to, including consultations with these communities' leaders. For this separation of church and state is also controversial when such issues are concerned. In other words, "we, the people" not only have various opinions about both existential issues, euthanasia and abortion, but also have various opinions about whether the separation of church and state applies to these issues.

To illustrate this latter kind of pluralism, consider an interesting finding of a study I conducted of the beliefs of 5,080 students in six North-Western European countries: Belgium, England and Wales, Germany, the Netherlands, Norway, and Sweden. The students were divided into 765 Catholics, 473 Protestants, 1409 Muslims, and 2433 nonreligious students on the basis of their own self-attribution. I determined their positions regarding the separation of church and state by asking them to what extent—on a five-point scale from 1 ("I totally disagree") to 5 ("I fully agree")—they believed that the politicians who represent them should decide on euthanasia and abortion irrespective of any religious leaders' will. The results, shown in table 1, reveal significant differences between Catholic, Protestant, and Muslim students, on the one hand, and nonreligious students, on the other: the former are ambivalent about (mean < 3.4) while the latter agree with (mean ≥ 3.4) politicians making decisions independently of religious leaders. In other words, regarding the issues of euthanasia and abortion the real supporters of the separation of church and state, including the equality of religious and nonreligious worldviews before the law, were not the religious but the nonreligious students.[61]

TABLE 7.1 Mean Opinions Regarding the Separation of Church and State Over Euthanasia and Abortion Among Catholic, Protestant, Muslim, and Nonreligious Students in Six North-Western European Countries

	Catholics		Protestants		Muslims		Nonreligious	
	Mean	st. dev.	Mean	st. dev.	Mean	st. dev.	Mean	st. dev.
Regarding euthanasia: politicians should decide irrespective of religious leaders	3.3	1.1	3.3	1.0	3.2	1.2	3.6	1.2
Regarding abortion: politicians should decide irrespective of religious leaders	3.2	1.2	3.4	1.1	3.0	1.2	3.7	1.3

Note: Range of scale: 1 ("I totally disagree") to 5 ("I fully agree"); st. dev. = standard deviation; Ambivalence: mean < 3.4; agree: mean ≥ 3.4.

RELIGIOUS QUESTIONS

To consider how Luke's narration of Paul's speech can illuminate Rawls's proviso, it is worth considering three specific questions that it raises from a religious perspective. The first is a religious question, the second concerns the concept of truth, and the third is of an ethical character. The religious question is that of whether faith in God is in fact reconcilable with public reason, or even with reason at all. Is there reason to be found in religion and, if so, is it such that it can and may be reduced to public reason? The "axial" religions, which include all the major religions, have all manner of political ideas, but because of their orientation to the transcendent, or divine, they cannot be reduced to these ideas.[62] And in the event of conflict between religious and public reason, does the former not have priority over the latter, at least from a religious perspective?

Resolving these questions falls beyond the scope of this chapter, but to mitigate them, I would suggest distinguishing practical from theoretical reason. Rawls defines religions as "comprehensive doctrines,"[63] thus relating them primarily to theoretical reason. But, as Paul's concern with Christianity and Hellenism as *paideiai* indicates, religions are better understood primarily as practical commitments. That is, they are primarily existential, spiritual, and moral practices with both a "vertical" dimension (an orientation of trust in God) and a "horizontal" one (an orientation toward fellow humans, including individual, social, and institutional relations, and with a special concern for those in distress). Hence while theoretical reason may speculatively explore whether God exists, who and what He is, or what divine revelation might be if it occurs, the question of the reasonability—a term Rawls cherishes[64]—of a religious practice is a matter of practical reason, something to be examined in practical terms.[65] In other words, in the order of priority religious practice comes first, while its practical-reasonable account of interrelated diachronic and synchronic practices is secondary, a product of its self-reflexive and transformative activity. Its theoretical, "comprehensive doctrine" is part of that account. Thus the implications of religion for public reason should primarily be examined in terms of its implications for the practice of individual and collective daily life in society and state,[66] particularly in terms of freedom and equality as codified in human rights, rather than in terms of its doctrinal claims.[67]

The second question pertains to the concept of truth. As I have mentioned, Rawls's epistemological notion of the burdens of judgment treats truth as perspectival. By juxtaposing religious and nonreligious worldviews in public debate, without subordinating one to the other, public reason puts religious truth on a par with other, equally "perspectival" truths. But religions tend to consider their worldviews as *the* truth, in the singular, and even as "the whole truth" or "the revealed truth." From their perspectives, public reason puts orthodoxy on a par with other orthodoxies, thus obliterating the distinction between orthodoxy and heterodoxy, and, indeed, undermining the very meaning of orthodoxy.[68]

This may be so, but Rawls does not deny that religious or any other citizens should present their truth as *the* truth. For this is what public debate is about: which truth claims hold water, and to what extent, in the forum of public reason? If adherents of religious and nonreligious worldviews are not prepared to engage in public dialogue—as is the case in both religious and nonreligious fundamentalisms—then there may be an exchange of information or a reciprocal attempt at conversion, but there is no scope for democratic dialogue, and thus for accepting democracy for the right reasons rather than merely as a modus vivendi. Rawls insists, then, not that any citizen abandon "their" truth, but just that they be prepared to translate and present it in public form.

Furthermore, outside their fundamentalist wings, religions are generally able to recognize mutual similarities and accept reciprocal additions. In other words, alongside or instead of purely exclusive orientations, they also display inclusive orientations, particularly regarding less prominent issues. One thinks of the Christian hierarchy of truths (*hierarchia veritatum*), comprising a scale of the truths that both Catholics and Protestants adhere to.[69] Even in the rather conservative Declaration of the Congregation for the Doctrine of the Faith of the Catholic Church of 2000, *Dominus Iesus*, by Cardinal Joseph Ratzinger (later Pope Benedict XVI), one finds some exclusive passages and some inclusive ones.[70] And, indeed, it is a general psychosocial fact about human beings that we transpose ourselves into others' perspectives, participating in their mental and experiential worlds, and thus become aware of similarities and differences.[71] It is therefore mistaken to think that in general there should be an absolute antithesis between insiders and outsiders of religions.[72] The many forms of—often unwitting—past and present syncretism are evidence of this, and Luke's narrative of Paul's speech to the Areopagus is a fine example, with its emphasis on the dialogue and mutual transformation of religious *paideiai*.

The third question is ethical, and concerns the distinction between teleological and deontological ethics. Rawls's sense of public reason would appear to reduce religious practice to deontological rights and freedoms, and to thus neglect the dense and particular teleological forms that religious life takes—its ideals, values, virtues, intentions, motivations, and loyalties, especially to one's community.[73] These forms are clearly Paul's focus in his speech to the Athenians. But the question is whether in the great religious traditions, teleology and deontology are really opposed. According to Paul Ricoeur, deontologically formulated rights and freedoms can be used to "sieve" teleological ideals, values, virtues, and loyalties to determine whether the latter infringe on the former, as, for instance, when religious customs oppress women, homosexuals, or minorities.[74] Once thus "sieved," Rawls's position appears to allow religious and other citizens' teleological orientations to guide their actions.

Considering these three questions regarding Rawls in light of the Lukan Paul's speech to the Areopagus thus helps to show how they might be answered, as well as to underline how the political common ground identified by Rawls serves a role analogous to that played by Hellenistic religious culture in Paul's speech. For, although it regards a shared democratic legal culture, rather than a shared religious one, Rawls's common ground nonetheless poses the same hermeneutic challenge as Hellenistic religious culture posed to Paul, namely, that of hermeneutically "translating" the common ground into the terms of those who do not share it, and thus potentially also transforming the common ground itself. And this is a task primarily of practical, rather than theoretical, reasoning, and one that involves transformations on both sides.

PUBLIC DELIBERATIVE REASONING BY RELIGIOUS CITIZENS

Besides illuminating the political common ground that Rawls envisions between religious and other citizens, developing the comparison with Paul's speech also serves to explain the kind of reasoning that Rawls thinks religious citizens must employ in developing this common ground. In particular, it brings out the need to employ terms that citizens with different worldviews can understand and the need to engage in a reciprocal exchange of perspectives.

Religious citizens may consider religious authority sufficient to justify their practical judgments. For instance, a Christian may consider God's will sufficient to justify the impermissibility of abortion in any circumstances. But irrespective of how persuasive such a justification may be for a Christian—notably, it neglects traditional Christian distinctions between life, human life, and the human person[75]—it is inappropriate to employ it in public debate for two reasons. First, it is not an argument, because it is tautological. For although the appeal to God's will is presented as an argument for the impermissibility of abortion, on closer examination it is revealed to be a mere clarification. The "argument" effectively says, "we are not free, because we are not free (being subject to God)"; the second phrase appears as an argument for what is claimed in the first phrase, but in fact only makes explicit what is already implied in the first phrase.[76] Second, a translation into public reason is lacking. Participants in public debate who do not share the Christian worldview that the justification presupposes may not be able to understand the statement, even if other Christians or other religious people do. For this reason, the religious citizen's argument must be translated into publicly understandable terms, in a way analogous to the Lukan Paul's translation of the Christian notion of God into the terms of his listeners' faith in the Hellenistic Zeus. Luke's Paul provides his Athenian listeners with an argument, not a tautology, and he articulates this argument in terms that his listeners, not only his fellow Christians, can understand.

Hugo Grotius makes a valuable distinction in this regard. He claims that an act may be considered good or justified in one of two ways: either simply because it is God's will (*justum esse, id est jure debitum, quia Deus voluit*) or because it is rational, which explains *why* God wills it (*ideo id Deum velle quia justum est*). In the first case, divine voluntarism takes priority over justification, and one arrives at the tautologies of the kind I mentioned. But in the second case, reason takes priority and has the task of explaining God's will, or, in the terms that I have been using, "translating" it into "public reasons," into a political "common ground." Grotius therefore holds that we should give reasons *as if* there is no God, despite the fact that he was a very religious person, belonging to the liberal wing of Dutch Protestantism. Thus he writes at the beginning of his *De jure belli ac pacis*, "What we have been saying [about law] would have validity even if we should concede [*etiamsi daremus*] that which cannot be conceded without the utmost wickedness, that there is no God, or that the affairs of men are of no concern to Him."[77]

Furthermore, having citizens give one another reasons as if there is no God does not mean that revealed truth and religious reason cannot also contribute to public debate in other, nonargumentative ways. They can "prime" public reasoning, by furnishing inspiring metaphors, myths, and rituals and thus tempering its possible harshness, abstractness, and cynicism, warming its coldness, bending its rigidity—in short, taking account of human measure. But they cannot play an argumentative role; their insights must be explained in terms that other citizens can understand.[78]

To make their justifications acceptable to others, religious citizens engaged in public debate must also take other citizens' perspectives, so as to relate their claims to others' different justificatory worldviews. In other words, a religious citizen must recognize what is "sacred" for others and construct an argument on the basis of it, such that others feel seen, heard, and understood, rather than neglected or, even worse, degraded.[79] Again, the analogy with the speech by the Lukan Paul is instructive. For by using Jewish-Hellenistic metaphors and concepts, he bridged the gap between Christian and Hellenistic religious culture, showing his listeners how their own Hellenistic religious ideas were also affirmed by Christianity. In the absence of such a religious "overlapping consensus," Rawls pursues a political one, but nonetheless requires religious citizens to take others' perspectives in making their claims understandable and acceptable to them.

This clearly involves some selectivity. In addressing himself to the Athenians, the Lukan Paul focuses on the ideas they share with Christians, such as the opposition to idolatry, human beings' inherence in God, and the unity of humanity. But he does not raise other central Christian notions that the historical Paul cherished, such as his negative view of mankind, including human weakness and sinfulness, his emphasis on the sacrifice of Jesus's death on the cross, the centrality of Jesus the risen Lord as well as the coming (*parousia*) of Christ, and the church as the God-given and Spirit-laden community of Christians.[80] He developed these notions in his letters to the Romans, the Corinthians, the Galatians, the Philippians, and the Thessalonians, but they are absent in the Lukan narrative of his speech in Athens. Even the figure of Christ—who plays the dominant role in the letters—is merely alluded to in the narrative, as an anonymous "man" raised from the dead and appointed by God to judge humankind.

To illustrate his proviso, Rawls refers approvingly to Catholic leaders like Cardinal Bernardin, archbishop of Chicago, who expressed his opposition to abortion not only in terms of religious ideas such as those of life as God's creation or gift, but also in the nonreligious terms of public peace, the human right to life, and commonly accepted standards of moral behavior. Rawls himself disagrees with Bernardin's view, but values his providing public reasons for his views.[81] In the same vein, other issues such as passive and active euthanasia and same-sex marriage can be discussed in public terms. Religious citizens may enrich public debate by calling attention to aspects for which religions may have a special sensitivity, like the limits of human control and choice, and thus may contribute to the reciprocal character of the debate and perhaps also adjust and revise it in some respects.

CONCLUSION

That was some weak hermeneutics.

In this chapter I have offered a hermeneutic analysis of the Lukan narrative of Paul's speech to the Areopagus, showing how the Lukan Paul attempts to establish common ground with his audience through deliberative rhetoric, including argumentation and perspective exchange. By bridging Jerusalem and Athens, Jewish religious culture and Hellenistic religious culture, the common ground he found was religious. In modern societies the common ground cannot be religious, but must instead be political. Nonetheless, just as the Lukan Paul translated Christian convictions into Jewish-Hellenistic ones by drawing on the legacy of the Jewish-Hellenistic diaspora in Asia Minor, so in contemporary public discourses the Christian legacy must be translated into public terms. In this sense, Rawls's answer to the question of how a Christian can support a democratic regime is a profoundly hermeneutic one.

Again, idk. What does he want to "get" by arguing that?

Notes

A previous version of this chapter was published as "Religion's Political Role in Rawlsian Key," *Religion and Theology* 19, nos. 1–2 (2012): 1–42 and *Balkan Journal of Philosophy* 1 (2012): 7–30. I thank Tom Bailey for his help in elegantly revising the text.

1. *PL* xxxvii.

2. See *PL* lv, 477; see also John Courtney Murray, *We Hold These Truths: Catholic Reflections on the American Propositions* (New York: Sheed and Ward, 1961); and Murray, "Natural Law and the Public Consensus," in *Natural Law and Modern Society*, ed. J. Cogley, R. Hutchins, and J. Murray (New York: Meridian, 1966), 48–81.

3. See van der Ven, *Human Rights or Religious Rules?* (Leiden: Brill, 2010), 187–226; and van der Ven, "From Natural Rights to Human Rights: A Cultural War in the Modern Era," *Religion, State and Society* 41, no. 2 (2013): 164–87.

4. Some scholars date Acts to before the destruction of Jerusalem in 70, others date it to the 70s or the early 80s on the basis of the discrepancy between Luke 21:20ff. and

188 ACCOMMODATING RELIGIONS WITH RAWLS

Mark 13:14–23, and others date it around 100 or later, on the basis of the use of Flavius Josephus's works on the wars of the Jews against the Romans (*Bellum Judaicum*) and on the history of the Jews (*Antiquitates Judaicae*). See Hans-Josef Klauck, *The Apocryphal Acts of the Apostles: An Introduction* (Waco, Tex.: Baylor University Press, 2008).

5. See Charlotte Schubert, "Der Areopag: Ein Gerichtshof zwischen Politik und Recht," in *Grosse Prozesse im Alten Athen*, ed. L. Burckhardt and J. von Ungern-Sternberg (München: Beck, 2000), 50–65.

6. Acts of the Apostles (hereafter, "Acts") 17:22–23. References to Acts are to chapter and verse numbers. The expression "to the unknown god" is not phrased in the usual polytheistic plural, "gods," but in the henotheistic or monotheistic singular. See Eduard Norden, *Agnosthos Theos: Untersuchungen zur Formengeschichte Religiöser Rede* (Darmstadt: Wissenschaftliche Buchgesellschaft, 1974), 121. It may be considered as performing an *ex voto* function (see Richard I. Pervo, *Acts: A Commentary* [Minneapolis: Fortress, 2009], 433) in a theodicy framework (see Pieter van der Horst, "The Altar of the 'Unknown God' in Athens [Acts 17:23] and the Cult of 'Unknown Gods' in the Hellenistic and Roman Period," *Aufstieg und Niedergang der Römischen Welt* 18, no. 2, [1989]: 1426–56; van der Horst, *De onbekende God* [Utrecht: Wever, 1988], 9–36; and Karel van der Toorn, *Sin and Sanction in Israel and Mesopotamia* [Assen: Van Gorcum, 1985], 94–97). It also may not be an inscription, but a dedication (see Martin Dibelius, *Paulus auf dem Areopag* [Heidelberg: Winter, 1939], 16; and O. Pesch, *Die Apostgeschichte (Apg 13–28)* [Köln: Benziger, 1986], 136), woven into Luke's narrative not as a statement of divine unknowability (see Martin Dibelius, *Aufsätze zur Apostelgeschichte* [Göttingen: Vandenhoeck & Ruprecht 1953], 21–22), but as a literary motif (see Adolf von Harnack, *Ist die Rede des Paulus in Athene ein ursprünglicher Bestandteil des Apostelgeschichte?* [Leipzig: Hinrich, 1913]), of which there are parallels in later books (Justin Taylor, *Les actes des deux apotres* [Paris: Gabalda, 1994], 289–94).

7. Acts 17:28.

8. Van der Horst, "The Altar of the 'Unknown God,'" 10.

9. See René Piettre, "Paul et les Épicuriens d'Athènes entre polythéismes, athéismes, et monothéismes," *Diogenes* 205 (2004): 62.

10. See Norden, *Agnosthos Theos*, 10 and 122.

11. See ibid., 127.

12. See Juhana Torkki, "Paul in Athens (Acts 17: 16–34): A Dramatic Episode," in *Lux Humana, Lux Aeterna: Essays on Biblical and Related Themes in Honour of Lars Aejmelaeus*, ed. A. Mustakallio (Göttingen: Vandenhoeck und Ruprecht, 2005), 338–40.

13. See Eckhard Plümacher, *Lukas als hellenistischer Schriftsteller: Studien zur Apostelgeschichte* (Göttingen: Vandenhoeck und Ruprecht, 1972), 20–22; Juhana Torkki, "The Dramatic Account of Paul's Encounter with Philosophy: An Analysis of Acts 17:16–34 with Regard to Contemporary Philosophical Debates" (PhD diss., University of Helsinki, 2004), 119–54; and Torkki, "Paul in Athens," 341–57.

14. See Plümacher, *Lukas als hellenistischer Schriftsteller*, 19 and 97–98.

15. See Plato, "Socrates' verdediging," in *Plato, Feest, Euthyfron, Socrates' verdediging, Kriton, Faidon* (Amsterdam: Atheneum, 2008), 99–139.

16. See Pervo, *Acts*, 425–28.

17. I quote from the New Revised Standard Version of the Bible (1989).

18. See Günther Bornkamm, *Early Christian Experience* (New York: Harper and Row, 1969); Ben Witherington, *The Acts of the Apostles: A Social-Rhetoric Commentary* (Grand Rapids, Mich.: Eerdmans, 1998); and Pervo, *Acts*, 432.

19. See Jan Assmann, *Herrschaft und Heil: Politische Theologie in Altägypten, Israel und Europa* (München: Hanser, 2000).

20. See Hans Conzelmann, *Die Apostelgeschichte* (Tübingen: Mohr, 1972), 107.

21. See Arthur Nock, *Essays on Religion and the Ancient World* (Oxford: Clarendon Press, 1986).

22. See Pesch, *Die Apostgeschichte*.

23. See Pervo, *Acts*.

24. See Norman DeWitt, *Epicurus and His Philosophy* (Westport, Conn.: Greenwood, 1976), 249.

25. See Pesch, *Die Apostgeschichte*, 137; and Pervo, *Acts*, 435.

26. See Norden, *Agnosthos Theos*, 16–17; Pesch, *Die Apostgeschichte*, 138; and Pervo, *Acts*, 430.

27. See Pervo, *Acts*, 436–38; and Conzelmann, *Die Apostelgeschichte*, 109.

28. See Dibelius, *Paulus*, 9–10.

29. See DeWitt, *Epicurus*, 250.

30. See Dibelius, *Paulus*, 31–32.

31. See Conzelmann, *Die Apostelgeschichte*, 109.

32. See Plato, *Timaeus*, 37c.

33. See Norden, *Agnosthos Theos*, 19–24.

34. See Piettre, "Paul et les Épicuriens," 60.

35. See Clare Clivaz, "L'analyse narrative signale-t-elle l'arrivée du muthos en exégèse? Histoire et Poétique autour d'Ac 17,28," in *Analyse narrative et bible*, ed. C. Focant and A. Wénin (Leuven: Peeters, 2005), 491.

36. In his *Phaenomena*, Aristobulus, a Jewish philosopher in second-century-B.C. Alexandria who linked Judaism with Hellenistic thought, quoted Aratos as saying of the intimate relation between God and humans, "we are all his children." See Conzelmann, *Die Apostelgeschichte*, 110; and Torkki, *Dramatic Account*, 162–65.

37. See Pesch, *Die Apostgeschichte*, 139n42.

38. See Dibelius, *Paulus*, 30–32.

39. See Nock, *Essays on Religion*, 58.

40. See ibid., 69.

41. See Witherington, *The Acts of the Apostles*, 518.

42. See Werner Kahl, "Paulus als kontextualisierender Evangelist beim Areopag," in *Der eine Gott und die fremde Kulte, Exklusive und inklusive Tendenzen in den biblischen Gottesvorstellungen*, ed. E. Bons (Neukirchen: Neukirchener, 2009), 73–94.

43. See Pesch, *Die Apostgeschichte*, 148.

44. See Paul Ricoeur, *The Conflict of Interpretations: Studies in Phenomenology and Existential Philosophy* (Evanston, Ill.: Northwestern University Press, 1992); and Ricoeur, *La memoire, l'histoire, l'oubli* (Paris: Seuil, 2000). In hermeneutics the "application model," which assumes a one-to-one relation between the original meaning of a text and its meaning today, is countered by intercontextual hermeneutics, which operates with a kind of quadratic equation: the present context relates to the present meaning of the text as the early context relates to the text's meaning in that age. On this, see Edward Schillebeeckx, *Theologisch geloofverstaan anno 1983* (Baarn: Nelissen, 1983); Schillebeeckx, *Mensen als verhaal van God* (Baarn: Nelissen, 1989); Clodovis Boff, *Theology and Praxis: Epistemological Foundations* (Maryknoll, N.Y.: Orbis Books 1987); van der Ven, *Human Rights*, 191–92; and Péter Losonczi, "Religion, Pluralism, and Politics: A Case for an Inter-Contextual Study on Europe and India," in *Secularism, Religion and Politics: India and Europe*, ed. P. Losonczi and W. van Herck (New York: Routledge, 2014).

45. See Jean-Pierre Wils, *Hermeneutiek en verlangen: Over godservaring en ethiek in het spoor van Friedrich D. E. Schleiermacher* (Nijmegen: Radboud Universiteit Nijmegen Press, 1997), 11; and Friedrich Schleiermacher, *Hermeneutik* (Heidelberg: Winter, 1974), 82.

46. See, for instance, Niklas Luhmann, *Die Wissenschaft der Gesellschaft* (Frankfurt: Suhrkamp, 1990); Luhmann, *Dar Recht der Gesellschaft* (Frankfurt: Suhrkamp, 1995); Luhmann, *Die Gesellschaft der Gesellschaft* (Frankfurt: Suhrkamp, 1998), chap. 2; and Luhmann, *Die Religion der Gesellschaft* (Frankfurt: Suhrkamp, 2000).

47. For a more detailed account, see van der Ven, *Human Rights*, 359–72.

48. See Pippa Norris and Ronald Inglehart, *Sacred and Secular: Religions and Politics Worldwide* (Cambridge: Cambridge University Press, 2005).

49. See Jean Porter, "Does the Natural Law Provide a Universally Valid Morality?," in *Intractable Disputes About the Natural Law: Alasdair MacIntyre and Critics*, ed. L. Cunningham (Notre Dame: University of Notre Dame Press, 2009), 53–95.

50. See van der Ven, "From Natural Rights to Human Rights."

51. See *JF* 223ff.

52. *LP* 123.

53. See *PL* xlvi, 6, and 156–57, and also Sebastiano Maffettone, *Rawls: An Introduction* (Cambridge: Polity, 2010), 52–99.

54. See *PL* xlvi, 54–58.

55. See *PL* xlvi, 249–250, 464–465.

56. Barack Obama, *The Audacity of Hope: Thoughts on Reclaiming the American Dream* (New York: Three Rivers Press, 2006), 218–19.

57. See Maffettone, *Rawls*, 287–88.

58. See *PL* 462.

59. See Jean-Pierre Wils, "Die hermeneutische Signatur der kommunitaristischen Liberalismuskritik," in *Kommunitarismus und Religion*, ed. M. Kühnlein (Berlin: Akademie Verlag, 2010), 17–38.

60. *PL* 476.

61. See van der Ven, *Human Rights*, 399–411.

62. The term "axial" is intended to distinguish previous religions, formerly known as "primitive religions," from those that came to be considered the axis of the history of religions, due to their supralocal expansion, religious abstraction, conceptualization, and social and political institutionalization. These religions date back to the fifth century B.C.E., with roots in the eighth century B.C.E. and offshoots in the third century B.C.E.. Because of their Judaic roots, Christianity and Islam are considered axial religions, albeit as secondary manifestations of them. On this, see Shmuel Eisenstadt, ed., *The Origins and Diversity of Axial Age Civilizations* (New York: SUNY Press, 1986); and Johan Arnason, Shmuel Eisenstadt, and Bjorn Wittrock, *Axial Civilizations and World History* (Leiden: Brill, 2005).

63. See *PL* 59.

64. See *LHMP* 164–65, 230–31, 240–41, and 331–32.

65. See Jan Walgrave, "Redelijke geloofsverantwoording," *Tijdschrift voor Theologie* 2, no. 2 (1962): 101–26; and Alessandro Ferrara, *The Force of the Example: Explorations in the Paradigm of Judgment* (New York: Columbia University Press, 2008), 62–79.

66. See Wolfgang Pannenberg, "Wie wahr is das Reden von Gott?," *Evangelische Kommentare* 4, no. 11 (1971): 629–33.

67. See van der Ven, *Human Rights*, 125–29.

68. See John Locke, *A Letter Concerning Toleration* (London: Routledge, 1991), 80–85.

69. After about five centuries the Catholic church accepted in the Second Vatican Council's *Decree On Ecumenism* (1964, number 11) the originally Protestant principle of the articles of faith being differentiated into an order of rank.

70. For exclusive passages, see Congregation for the Doctrine of the Faith, *Dominus Iesus: On the Unicity and Salvific Universality of Jesus Christ and the Church*, 2000, paragraphs 6 and 15, and for inclusive ones, see paragraphs 8, 14, and 22, www.vatican.va /roman_curia/congregations/cfaith/documents/rc_con_cfaith_doc_20000806 _dominus-iesus_en.html. See also van der Ven, *Human Rights*, 72–73.

71. See John T. Cacioppo and William Patrick, *Loneliness: Human Nature and the Need for Social Connection* (New York: Norton, 2009).

72. See Jeppe Jensen, "Revisiting the Insider-Outsider Debate: Dismantling a Pseudo-Problem in the Study of Religion," *Method and Theory in the Study of Religion* 23, no. 1 (2011): 29–47.

73. See Michael Walzer, *Spheres of Justice* (New York: Basic, 1983); Jean-Pierre Wils, "Universality of Human Rights and the Need for Parsimony," in *Tensions Within and*

192 ACCOMMODATING RELIGIONS WITH RAWLS

Between Religions and Human Rights, ed. J. A. Van der Ven and H.-G. Ziebertz (Leiden: Brill, 2011), 9–26; and Michael Reder, "Wie weit können Glaube und Vernunft unterscheiden werden," in *Ein Bewusstsein von dem, was fehlt: Eine Diskussion mit Jürgen Habermas*, ed. M. Reder and J. Schmidt (Frankfurt: Suhrkamp, 2008), 51–68.

74. See Paul Ricoeur, *Oneself as Another* (Chicago: University of Chicago Press, 1992), 169–296.

75. See Charles Curran, "Abortion: Its Moral Aspects," in *Abortion: The Moral Issues*, ed. E. Batchelor Jr. (New York: Pilgrim, 1982), 115–28.

76. See Bruno Schüller, "Zur Problematik allgemein verbindlicher ethischen Grundsätze," *Theologie und Philosophie* 45 (1970): 1–23; Schüller, *Die Begründung sittlicher Urteile: Typen ethischer Argumentation in der katholischen Moraltheologie* (Düsseldorf: Patmos, 1973), 182–98; and Harry Kuitert, "Hebben christenen het recht om zichzelf te doden?," *Concilium* 21, no. 3 (1985): 96.

77. Hugo Grotius (Hugo de Groot), *De jure belli ac pacis* (Oxford: Clarendon Press, 1625), prolegomena 11.

78. See Jürgen Habermas, *Zwischen Naturalismus und Religion* (Frankfurt: Suhrkamp, 2005), 119–54.

79. See Axel Honneth, *Kampf um Anerkennung: Zur moralischen Grammatik sozialer Konflikte* (Frankfurt: Suhrkamp, 1994), 107–225; Honneth, *Unsichtbarkeit: Stationen einer Theorie der Intersubjektivität* (Frankfurt: Suhrkamp, 2003), passim; and Paul Ricoeur, *The Course of Recognition* (Cambridge, Mass.: Harvard University Press, 2005), 171–219.

80. See James Dunn, *The Theology of Paul the Apostle* (Grand Rapids, Mich.: Eerdmans, 1998), passim; and Gerd Lüdemann, *Paul: The Founder of Christianity* (New York: Prometheus Books, 2002), passim.

81. See *PL* livn32, 243n32, and 480n82.

PART III

TRANSCENDING RAWLS

8

E Pluribus Unum

JUSTIFICATION AND REDEMPTION
IN RAWLS, COHEN, AND HABERMAS

JAMES GLEDHILL

An ideal of intersubjective relations of community runs through-out John Rawls's work. The publication of his undergraduate senior thesis, submitted at Princeton in 1942 and titled *A Brief Inquiry Into the Meaning of Sin and Faith: An Interpretation Based on the Concept of Community*, offers an important new perspective on this theme. The assurance with which the young Rawls declares that the "dichotomy between the individual and society which recent Western thought has puzzled over is really no dichotomy at all" suggests that we should reassess his mature work beyond the standard dichotomy of "liberal-ism" versus "communitarianism."[1] In particular, I will argue, his early religious concern with redemption through community was not so much abandoned in his mature work as reinterpreted within a non-theistic, but nonetheless not secular, philosophical framework.[2]

To bring out and evaluate this sense of redemption through com-munity, I will consider it in light of the arguments made by two of Rawls's most significant critics, G. A. Cohen and Jürgen Habermas. In particular, I will show how these three thinkers offer contrasting models of the creation of social harmony out of plurality that stand in complex relations to religious ideas of community. Following Cohen,

I will refer to the sense of community involved as "justificatory community," and show how such community is a communicative relation, one that either makes it possible for persons to say something to one another or itself consists in a reciprocal practice of communication.[3]

For purposes of comparison, I will focus on two analogies that Rawls employs in describing a well-ordered society, one with a symphony orchestra and the other with a well-constituted and well-played game. I will begin by comparing the analogy of a symphony orchestra with Cohen's own analogy between socialist community and a jazz band, drawing upon Rawls's senior thesis to show why he would reject Cohen's model of justificatory community. I will then turn to Rawls's analogy with a game and show how Stanley Cavell's related critique of Rawls is more successful than Cohen's in identifying both the aspirations and the limitations of Rawls's approach. Finally, turning to Habermas, I will argue that Habermas's discourse theory, which I present in terms of Hans-Georg Gadamer's analogy between communication and play, is able to respond to what is valid in Cavell's criticisms while maintaining fundamental commitments of Rawls's model of justificatory community. To use the young Rawls's distinction between communities formed by a vertical relation to God and those formed by horizontal relations to other persons,[4] my overall story will be of a move from Cohen's sense of a justificatory community involving individuals standing in vertical relations to principles of justice, to Rawls's model of "conversion" in which vertical relations to principles of justice open persons up to horizontal relations of community with others, and finally to Habermas's fully intersubjective model of justificatory community, consisting in horizontal relations of communicative justification that nevertheless preserve a moment of transcendence.

COHEN: SOCIALIST COMMUNITY AS A JAZZ BAND

Cohen describes the development of his socialist commitments as a move from the economic point of view of historical materialism to a moral point of view. Both points of view reject the political point of view adopted by Rawls, according to which achieving equality is a matter of constitution-making. Cohen takes Rawls's view to founder on the fact that "we cannot make a constitution *together* unless and until we are already equals."[5] But, while Cohen remains committed to a socialist ideal of community as overcoming both distributive inequality and the alienated political idea of constitution-making between abstract legal persons,[6] there is a change in the way in which he sees such community as coming about. From the point of view of historical materialism, this was a question of the teleological development of material productive forces independent of control by social structures and how this would create the material abundance that facilitates proletarian revolution.[7] But in his normative theory of justice, Cohen abandons hope of such material abundance and instead views "rules of regulation" as teleological devices for promoting fundamental fact-independent principles of justice. Having given up the idea of a society beyond the circumstances of justice, Cohen turns to fundamental principles of justice understood as situated beyond facts about society. From this new moral point of view, community comes about through something like the Christian conception of "a moral revolution, a revolution in the human soul."[8]

In order to understand the ideal of justificatory community that Cohen articulates in opposition to Rawls, it is helpful to look first at the model of community that Cohen thought would be facilitated by material abundance. According to this model, community is instrumental to the achievement of persons' independently specified goals. It is a "concert of mutually supporting self-fulfilments, in which no one takes promoting the fulfilment of others as any kind of obligation."[9] As a way of picturing Marx's idea of a society in which the "free development of each is the condition for the free development of all," Cohen draws an analogy with a jazz band.[10] He asks that one

> imagine a jazz band each player in which seeks his own fulfilment as a musician. Though basically interested in his own fulfilment, and not in that of the band as a whole, or of his fellow musicians taken severally, he nevertheless fulfils himself only to the extent that each of the others also does so, and the same holds for each of them.[11]

In discussing this model, Daniel Brudney offers a helpful twofold distinction for analyzing how individuals may share ends in community.[12] First of all, Cohen's jazz musicians may be said to have an externally oriented as opposed to an internally oriented shared end. The musicians share an end of playing jazz that each of them has as an individual, antecedently to engaging in cooperation with others. They do not share the end of playing together. Moreover, theirs is an overlapping rather than an intertwined shared end. The fact that each musician fulfills himself only to the extent that the others also do so is contingent upon factors that lie beyond their practice of cooperation and that lead their individual ends to overlap. In an intertwined end, by contrast, attaining the end with and through others is a necessary condition of realizing the end. I will return to this twofold distinction in analyzing the models of justificatory community offered by Rawls and Habermas.

Although Cohen presents his critique of Rawls's model of justificatory community as an internal critique, it might rather be thought to presuppose his own conception of justice.[13] On Cohen's view, "something transcending human will must figure in morality if it is to have an apodictic character."[14] Fundamental principles of justice, for one, "transcend the facts of the world."[15] This sense of vertical relations to principles of justice might seem to stand in tension with the "interpersonal test" to which Cohen appeals in criticizing Rawls's difference principle, which might appear to be a purely horizontal criterion of interpersonal justification.[16] However, Cohen's model of justificatory community can rather be seen as following from his own vertical conception of justice.

On Cohen's view, for justificatory community to exist, all policies, and their attendant justifications, must be capable of a comprehensive justification. That is, any policy must pass an interpersonal test that "asks whether the argument could serve as a justification of a mooted policy when uttered by any member of society to any other member."[17] Cohen famously argues that the incentives argument often seen as permitted by Rawls's difference principle fails this interpersonal test. When the rich argue in favor of material incentives, they present themselves in the third person: "they (the rich) will only work harder if they receive material incentives." But when the argument is presented in the first person, justification breaks down: "We (that is, I and other rich people like me) won't work harder without material incentives." If everyone were to freely endorse true fundamental principles of justice, and follow them in their personal behavior, the interpersonal test would be met and comprehensive justification achieved. In his model of socialist community, where an egalitarian ethos obtains, individuals share the externally oriented end of acting in accordance with true fundamental principles of justice, not the internal end of establishing rules for living together. And since justice is fundamentally a matter of achieving the correct distributive pattern, the fact that all individuals must follow principles of justice in their personal behavior is a contingent means for bringing about an overlapping end, one made necessary by the fact that material abundance is not a realistic prospect.

There is some ambiguity as to how the interpersonal test that Cohen employs in his critique of Rawls relates to the socialist idea of community that he defends in *Why Not Socialism?* In the latter work, Cohen describes socialist community as achieving communal reciprocity, which might be taken to involve a commitment to an intersubjective model of community.[18] But Cohen presents this idea of communal reciprocity in second-person-singular, "I-you" terms: I serve you because I find intrinsic value in doing so, as opposed to the instrumental value that motivates market relations, even if I also expect that you will serve me. Cohen's moral model of socialist community thus remains a concert of mutually supporting self-fulfillments, in which no one takes promoting the fulfillment of others as any kind of obligation. For Rawls, as I will show, reciprocity is rather a matter of a first-person-plural perspective, of acting in accordance with reasons "we" can mutually acknowledge as free and equal citizens.

How does Cohen's conception of justificatory community relate to religious ideas? In connecting his critique of Rawls with his reading of the Gospels, Cohen comments that Jesus would rightly have "spurned the liberal idea that the state can take care of justice for us, provided only that we obey the rules it lays down."[19] However, Cohen's model of justificatory community might be more illuminatingly compared to the Jewish understanding of the relationship between justice and love articulated by Franz Rosenzweig. On Rosenzweig's interpretation of the golden rule to love one's neighbor as oneself, "the neighbor is only a representative. He is not loved for his own sake, nor for his beautiful eyes, but only because he just happens to be standing there, because he happens to be nighest to me. Another could easily stand in his place—precisely at this place nearest me. The neighbor is the other."[20]

On this view, as on Cohen's, the horizontal relations of justification in which one stands to the other result from, and can be used to test for, appropriate vertical relations to justice.[21] Thus there are also Platonic resonances in the idea of a revolution in the human soul that achieves justice in the community as a whole, something that helps to explain why Cohen's interest in fact-independent fundamental principles of justice is not a purely theoretical one, but serves a revolutionary socialist doctrine. As Habermas notes, for Plato "nothing is more practical than theory itself": knowledge promises salvation.[22] Put another way, unless faith that there exists a substantive truth about justice is maintained, justificatory community as Cohen conceives of it will be impossible.

But this means that Cohen fails to provide a genuinely intersubjective model of justificatory community. Indeed, his rejection of Rawls's political point of view of constitution-making extends to a wholesale rejection of internally oriented ends. In particular, he rejects the idea of socialization into a shared internally oriented end that he acknowledges Karl Marx relies upon in his early writings, but which, he argues, Marx's later historical materialism repudiates. On an alternative humanist interpretation, however, Marx's model of community can be seen as involving an internally oriented and intertwined end. On this view, a shared internally oriented end is a matter of establishing a general will, and the maintenance of a general will depends upon its being an intertwined end: persons' interests as citizens do not exist atomistically, but only as a result of internal relations between persons acting as integral parts of the community they constitute.[23] It is just such a conception of justificatory community that is articulated by Rawls.

RAWLS: A WELL-ORDERED SOCIETY AS A SYMPHONY ORCHESTRA

When describing Jean-Jacques Rousseau's conception of a well-ordered society along with his own model of how social harmony is created out of plurality, Rawls draws an analogy with a symphony orchestra. Specifically, he compares the idea of a well-ordered society to a "group of musicians every one of whom could have trained himself to play equally well as the others any instrument in the orchestra, but who each have by a kind of tacit agreement set out to perfect their skills on the one they have chosen so as to realize the powers of all in their joint performances."[24] Rawls's classical musicians commit themselves to a joint performance and therefore have an internally oriented shared end. In the terms of theories of collective intentionality, a symphony orchestra is not simply an aggregation of "I intentionality," but a matter of "We intentionality." As John Searle puts it, "If I am a violinist in an orchestra I play my part in our performance of the symphony."[25] This analogy suggests that Michael Sandel is mistaken to admonish Rawls for forgetting that "when politics goes well, we can know a good in common that we cannot know alone."[26] Moreover, unlike a contract for mutual advantage, the internally oriented end that Rawls's musicians share is an intertwined end. This means that they can only fulfill their individual ends in and through a collective end.[27] By rejecting ideas of justificatory community that depend upon the socialization of individuals into adopting a shared point of view and transcending individualism, Cohen reduces eligible conceptions of community to a dichotomy between self-interested bargaining and a shared commitment to an external end.[28] Like Sandel, Cohen does not consider that among internally oriented ends, intersubjective relations can take the form of intertwined ends, rather than simply overlapping ones.

In *A Theory of Justice*, Rawls claims that the "public realization of justice is a value of community." In a note, he elaborates on this as follows: "persons need one another since it is only in active cooperation with others that one's powers reach fruition. Only in a social union is the individual complete."[29] By contrast, on Cohen's Marxian view of full communism, "if we were musicians we might want to take turns playing all the instruments in the orchestra."[30] Rawls recognizes that on a Hegelian interpretation, Marx might be seen as endorsing the orchestra model, but he tends to follow a more revolutionary, utopian interpretation of Marx, claiming of it that "a society in which all can achieve their complete good, or in which there are no conflicting demands and the wants of all fit together without coercion into a harmonious plan of activity, is a society in a certain sense beyond justice."[31] In such a society, persons would no longer have to act from a sense of justice, which develops only in response to the factual circumstances of justice. Of course, Cohen considers it impossible to move "beyond justice," since he understands justice to consist in a patterned egalitarian distribution, however this is produced.[32] But Rawls's point still holds against Cohen's normative theory of justice. By denying that justice is a virtue of citizens, and thus rejecting both a Marxian idea of socialization and the Humean idea of benevolence as vehicles for the realization of justice, Cohen's egalitarian ethos is an externally oriented, overlapping end, and not a matter of intersubjective virtues of social cooperation.

Cohen may well be right to hold that justice cannot be adequately understood as a matter of Christian charity or Humean benevolence. However, he does not explore in any detail how Rawls follows the lead of Rousseau and Immanuel Kant, who, both reinterpreting Christian ideas, understand justice as an intersubjective relationship between free and equal persons. Indeed, Rawls's rejection of models of justificatory community such as Cohen's that appeal to vertical relations to external ends can be traced back to his senior thesis. There the contrast I have employed between externally oriented and internally oriented ends is echoed by Rawls's distinction between "natural" and "personal" relations: while natural relations are relations to objects, personal relations are relations to other persons. In Rawls's words, "proper ethics" involves not natural relations to the Form of the Good, Truth, or God, but "the relating of person to person and finally to God."[33]

Indeed, it is striking how much of the structure of the young Rawls's religious model of community finds its way into his mature work.[34] In his senior thesis, Rawls suggests that "the chief problem of politics is to work out some scheme of social arrangements which can so harness human sin"—which Rawls understands in terms of egoism and pride—"as to make the natural correlates of community and personality possible."[35] In his mature work, the process of reflective equilibrium can be seen as directed toward discovering a shared "incipient if latent sense of community waiting to be brought to light, elaborated, and self-consciously strengthened through reflection."[36] A political conception of justice appeals to a sense of justice that persons share as citizens, the difference principle requiring persons to pursue their own conceptions of the good only on terms consistent with the common good. Rawls acknowledges that Cohen's socialist ideal of equality is incompatible with this understanding of the difference principle. He writes that, on Cohen's view, "no one can be required"—that is, required by coercive rules—"to benefit himself only in ways that contribute to others' well-being," since this would be to encroach on persons' freedom to direct their own labor.[37] From this, Cohen concludes that the commitment to principles of justice must be a free individual choice. But the difference principle testifies to Rawls's alternative, Rousseauian strategy of elevating humankind by "curing the malady from within,"[38] redirecting individuals' particular ends in such a way that they contribute toward the common good. In other words, as a principle of reciprocity, the difference principle realizes the shared intertwined end of the good of a well-ordered society.

The end toward which Rawls looks in his senior thesis is the "reconciliation between person and community," the "personal relations" of person to person and finally to God.[39] The problem of political liberalism that he raises in his later work is that of whether citizens who hold a plurality of comprehensive doctrines can achieve reconciliation by public reason. There are limits to reconciliation by public reason, of course, the most crucial being the fact that "comprehensive doctrines are, politically speaking, unreconcilable."[40] But, while the differences between citizens that result from their differing comprehensive doctrines cannot be reconciled, citizens can be reconciled to conflicts produced by differences in status, class position, and occupation or in ethnicity, gender, and race, when they accept a reasonable political conception of justice and know that their social institutions conform to it. In Rawls's senior thesis, God restores man to community, for man must wait for God to speak to him before he can communicate with the "other" in community.[41] In his later work, holders of comprehensive doctrines undergo a nontheistic but structurally similar process of conversion, since only by accepting a political conception of justice can they deliberate in accordance with shared public reasons. In reconciliation by public reason, we become reconciled to our social world, affirming reasonable pluralism as constitutive of social freedom.

Rawls develops the idea of an overlapping consensus as part of a Kantian "defense of reasonable faith in the real possibility of a just constitutional regime."[42] Seeing such consensus as achieving the intertwined end of a well-ordered society avoids some of the misleading connotations that he sought to correct by emphasizing that a reasonable overlapping consensus achieves "stability for the right reasons." Far from seeking to challenge religious views, political liberalism is better understood as relying upon the transformation of the transcendent ends of comprehensive doctrines in the "conversion" experience of wide and general reflective equilibrium, through which an overlapping consensus on a political conception of justice is formed. Indeed, in Rawls's model of overlapping consensus there are resonances of the "dialectical quality" of conversion he emphasizes in his senior thesis, a process that he describes as "a being burst in upon and being bent back" through which persons are "not lifted out of the earthly community," not "abstracted from [their] fellow men and assumed into heaven," but "planted more firmly into that earthly community."[43] Ultimately, I think it is difficult to understand the possibility of an overlapping consensus in Rawls's sense without recognizing that it demands such a "leap of faith" on the part of citizens who hold comprehensive doctrines, as they accept the very great value of the good of political community.[44]

I have argued that political liberalism has a conception of justificatory community structurally similar to Rawls's senior thesis. The integration of personality into community involves a vertical relation— whether to God or to a political conception of justice—but this is required and ultimately justified by the horizontal relations with others that it facilitates. That being said, the vestiges of Rawls's religious conception of community that remain in political liberalism render the idea of an overlapping consensus problematic from the point of view of an intersubjective conception of justificatory community. This may be illustrated by returning to his orchestra analogy. The intersubjective relation formed in a symphony orchestra, like Rawls's model of a "social union of social unions," is a harmony between harmonious sections. Musicians have a place at a desk as a member of the strings, brass, woodwind, or percussion section, and they cannot coordinate their playing with all other members of the orchestra. A conductor is required to coordinate the performance. While not a member of the orchestra, the conductor determines the overall shape of how the piece will be played and the nature of the contributions of the players. In a performance, the "We intentionality" of a symphony orchestra depends to a significant degree upon the higher-level "I intentionality" of the conductor.

The ambiguous position of the conductor of a symphony orchestra recalls the ambiguous role of Rousseau's figure of the "lawgiver." Rawls describes this figure, "the mechanic who invents the machine," as a deus ex machina required to explain the origins and stability of the social contract.[45] Rousseau appeals to the figure of the lawgiver in response to a problem of utopianism, a problem of constitutional founding that generates a political circle:

For a nascent people to be capable of appreciating sound maxims of politics and of following the fundamental rules of reason
of State, the effect would have to become the cause, the social
spirit which is to be the work of the institution would have to
preside over the institution itself, and men would have to be
prior to laws what they ought to become by means of them. Thus
since the Lawgiver can use neither force nor reasoning, he must
of necessity have recourse to an authority of a different order,
which might be able to rally without violence and to persuade
without convincing.[46]

Rawls observes that principles and institutions may be introduced for
different reasons than those that later generations have for accepting
them. Rousseau's social contract could come about in a way similar
to that in which after the Wars of Religion religious toleration was
accepted as a modus vivendi.[47] From the point of view of his own conception of the social contract, Rawls describes how a modus vivendi
might develop into a constitutional consensus, and from there into
an overlapping consensus.[48] Since he does not appeal to a Hegelian
teleological philosophy of history, however, the problem remains
of how exactly the social contract of an overlapping consensus may
come about and of the authority to which a political conception of
justice that offers the promise of realizing an overlapping consensus
can appeal.

Rousseau asks how citizens can obey when no one commands. He
answers: "It is to law alone that men owe justice and freedom. It is this
salutary organ of the will of all that restores in [the realm of] right
the natural equality among men. It is this celestial voice that dictates
the precepts of public reason to every citizen, and teaches him to act
in conformity with the maxims of his own judgement, and not to be
in contradiction with himself."[49] On Rousseau's view, it would require
gods to give men such laws. It is hard not to conclude that Rawls's
political conception of justice for the basic structure of society, which
gives the content of public reason, must also appeal to "an authority
of a different order" so as to "persuade without convincing."[50] That is,
Rawls's political conception of justice presupposes, but cannot reflexively justify, the authority of a perspective beyond the rules of social
institutions required to bring about the intersubjective relationship of

an overlapping consensus. In pursuing these issues further, it is worth turning to Cavell's critique of Rawls.

THE RULES OF THE "CONVERSATION OF JUSTICE" LANGUAGE GAME

Cohen's "interpersonal test" concerns the utterances that persons are able to make to one another. Like Cohen, Cavell considers what citizens in a Rawlsian well-ordered society are able to say to one another—what he calls the "conversation of justice" in Rawls's work—and criticizes Rawls's focus on the basic structure of society, in favor of an ethic of personal behavior.[51] However, Cavell's critique offers a very different view of the aspirations and limitations of Rawls's model of justificatory community.

Cavell focuses on the relationship between two standpoints and what persons can say to one another when acting from these two different standpoints. The first standpoint is that of the original position in which parties agree upon principles of justice for the basic structure of society. Rawls says of the principles of justice chosen in the original position that they are those such that, when realized in institutions, persons "can say to one another that they are cooperating on terms to which they would agree if they were free and equal persons whose relations with respect to one another were fair."[52] The second standpoint is that of deliberative rationality, from which persons pursue their conceptions of the good. When discussing this standpoint, Rawls argues that the "parties cannot agree to a conception of justice if the consequences of applying it may lead to self-reproach should the least happy possibilities be realized. They should strive to be free of such regrets." In the words Cavell focuses on, in the society of justice as fairness we could act from the point of view of deliberative rationality so as to ensure that our conduct is "above reproach."[53]

As Cavell recognizes, the problem is not so much that Rawls thinks that focusing on the basic structure as the primary subject of justice allows individuals to pursue their own ends without being concerned about justice, but that Rawls sees the constitutive rules of social institutions as serving a utopian function. Where Cohen finds an excess of realism in Rawls's focus on the basic structure, Cavell finds an excess of utopianism. In the realistic utopia of a society well-ordered by the principles of justice as fairness, the intersubjective relations of Kant's kingdom of ends are realized as a democratic realm of ends in our social world. We achieve a society that we could give our consent to once and for all, and are thus reconciled to our social world.

This is where Rawls's second analogy is relevant. Essential to the idea of justice as fairness is the idea that principles of justice for a well-ordered society are like the rules of a well-constituted and well-played game. Rawls describes a shared end, "the common desire of all the players that there should be a good play of the game," that "can be realized only if the game is played fairly according to the rules, if the sides are more or less evenly matched, and if the players all sense that they are playing well. But when this aim is attained, everyone takes pleasure and satisfaction in the very same thing. A good play of the game is, so to speak, a collective achievement requiring the cooperation of all."[54] Cavell's analysis of the "conversation of justice" in *A Theory of Justice* builds upon his earlier critique of the understanding of rules Rawls presents in "Two Concepts of Rules."[55] There Rawls considers rules from two standpoints that parallel his later discussion of the standpoints of the original position and of deliberative rationality: first from the standpoint of the role of rules in constituting social practices, and then from the standpoint of the following of rules within a practice. For Cavell, Rawls's mistake is to assimilate the two standpoints, by assimilating "actions *in accordance with* rules to actions *determined* by rules."[56] That is, Rawls thinks that the rules that define a practice also determine how one must act within the practice. But, Cavell argues, the practice of promise-keeping with which Rawls is concerned is not adequately explained by claiming that the rules of the practice of promising determine that promises ought to be kept; promising is not akin to a contractual act. And Cavell points out that Rawls's analysis of the practice of promise-keeping in "Two Concepts of Rules" problematically reappears in the context of his discussion of political obligation in *A Theory of Justice*. There he mistakes the rules that frame politics (determined from the standpoint of the original position) for those governing our behavior in politics (in deliberatively pursuing our conceptions of the good).[57] For Cavell, this constitutes Rawls's utopianism.

Intriguing support for the view that Rawls understands games in this way is provided by a letter in which he describes why baseball might be regarded as "the best of all games." There he describes how in baseball "the rules of the game are in equilibrium: that is, from the start, the diamond was made just the right size, the pitcher's mound just the right distance from home plate, etc., and this makes possible the marvelous plays, such as the double play. The physical layout of the game is perfectly adjusted to the human skills it is meant to display and to call into graceful exercise."[58] This idea of calling human skills into complementary and graceful exercise is just the idea that is present in Rawls's symphony orchestra analogy. To mix metaphors, the conductor of the orchestra is required to establish the "rules of the game" that determine the shared end that makes a well-ordered society.

Cavell thus draws attention to a utopian aspiration for transcendence in Rawls's work. Rawls's aspiration that we be able to conduct ourselves in a manner that is above reproach is reflected in the unrealistic demands that he makes of the rules of social practices. I will now proceed to consider a third model of justificatory community, that offered by Habermas, which conceives of justificatory community in a way that can avoid these criticisms.

HABERMAS: TRANSCENDENCE FROM WITHIN LANGUAGE GAMES

Habermas is known as a critic of Gadamer. However, while he rejects the conservative implications of Gadamer's hermeneutics, he takes inspiration from its model of linguistic intersubjectivity. Of particular relevance in the present context is the analogy between language and playing a game. Gadamer describes the shared end that takes place in language as the ongoing playing of a language game in which "all playing is a being-played."[59] This analogy becomes for him a way of examining the relationship between faith and understanding. While initially this might appear to be an unlikely analogy, what is essential to it is the idea of a movement of a whole that transcends individual subjectivity. As Gadamer puts it,

> The back and forth movement that takes place within a given field of play does not derive from the human game and from

playing as a subjective attitude. Quite the contrary, even for human subjectivity the real experience of the game consists in the fact that something that obeys its own set of laws gains ascendency in the game. . . . The back and forth movement of the game has a peculiar freedom and buoyancy that determines the consciousness of the players. . . . [T]he individual self, including his activity and his understanding of himself, is taken up into a higher determination.[60]

As Habermas explains, instead of seeking a "meta-theory" beyond existing practices that can unify divergent ends, Gadamer seeks to preserve "the unity of reason in the pluralism of languages" by appealing to "the tendency to self-transcendence that is inherent in the practice of language."[61] In learning our native language we also learn how to learn languages in general. Similarly, in learning a rule we learn how to interpret, and not merely apply, that rule.

This is another way of bringing out the limits of Rawls's understanding of rules as an external determining framework that brings about an ideal shared end. Focusing on the idea of play highlights how rules establish a space or field of play that enables individuals to pursue their ends in a manner that cannot be externally predetermined or consciously controlled by the individual players. Rather than the rules of the game defining a shared end, a shared end develops in and through playing the game.[62]

Crucially, while Habermas's idea of communicative rationality can be seen as adopting a Gadamerian understanding of language, he rejects the idea that discourse has a substantive higher end into which individuals are taken up. This is reflected in his nuanced view of the relationship between postmetaphysical reason and religion.[63] Thus, with Habermas as with Rawls, a model of intersubjectivity and the transcendence of individuality through justificatory community stands in a complex relationship with religious ideas. Yet Habermas's alternative model succeeds in maintaining an idea of transcendence without raising the problems that Rawls's model does.

In reflecting upon the significance of Rawls's senior thesis, Habermas identifies parallels between Rawls and Kant. He remarks that the history of Rawls's work "exhibits a philosophical reshaping of religious ideas comparable to that first undertaken by Kant":

The principal features of the religious ethics of community could be sublimated into secular deontology because the triadic pattern of relations we find in monotheistic communities remains intact in the "kingdom of ends." . . . In this case members do not stand in a direct relation to each other either. Instead all interpersonal relations are mediated by the relation of each to the authority of an impartial "third," namely that of the moral law. The relation of the individual to the single transcendent and unifying God is now replaced by the moral point of view from which all autonomous actors deliberate equally on how they shall behave in cases of conflict.[64]

For Kant the moral law takes the place of God. What does Rawls put in place of the impartial third point of view of Kant's moral law? He rejects Kant's metaphysics and lacks the reassurance of Hegel's teleological philosophy of history. Yet, he takes it to be possible for citizens to adopt an impartial, public point of view beyond their particular ends because of the sense of justice they share in sharing a social world. To mediate interpersonal relations by a political conception of justice therefore presupposes a transcendent point of view. Viewing Rawls's project from Habermas's perspective, one can question whether Rawls fully sublimates a religious ethic of community into a secular deontology.

In his debate with Rawls, Habermas argues that the way in which Rawls establishes the "rules of the game" of constitutional democracy through the original position represents an external limitation upon the political autonomy of citizens. Rawlsian citizens, he argues, "cannot reignite the radical democratic embers of the original position in the civic life of their society."[65] Habermas's alternative view of constitutional democracy puts him in a position to respond to concerns, such as those expressed by Cavell, about the utopian role of the original position. He rejects the view that political obligation derives from seeing democracy as a current counterpart to a promise of the Founding Fathers. Echoing Cavell's criticism of Rawls's use of a contractual model of promising in his account of political obligation, he emphasizes that promises are illocutionary acts which establish interpersonal relations, and that it is a consequence of persons' autonomy that the duties they generate can have only a specific content and not the binding character of obligation as such.[66] Habermas therefore rejects Rawls's dualistic model of the rules that define a social practice and those that govern moves within that practice, the model that originates in Rawls's analysis in "Two Concepts of Rules" and is maintained in his view of the relationship between the point of view of parties in the original position and that of citizens in a well-ordered society. To redeem the idea of "E pluribus unum" in a radical-democratic practice of collective self-legislation, it is not enough to alternate between moments of constitutional reconstruction and a normal politics of pledging allegiance to "one nation under God." Instead, it is necessary to maintain the performative standpoint of "we the people" in the ongoing procedures through which the shared end of justificatory community is reproduced.[67]

Habermas's communicative model of intersubjectivity does not face Rawls's problem of understanding a process of "conversion" from a subjective to an intersubjective perspective. The way in which Habermas draws upon this idea of intersubjectivity as the basis for an alternative model of justificatory community is most clearly evident in his reconstruction of George Herbert Mead's approach.[68] On Mead's model, persons are seen as individuated through being socialized, and the reproduction of social order is then seen as dependent upon the intersubjective actions of individuals. This provides a way of understanding how the unity that is preserved through language is a unity of differentiated selves. In Habermas's words, "Rousseau's universalized public and Kant's intelligible world are rendered socially concrete and temporally dynamic . . . by Mead; in this way, the anticipation of an idealized form of communication is supposed to preserve a moment of unconditionality for the discursive procedure of will formation."[69] In practical discourse, as Mead puts it, we construct an "ideal world, not of substantive things but of proper method."[70] This is fundamental to why Habermas is able to present his communicative philosophical paradigm as occupying a conceptual space "between naturalism and religion." While an idea of transcendence is maintained in postmetaphysical thinking, it is an idea of "transcendence from within" that does not subsume the perspective of individuals. Habermas describes this simultaneously contextual and context-transcending status of communicative validity claims as follows:

As agents of communicative action, we are exposed to a transcendence that is integrated in the linguistic conditions of reproduction without being delivered up to it. . . . Linguistic intersubjectivity goes beyond the subjects without putting them *in bondage* [*hörig*]. It is not a higher-level subjectivity and therefore, without sacrificing a transcendence from within, it can do without the concept of an Absolute.[71]

Rawls rejects Habermas's approach because he sees it as a comprehensive Hegelian doctrine. On Rawls's interpretation of Habermas,

once the form and structure of the presuppositions of thought, reason, and action—both theoretical and practical—are properly laid out and analyzed by his theory of communicative action, then all the alleged substantial elements of those religious and metaphysical doctrines and the traditions of communities have been absorbed (or sublimated) into the form and structure of these presuppositions.[72]

But, if anything, it is Rawls who follows a Hegelian approach in which philosophy absorbs and sublimates the substantial elements of religious and metaphysical doctrines. Habermas distinguishes "*rationalist* approaches that (in the Hegelian tradition) *subsume* [*aufheben*] the substance of faith into the philosophical concept, from *dialogical* approaches that (following Karl Jaspers) adopt a critical attitude toward religious traditions while at the same time being open to *learning* from them."[73] To be sure, Habermas asks whether the Wars of Religion could have been "brought to an end if the principle of tolerance and freedom of belief and conscience had not been able to appeal, with good reasons, to a moral validity *independent* of religion and metaphysics."[74] But postmetaphysical philosophy for Habermas "neither announces the absence of consolation in a world forsaken by God, nor does it take it upon itself to provide any consolation." The idealizing presuppositions of the communicative use of reason offer a glimmer of an ideal of justificatory community, but this is not "filled in as the totality of a reconciled form of life and projected into the future as a utopia."[75]

Whereas Rawls's model of justificatory community involves a substantive internally oriented, intertwined end, then, Habermas's model of intersubjective communication involves a procedural internally oriented, intertwined end. That is, whereas Rawls constructs a substantive conception of justice for a well-ordered society that seeks to determine the shared end of the practice of social cooperation between citizens, Habermas reconstructs the idealizing presuppositions of procedures oriented toward establishing shared ends through which the practices of morality and constitutional democracy are reproduced.

CONCLUSION

Rawls, Cohen, and Habermas offer three models of justificatory community that stand in different relationships to religious ideas of redemption. Because of the way Cohen and Habermas both criticize Rawls's model of justificatory community as an overlapping consensus for grounding principles of justice in factual contingencies, it is easy to overlook the profound differences between the alternative models of justificatory community that they offer. Both object to Rawls's aspiration for reconciliation to our social world, but whereas for Cohen Rawls succumbs to excessive realism, I have argued that, properly interpreted with the aid of Cavell, from a Habermasian perspective Rawls's model of justificatory community is excessively utopian.

While Cohen argues that vertical relations to external substantive principles of justice are a prerequisite for horizontal relations of interpersonal justification, Habermas rejects any appeal to external substantive principles of justice, denying any conceptual space for an external perspective beyond intersubjective communicative practice. His model of justificatory community maintains an idea of transcendence, but of transcendence from within the facts of this world—it therefore abandons the utopian aspiration for a reconciled form of life. While Rawls's intersubjective procedure of the original position remains dependent upon, while "sublimating," the transcendent orientations of comprehensive doctrines toward substantive ideas of the good, the intertwined end that Habermas sees as established through language and law is purely procedural. As Habermas insists, this is necessary in order to vindicate the idea that the constitutional democratic state does not depend upon a prepolitical idea of the good, but is rather capable of reproducing the motivations on which it depends from its own secular resources.[76]

Notes

I am grateful to the editors and to Stephen Mulhall for helpful comments, and to the participants at the "Between Rawls and Religion" conference held at LUISS University and John Cabot University in December 2010, and particularly Sebastiano Maffettone, for helpful discussion.

1. *BI* 127.

2. See David Reidy, "Rawls's Religion and Justice as Fairness," *History of Political Thought* 31, no. 2 (2010): 309–43. In his autobiographical reflections "On My Religion" Rawls describes how, although he abandoned his orthodox Episcopalian beliefs after his experiences in the Second World War, he did so out of moral doubts about Christian doctrines such as original sin and predestination, rather than out of a loss of faith per se. As he puts it, "my fideism remained firm against all worries about the existence of God" (*MR* 263).

3. As well as describing Rawls's idea of overlapping consensus, and its acceptance of "the fact of democratic unity in diversity" (*LP* 124–25), my use of the motto "E pluribus unum," from the Seal of the United States, alludes to W. V. O. Quine's use of the phrase to describe the objective pull of language. Quine, *Word and Object* (Cambridge, Mass.: MIT Press, 1960), 5–9. See also Jürgen Habermas, "The Unity of Reason in the Diversity of Its Voices," in *Postmetaphysical Thinking* (Cambridge: Polity, 1992), 115–48, which brings together the metaphysical, religious, and linguistic themes.

4. *BI* 243–46.

5. G. A. Cohen, *If You're an Egalitarian, How Come You're So Rich?* (Cambridge, Mass.: Harvard University Press, 2000), 3.

6. G. A. Cohen, *Self-Ownership, Freedom, and Equality* (Cambridge: Cambridge University Press, 1995), 138; Cohen, *Rescuing Justice and Equality* (Cambridge, Mass.: Harvard University Press, 2008), 116. The historical reference point here is Karl Marx, "On the Jewish Question," in *Karl Marx: Selected Writings*, ed. D. McLellan, 2nd ed. (Oxford: Oxford University Press, 2000), 46–70.

7. G. A. Cohen, *Karl Marx's Theory of History: A Defence*, expanded ed. (Princeton: Princeton University Press, 2001).

8. Cohen, *If You're an Egalitarian, How Come You're So Rich?*, 2. In this context it is worth noting that, after an antireligious communist Jewish upbringing, in later life

Cohen described himself as an agnostic, as being "very Jewish" while not believing in the God of the Old Testament. In his Gifford Lectures, intended to promote "knowledge of God," he reflects upon the development of his "deep interest and sympathy" with the teachings of Jesus in the Gospels (ibid., 2–6). See also his posthumously published reflections on spirituality in Cohen, *Finding Oneself in the Other*, ed. M. Otsuka (Princeton: Princeton University Press, 2013), 201–7.

9. Cohen, *Self-Ownership, Freedom, and Equality*, 123.

10. Karl Marx, "The Communist Manifesto," in *Karl Marx: Selected Writings*, 262.

11. Cohen, *If You're an Egalitarian, How Come You're So Rich?*, 122. For criticism of this analogy, see Keith Graham, "Self-Ownership, Communism and Equality," *Proceedings of the Aristotelian Society*, supp. vol. 64 (1990): 53. For an appeal to Cohen's idea of a jazz band as a key to explaining "the meaning of life," see Terry Eagleton, *The Meaning of Life* (Oxford: Oxford University Press, 2007), 174–75.

12. Daniel Brudney, "Community and Completion," in *Reclaiming the History of Ethics: Essays for John Rawls*, ed. A. Reath, B. Herman, and C. M. Korsgaard (New York: Cambridge University Press, 1997), 397–98.

13. Here I follow the reading in Elizabeth Anderson, "Cohen, Justice, and Interpersonal Justification," APSA 2010 Annual Meeting Paper (2010), in contrast to that of Nicholas Vrousalis, "Jazz Bands, Camping Trips and Decommodification: G. A. Cohen on Community," *Socialist Studies* 8, no. 1 (2012): 1–20.

14. G. A. Cohen, "Reason, Humanity, and the Moral Law," in *The Sources of Normativity*, by Christine M. Korsgaard, with G. A. Cohen, Raymond Geuss, Thomas Nagel, and Bernard Williams, ed. O. O'Neill (Cambridge: Cambridge University Press, 1996), 188.

15. Cohen, *Rescuing Justice and Equality*, 291. As Anderson suggests, Cohen's luck egalitarian conception of justice presupposes a "God's eye" point of view on the world. According to luck egalitarianism, natural as well as social inequalities are unjust and not simply natural facts, as they are for Rawls. Complaining that the distribution of native endowments is unjust is not far from claiming that the Portuguese suffered an injustice, rather than a natural disaster, in the Great Lisbon Earthquake, one of the events that led Voltaire to satirize Leibniz's theodicy. Rawls rejects Leibniz's metaphysical perfectionism and its ethics of creation, according to which, Rawls writes, "even the general facts of nature are to be chosen" (*TJ* 159/*TJ* (rev.) 137; see also *LHMP* 109). Cohen glosses this as the idea that "the function of fact-independent principles is to determine what the general facts of nature are to be," to which he responds that "they might have that function for God, but they need not therefore have that function for us" (Cohen, *Rescuing Justice and Equality*, 261n50). Nonetheless Cohen's luck egalitarianism presupposes such a God's eye point of view, even if it is not one that we can adopt.

16. For this argument, see Anderson, "Cohen, Justice, and Interpersonal Justification."

17. Cohen, *Rescuing Justice and Equality*, 42.

18. G. A. Cohen, *Why Not Socialism?* (Princeton: Princeton University Press, 2009), 38–45; Vrousalis, "Jazz Bands, Camping Trips and Decommodification." Elsewhere, in Vrousalis, "G. A. Cohen's Vision of Socialism," *Journal of Ethics* 14, nos. 3–4 (2010): 213, Vrousalis equates Cohen's interpersonal test with Habermas's discourse ethics. As will become clear, I do not believe that this equation can be sustained.

19. Cohen, *If You're an Egalitarian*, 6.

20. Franz Rosenzweig, *Star of Redemption* (Notre Dame: University of Notre Dame Press, 1985), 218. On the synthesis of Judaism and German Idealism in Rosenzweig's work, see Jürgen Habermas, "The German Idealism of the Jewish Philosophers," in *Philosophical-Political Profiles* (Cambridge, Mass.: MIT Press, 1983), 21–43.

21. This judgment is unaffected by Cohen's posthumously published notes on the idea of regarding people as equals and the Hegelian idea of "finding oneself in the other," ideas that he argues for in matters other than justice. See Cohen, *Finding Oneself in the Other*, 143, 193–200.

22. Jürgen Habermas, "The Relationship Between Theory and Practice Revisited," in *Truth and Justification* (Cambridge: Polity, 2003), 278.

23. Brudney, "Community and Completion." See also Andrew Levine, *The General Will: Rousseau, Marx, Communism* (Cambridge: Cambridge University Press, 1993).

24. *TJ* 524n/*TJ* (rev.) 459n. See also *PL* (pbk.) 320–24. In *TJ*, Rawls only refers to Wilhelm von Humboldt and Kant as suggesting such a model. However, in describing how for Rousseau citizens achieve moral freedom through recognition of others, he remarks: "Think of how the trained powers of musicians reach their fullest fruition only when exercised with other musicians in chamber music and orchestras" (*LHPP* 240). For Hegel too, "magnificent instrumentalists as we may be, we can only achieve the consummation of our skills alongside others in the social orchestra." Dudley Knowles, *Routledge Philosophy Guidebook to Hegel and the Philosophy of Right* (London: Routledge, 2008), 56. On Rawls's use of the orchestra analogy, see Nancy S. Love, "Rawlsian Harmonies: Overlapping Consensus Symphony Orchestra," *Theory, Culture and Society* 20, no. 6 (2003): 121–40.

25. John Searle, *The Construction of Social Reality* (London: Penguin, 1995), 23.

26. Michael Sandel, *Liberalism and the Limits of Justice*, 2nd ed. (Cambridge: Cambridge University Press, 1998), 183.

27. Brudney, "Community and Completion," 414n43.

28. Cohen, *Self-Ownership, Freedom, and Equality*, 134.

29. *TJ* 529, 525n/*TJ* (rev.) 463, 460n.

30. *LHPP* 369.

31. *TJ* 281, 524n/*TJ* (rev.) 249, 460n.

32. Cohen, *Self-Ownership, Freedom, and Equality*, 138–43.

33. *BI* 114–15. This emphasis on personal relations as the basis of ethics helps to explain Rawls's later loss of faith in God. As he puts it on "On My Religion," "the

content of the judgments of practical reason depends on social facts about how human beings are related in society and to one another. . . . Given these facts as they undeniably are in our social world, the basic judgments of reasonableness must be the same, whether made by God's reason or by ours" (MR 268).

34. On Rawls's engagement with the relationship between religion and politics throughout his work, see Daniel A. Dombrowski, *Rawls and Religion: The Case for Political Liberalism* (Albany: SUNY Press, 2001).

35. *BI* 127–28.

36. Gerald D. Doppelt, "Beyond Liberalism and Communitarianism: Towards a Critical Theory of Social Justice," in *Universalism vs. Communitarianism*, ed. D. Rasmussen (Cambridge, Mass.: MIT Press, 1990), 49.

37. *LHPP* 368.

38. Frederick Neuhouser, *Rousseau's Theodicy of Self-Love* (Oxford: Oxford University Press, 2008), 185–264.

39. *BI* 127.

40. *PL* (pbk.) 91.

41. *BI* 224–25.

42. John Rawls, "The Idea of an Overlapping Consensus," in *CP* 448. See also *PL* (pbk.) 172.

43. *BI* 233, 244.

44. See also Paul Weithman, "John Rawls and the Task of Political Philosophy," *Review of Politics* 71, no. 1 (2009): 113–25.

45. *LHPP* 237–41.

46. Jean-Jacques Rousseau, "The Social Contract," in *The Social Contract, and Other Later Political Writings*, ed. V. Gourevitch (Cambridge: Cambridge University Press, 1997), 71.

47. *LHPP* 240–41.

48. *PL* (pbk.) 158–68.

49. Jean-Jacques Rousseau, "Discourse on Political Economy," in *The Social Contract, and Other Later Political Writings*, 10.

50. See also Patrick Neal, "Does He Mean What He Says? (Mis)understanding Rawls's Practical Turn," *Polity* 27, no. 1 (1994): 77–112; Paul Ricoeur, "Is a Purely Procedural Theory of Justice Possible?," in *The Just* (Chicago: University of Chicago Press, 2000), 36–57; Peter Lassman, "Political Theory as Utopia," *History of the Human Sciences* 16, no. 1 (2003): 49–62; and Matthew Scherer, "Saint John: The Miracle of Secular Reason," in *Political Theologies: Public Religions in a Post-Secular World*, ed. H. de Vries and L. E. Sullivan (New York: Fordham University Press, 2006), 341–62. Scherer offers an insightful, if unsympathetic, analysis of Rawls's work, and the rhetorical strategies it adopts, from the perspective of the Rousseauian paradox of politics and its relationship to a Christian problematic of conversion. As he puts it, "A large part of Rawls's saintly measure inheres in the force of his personal character and the power of his

emotional appeals to inspire conviction in a reader who would otherwise be unprepared for it, thus producing a conversion of interest that cannot be explained with reference to argumentative force alone." Scherer, "Saint John," 353.

51. Cavell's perfectionism is indebted to Ralph Waldo Emerson, but, like Cohen, his concern can be described as being with the state of the individual's soul, articulating a vision, originating in Plato, of the soul's being transformed by a Good that sustains the promise of utopia. See Stephen Mulhall, "Perfectionism, Politics and the Social Contract: Rawls and Cavell on Justice," *Journal of Political Philosophy* 2, no. 3 (1994): 224–25.

52. *TJ* 13/TJ (rev.) 12.

53. *TJ* 422–23/TJ (rev.) 371. For Cavell's view, see Stanley Cavell, *Conditions Handsome and Unhandsome* (Chicago: University of Chicago Press, 1990), 18, 113; and Cavell, *Cities of Words* (Cambridge, Mass.: Harvard University Press, 2005), 171.

54. *TJ* 525–26/TJ (rev.) 461.

55. John Rawls, "Two Concepts of Rules," in *CP* 20–46.

56. Stanley Cavell, *The Claim of Reason*, 2nd ed. (Oxford: Oxford University Press, 1999), 307, 304. As Stephen Mulhall puts it in elaborating on Cavell's point: "The point of games lies not in the framework of prescription that makes up its rules of play, but in the space the rules of play define; within that space, those who can marry a grasp of strategy to the necessary talent and physical condition, who can see what ought to be done and are in a position to do it, are set free to achieve forms of human excellence. Rawls's vision of games mistakes the framework for the space, the prescriptive means for the celebratory ends they subserve." Mulhall, "Promising, Consent, and Citizenship: Rawls and Cavell on Morality and Politics," *Political Theory* 25, no. 2 (1997): 177.

57. *TJ* 342–50/TJ (rev.) 301–8.

58. *BG*. This letter, written in 1981, relates the details of a conversation that Rawls had with Harry Kalven twenty years earlier. The similarities with Rawls's own view make it unlikely that it does not represent his own outlook.

59. Hans-Georg Gadamer, *Truth and Method*, 2nd rev. ed. (New York: Continuum, 1989), 106.

60. Hans-Georg Gadamer, "On the Scope and Function of Hermeneutical Reflection," in *Philosophical Hermeneutics* (Berkeley: University of California Press, 1977), 53–54.

61. Jürgen Habermas, *On the Logic of the Social Sciences* (Cambridge: Polity, 1988), 144. Another way of stating my central argument would be to compare the move from Rawls to Habermas with that of W. V. O. Quine to Donald Davidson. On the similarities between the conceptions of intersubjectivity of Gadamer and Davidson, see Habermas, "From Kant's 'Ideas' of Pure Reason to the 'Idealizing' Presuppositions of Communicative Action: Reflections on the Detranscendentalized 'Use of Reason,'" in *Truth and Justification*, 120.

62. It is important here to distinguish Habermas's idea of the "rules" of moral discourse from the idea of constitutive rules of a game. Discourse rules do not determine

what are to count as acceptable moves within discourse, but are "merely the form in which we present the implicitly adopted and intuitively known pragmatic presuppositions of a special type of speech." Habermas, "Discourse Ethics: Notes on a Program of Philosophical Justification," in *Moral Consciousness and Communicative Action* (Cambridge: Polity, 1990), 91. Habermas's idea of the practice of argumentation as the reflexive form of communicative action can be seen as sharing Pierre Bourdieu's concern with understanding the "conductorless orchestration" of social practices. As Bourdieu puts it, "objectively 'regulated' and 'regular' without being in any way the product of obedience," the relationship between principles and practices "can be collectively orchestrated without being the product of the organizing action of a conductor." Bourdieu, *The Logic of Practice* (Cambridge: Polity, 1990), 59, 53.

63. Habermas's concern with understanding how social cooperation between religious and secular citizens is possible has led him to recognize the importance of Rawls's political liberalism. His recent engagement with the continuing importance of religion in postsecular societies has been seen as a reversal of an earlier, more negative attitude. But from a philosophical rather than a sociological standpoint, Habermas was always clear that, for a philosopher who grows up steeped in the tradition of German Idealism and its theoretical appropriation of ideas of God and salvation, there is "excluded from the start an approach that would merely objectify Jewish and Christian traditions." Habermas, "Transcendence from Within, Transcendence in This World," in *Religion and Rationality: Essays on Reason, God, and Modernity*, ed. E. Mendieta (Cambridge: Polity, 2002), 68–69. While postmetaphysical thinking cannot support a theological idea of the Absolute, for Habermas it equally cannot support a methodical atheism, such as Hegel's, that seeks to sublate the content of religious ideas. Both the Old Testament Hebrew morality of justice and the New Testament Christian ethics of love remain part of the genealogy of postmetaphysical morality. Habermas, "A Genealogical Analysis of the Cognitive Content of Morality," in *The Inclusion of the Other: Studies in Political Theory*, ed. C. Cronin and P. De Grieff (Cambridge: Polity, 1999), 7–11.

64. Jürgen Habermas, "The 'Good Life'—a 'Detestable Phrase': The Significance of the Young Rawls's Religious Ethics for His Political Theory," *European Journal of Philosophy* 18, no. 3 (2010): 448–49.

65. Jürgen Habermas, "Reconciliation Through the Public Use of Reason," in *The Inclusion of the Other*, 69. Rawls asks in reply, "are the citizens of Rousseau's society of *The Social Contract* never fully autonomous because the Legislator originally gave them their just constitution under which they have grown up?" Rawls, "Reply to Habermas," in *PL* (pbk.) 402.

66. Jürgen Habermas, *Between Facts and Norms: Contributions to a Discourse Theory of Law and Democracy* (Cambridge: Polity, 1996), 548n76.

67. I have pursued this contrast in more detail, and with greater reference to the Rawls-Habermas debate, in Gledhill, "Procedure in Substance and Substance in

Procedure: Reframing the Rawls-Habermas Debate," in *Habermas and Rawls: Disputing the Political*, ed. J. G. Finlayson and F. Freyenhagen (New York: Routledge, 2011), 181–99.

68. George Herbert Mead also focuses upon games as providing a model of intersubjectivity. See Mead, *Mind, Self, and Society* (Chicago: University of Chicago Press), 150–64.

69. Jürgen Habermas, "Individuation through Socialization: On George Herbert Mead's Theory of Subjectivity," in *Postmetaphysical Thinking*, 184.

70. Ibid.

71. Habermas, "Transcendence from Within, Transcendence in This World," 91.

72. Rawls, "Reply to Habermas," in *PL* (pbk.) 432.

73. Jürgen Habermas, "The Boundary Between Faith and Knowledge: On the Reception and Contemporary Importance of Kant's Philosophy of Religion," in *Between Naturalism and Religion* (Cambridge: Polity, 2008), 245.

74. Habermas, "Reconciliation Through the Public Use of Reason," 67.

75. Habermas, "The Unity of Reason in the Diversity of Its Voices," 145.

76. Jürgen Habermas, "Pre-Political Foundations of the Constitutional State?" in *Between Naturalism and Religion*, 101–13.

9

A Reasonable Faith?

POPE BENEDICT'S RESPONSE TO RAWLS

PETER JONKERS

In a much-quoted passage, John Rawls formulates the guiding question of *Political Liberalism* as follows: "How is it possible for those affirming a religious doctrine that is based on religious authority, for example, the Church or the Bible, also to hold a reasonable political conception that supports a just democratic regime?"[1] In this chapter I want to evaluate Rawls's answer to this question by comparing it with that offered by the former head of the Catholic Church, Pope Benedict XVI.[2] This comparison is illuminating in three ways. First, Pope Benedict was not only an outstanding intellectual with strong opinions about, among many other things, the role of religion in the public sphere, but as the highest authority in the Catholic Church, he also defined the Church's official position in this debate. Second, he defined the reasonable apologia of Christian faith in the secular world as one of the most important priorities of his pontificate. He therefore did not limit himself to preaching to the converted, but wished to discuss the Church's position on these issues with the world at large in a critical and yet constructive way. In particular, when he addressed a secular audience he consistently defended the Catholic position as far as possible on the basis of reasonable, rather than strictly theological, arguments.[3] This approach makes it methodically feasible to compare his position with Rawls's political liberalism. Finally, Pope Benedict's position presents a fascinating case for examining Rawls's claim that reasonable comprehensive doctrines should endorse his idea of political liberalism. Roman Catholicism is clearly a "comprehensive doctrine" in Rawls's sense. But can Pope Benedict be expected to answer Rawls's guiding question positively, and if not, does he have good reasons for his refusal?

Pope Benedict's basic answer is that, although modern principles of political freedom, democracy, equality, and reasonable argument are to be affirmed, a free state rests on "pre-political moral foundations," which serve as normative points of reference for every regime and must be held in common by all religions and secular worldviews.[4] This answer reflects the fact that Pope Benedict disagrees with Rawls on at least two fundamental issues, which constitute the core of the debate between them and to which I shall refer regularly in the course of my analysis. In the first place, Pope Benedict does not share Rawls's trust in fundamental human reasonableness as a guarantee for political fairness. For Rawls, persons are reasonable when "they are ready to propose principles and standards as fair terms of cooperation and to abide by them willingly, given the assurance that others will likewise do so. Those norms they view as reasonable for everyone to accept and therefore as justifiable to them; and they are ready to discuss the fair terms that others propose."[5] This idea of reasonableness informs the whole project of Rawls's political liberalism, because "the form and content of this reason . . . are part of the idea of democracy itself."[6] In contrast, Pope Benedict, although consistently stressing the importance of reason in all human affairs, is much more pessimistic about Rawls's claim that human beings, who are always children of their own time and cultural situation, are reasonable enough to provide the general principles or standards that are necessary for specifying fair cooperation. The kernel of his first disagreement with Rawls therefore concerns whether reason has this capacity—as Rawls tries to show with, for instance, his distinction between the reasonable and the rational[7]—or rather risks being merely a social or inherently ethnocentric construction, such that it cannot provide such general standards and reasonable consensus is unfeasible, as Pope Benedict argues.[8] Pope Benedict's pessimism about the plausibility of reason's universality and impartiality leads him to refer to notions like "intrinsic truth" and "goodness" as necessary referents for reason, and as offering fundamental norms underlying reasonable political consensus.

This brings me to the second point of disagreement between Pope Benedict and Rawls. Rawls wishes to exclude views on intrinsic truth and goodness from political philosophy because they introduce transcendent, or metaphysical, notions that cannot be reasonably examined. Religious comprehensive doctrines rest on religious authority, while metaphysics presents itself as a pseudo-rational kind of knowledge about supersensible things. But, like many other contemporary philosophers, Rawls puts metaphysics (represented paradigmatically by Plato and Aristotle) on a par with the Christian tradition (represented by Augustine and Aquinas) by interpreting them both as claiming "that there is but one reasonable and rational conception of the good."[9] Because of the transcendent and hence dogmatic character of Christian and metaphysical ideas about the true and the good, Rawls insists on distinguishing political liberalism as clearly as possible from religious and metaphysical conceptions of justice. For Pope Benedict, by contrast, it is essential to hold to the ideas of intrinsic truth and goodness as a prepolitical normativity, not because they are God's commandments, but because they are exemplifications of the rationality that inheres in the world, such that they are the only true general standards for fair cooperation and justice. From this perspective he poses some crucial questions to Rawls and others who place reasonable consensus at the basis of a democratic polity. For example, he asks, "the consensus of whom?" and "what is reasonable? how is reason shown to be true?" as well as asking "whether there is something . . . that is antecedent to every majority decision and must be respected by all such decisions."[10]

Despite these two major divergences, Pope Benedict and Rawls implicitly agree on a crucial point, namely, the reasonableness of reason. In particular, in this regard both refer to Kant's idea of a reasonable faith, according to which faith is never solely reason's belief in its own capacities, but is also the belief that reasonableness is inherent in reality itself. This congruence between Pope Benedict's and Rawls's views is rarely noted by commentators, but I will attempt to show that it constitutes the essence of debates over what makes a polity just and, hence, humane.[11]

The structure of my chapter is the following. I shall begin by discussing the issues of (non)public reason and justification that are the major points of disagreement between Pope Benedict and Rawls. Then, in the second section, I will turn to Pope Benedict's idea of wisdom as an alternative common ground for political life. In the third section I will discuss the enigmatic issue of a philosophical faith in reason. In the following section, I will comment on Pope Benedict's and Rawls's divergent ideas about reasonable pluralism. I will conclude by briefly pointing out the resulting aporia, one that underlies a great deal of contemporary political thinking and for which neither Rawls nor Pope Benedict has a convincing solution.

REASONABLE JUSTIFICATION IN POLITICS

As my point of departure, I take the speech that Pope Benedict prepared to give at the "La Sapienza" University of Rome in January 2008, and in which he gives a short, interesting response to Rawls's philosophical project.[12] From the beginning of the lecture, he addresses the tricky question of whether he, as pope, has anything meaningful to say to a secular audience. His basic answer is that the Church, whose history, example, and message inevitably influence the entire human community, is "increasingly becoming a voice for the ethical reasoning of humanity."[13] Of course, Pope Benedict realizes that to this it will be objected that he "draws his judgments from faith and hence cannot claim to speak on behalf of those who do not share this faith." But he defends himself by referring approvingly to Rawls, who, he writes, while "denying that comprehensive religious doctrines have the character of 'public' reason, nonetheless at least sees their 'non-public' reason as one which cannot simply be dismissed by those who maintain a rigidly secularized rationality, because these doctrines derive from a responsible and well-thought-out tradition in which, over lengthy periods, satisfactory arguments have been developed in support of the doctrines concerned."[14] Thus, surprisingly perhaps, Pope Benedict borrows an argument from the liberal thinker Rawls to criticize rigidly secularized rationality for its parochiality and, paradoxically, to reverse the standard Enlightenment objection to religion.

Although this passage shows that Pope Benedict appreciates Rawls's definition of religious traditions as reasonable comprehensive doctrines, it should not obscure the differences between Pope Benedict's and Rawls's conceptions of (non)public reason and justification. Regarding the idea of reasonableness, Pope Benedict interprets Rawls as acknowledging "that down through the centuries, experience and demonstration—the historical source of human wisdom—are also a sign of its reasonableness and enduring significance. . . . Humanity's wisdom—the wisdom of the great religious traditions—should be valued as a heritage that cannot be cast with impunity into the dustbin of the history of ideas."[15] Certainly, Pope Benedict would agree with Rawls's claim that "the roots of democratic citizens' allegiance to their political conceptions lie in their respective comprehensive doctrines."[16] But by defining the great religious traditions as expressions of "humanity's wisdom," and by interpreting their long-standing experience and demonstrative capacities in existential issues as a sign of their reasonableness as such, Pope Benedict makes clear that he does not accept Rawls's distinction between public and nonpublic reason. At the end of his speech, he even states that "the history of the saints, the history of the humanism that has grown out of the Christian faith, demonstrates the truth of this faith in its essential nucleus, thereby giving it a claim upon public reason." This leads him to conclude that "the message of the Christian faith is never solely a 'comprehensive religious doctrine' in Rawls's sense, but is a purifying force for reason, helping it to be more fully itself. On the basis of its origin, the Christian message should always be an encouragement towards truth, and thus a force against the pressure exerted by power and interests."[17] Pope Benedict's basic reason for this statement is that for Christianity, as a religion of the Logos, the world comes from reason, such that reason is the world's criterion and goal.[18] On the grounds that the particular tradition he represents participates in the universal reasonableness of God's creation, therefore, Pope Benedict claims the right to participate in the ethical reasoning of our time, and this not only at the level of nonpublic reason, but also, and more importantly, at that of public reason proper.

This also reveals that Pope Benedict understands public justification in a very different way from Rawls. For Rawls, "public justification is not simply valid reasoning, but argument addressed to others:

it proceeds correctly from premises we accept and think others could reasonably accept to conclusions we think they could also reasonably accept."[19] Regarding this process of reasonable justification of comprehensive doctrines, he insists that "there are no restrictions or requirements on how religious or secular doctrines are themselves to be expressed; these doctrines need not, for example, be by some standards logically correct, or open to rational appraisal, or evidentially supportable."[20] However, for the "proviso" to be fulfilled—that is, for the nonpublic justifications of comprehensive doctrines to become truly political justifications, based on public reason—the reasonableness of these doctrines must depend on the reason that those who present the justification of their doctrines share with those to whom these justifications are addressed, and this reasonableness is primarily to be decided not by the former group, but by the latter.

Rawls's idea of public justification denies that religious traditions may participate in this process as long as they have not fulfilled the proviso. In opposition to this, as I have shown, Pope Benedict first argues that comprehensive doctrines (both religious and secular) are actually part of public reason, such that they must always already have satisfied Rawls's proviso. Second, Pope Benedict takes the normativity of these doctrines to have priority over the idea of overlapping consensus. His basic reason for this is that he understands these doctrines as traditions of wisdom with long histories as purifying forces for reason, particularly with respect to the partial rationality of interest groups. Hence, these traditions not only can but also *should* participate in the process of ethical reasoning. The upshot of these two arguments is that Pope Benedict proposes the notion of wisdom as a normative point of reference for consensus and hence as an alternative common ground for *public* justification.

It is important to note that Pope Benedict's reasons for adopting this position are philosophical rather than religious, although his philosophical frame of reference is clearly at odds with Rawls's. Nonetheless, it is also worth examining some of the theological reasons for this aspect of Pope Benedict's disagreement with Rawls, and how they compare with Rawls's own views on theology. In his autobiographical essay "On My Religion," Rawls explains why he abandoned his orthodox Christian beliefs in spite of the deeply religious temperament that informed his life and writings.[21] In particular, he recounts how his personal experiences during the Second World War, and especially his awareness of the Holocaust, led him to question whether prayer was possible. "To interpret history as expressing God's will, God's will must accord with the most basic ideas of justice as we know them. For what else can the most basic justice be? Thus, I soon came to reject the idea of the supremacy of the divine will as [like the Holocaust] also hideous and evil."[22] Furthermore, by studying the history of the Inquisition Rawls came to "think of the denial of religious freedom and liberty of conscience as a very great evil," such that "it makes the claims of the Popes to infallibility impossible to accept."[23] Finally, his reading of Jean Bodin's thoughts about toleration led him to claim that religions should be "each reasonable, and accept the idea of public reason and its idea of the domain of the political."[24] Against this background, it is no wonder that Rawls considers the very concept of religious truth as authoritarian and intolerant, and the ensuing persecution of dissenters as the curse of Christianity. Instead, he argues, one has to accept "that politics in a democratic society can never be guided by what we see as the whole truth." Ultimately, there is no other option for a democratic society than "to live politically with others in the light of reasons all might reasonably be expected to endorse."[25]

These remarks, albeit autobiographical, suggest that Rawls's main reason for rejecting the notion of (religious) truth as the basis of public justification is that it is exclusivist with regard to other comprehensive doctrines and claims an a priori superiority over the reasonable political values of a constitutional democracy. If a religion upholds such a notion of truth, it no longer qualifies as a *reasonable* comprehensive doctrine. Rawls links this exclusivist conception of truth with the idea of a voluntarist God, whose absolute free will is the only source of all being and all moral and political values, such that only people who believe in the true God will be saved. Rawls admits that if the Christian religion were to accept the idea of a reasonable, nonvoluntarist God, according to which "the ground and content of those values is God's reason, . . . then God's will serves only a subordinate role of sanctioning the divine intentions now seen as grounded on reason."[26] Such an idea of God would avoid exclusivism and would allow for the possibility that God's salvation extends to people who do not believe in Him, but who nevertheless accept essential moral and political values on the basis of a reason that they share with the faithful. But, while admitting this possibility, Rawls nonetheless equates the idea of religious truth with exclusivism, a voluntarist God, and an authoritarian Church.

By interpreting religious and secular traditions as expressions of wisdom, Pope Benedict wants to show that Rawls's sharp distinction between nonpublic and public reason not only is inadequate on philosophical grounds, in the ways that I have mentioned above, but also results from theological reasons that are at odds with Catholicism.[27] A first reason for the (post–Vatican II) Catholic Church to reject the exclusivist position is that it would deny salvation to all non-Christians. Furthermore, Pope Benedict repudiates the idea of a voluntarist God, because this would eventually lead to "a capricious God, who is not even bound to truth and goodness." Instead, as I have mentioned, he argues that Christianity is fundamentally a religion of the Logos, such that it is "a religion in keeping with reason."[28] Therefore, he cannot accept a separation of faith and reason, or, phrased positively, he holds that God's will is subordinate to and grounded in His reason. Indeed, the idea of the unity of faith and reason provides Pope Benedict with a theological argument for his claim that Christianity cannot be expected to justify itself before the tribunal of secular reason, whose authority it cannot accept precisely because it rests on a separation of faith and reason.

Rawls's view of the Christian religion thus relies too heavily on his negative ideas of an authoritarian Church, an exclusivist religious truth, and a voluntarist God. This is not only indicated by his autobiographical remarks; it is also reflected in the guiding question of *Political Liberalism*, which refers to a "religious doctrine that is based on religious *authority*, for example, the Church or the Bible," and in his claim later in the book that Churches are inherently exclusivist, since they hold "that there is but one reasonable and rational conception of the good."[29] This exclusivist and authoritarian interpretation of Christianity is theologically problematic and surely at odds with the Catholic view on the matter, which puts God's reason prior to His will.

THE IDEA OF WISDOM AS AN ALTERNATIVE COMMON GROUND

In order to fully understand Pope Benedict's view of Christianity as a tradition of wisdom, it is important to further examine the idea of the unity of faith and reason. Generally speaking, wisdom can be defined as a life-orientating kind of knowledge that is based on human experience, but that also has a divine origin.[30] In other words, wisdom departs from our concrete historical and cultural situation as humans, while nonetheless orientating it toward attaining "our destiny and thereby realizing our humanity."[31] Through its divine origin, wisdom refers to transcendent truths and values, which are normative points of reference with regard to all our reasonable deliberations and consensus-building. Whereas reason primarily refers to a human capacity, offering a common ground for consensus between the ideas of people who are in principle equally reasonable, wisdom refers to a much broader kind of reasonableness, because it results from those ways of life that, through the ages, have proved themselves to be fruitful, that is, to orientate the lives of individuals and communities toward truth and goodness. Phrased philosophically, a wise person is able to see things, and particularly existential issues, in a larger perspective—*sub specie aeternitatis,* as it were. This implies that true wisdom transcends the reasonable deliberations of individuals, which are always embedded in the contingencies of place and time, and is thus able to serve as a purifying force for reason. Hence, it is no wonder that wisdom is something that all humans, regardless of their cultural and religious affiliations, strive for, and that all religious and secular traditions claim to be the source of true wisdom. In sum, wisdom can be considered as knowledge that has a transcultural, universally human character.[32] Yet, precisely because humans are not divine, nobody can claim to "possess" wisdom absolutely—a finitude that is expressed by Socrates's contrast between the Gods, who *are* wise, and humans, who can only strive after wisdom,[33] as well as by Paul's saying that God has made foolish the wisdom of the world.[34] Obviously, this insight applies equally to religious and secular traditions: although all of them claim to be treasure-houses of wisdom, the very transcendent character of wisdom prevents them from being able to rightly claim that they possess it completely.

It is on these grounds that Pope Benedict criticizes Rawls's proposal to replace the idea of truth with that of reason: in his view, it makes the question of how reason is shown to be true impossible to answer.[35] In particular, without a broader perspective reason is unable to adequately assess the different claims of parties and interest groups when issues of justice are at stake. In other words, since reason is essentially a human capacity, Pope Benedict insists that the idea of reason risks being reduced to that of the rationality of a coincidental majority. Whereas this danger might be avoided in a small, well-organized, and socially cohesive community, it has become ever more difficult to reach reasonable consensus in a globalized world. Nowadays, every proposal for consensus is more often than not faced with the unsettling question, "the consensus of whom?"[36] Philosophically speaking, the deconstruction of reason, which results in its being characterized as inherently ethnocentric or as a social construction, has become a real threat to the possibility of reasonable consensus. With these problems in mind, Pope Benedict proposes the idea of wisdom as an alternative common ground, one that treats traditions of wisdom as concretizations of this idea, and therefore as suitable contributions to public reasoning over the normative basis for a just society, since they broaden reasonableness by connecting it with truth and by including long-standing insights. Pope Benedict does not say that Christianity is the only tradition of wisdom, or that Christians possess wisdom completely, and hence that their specific ideas about right and wrong could be enforced on a pluralist society. But he does claim that only the idea of wisdom is able to free consensus from spatiotemporal and cultural limitations, and reason from its inevitable finitude and subjectivity. Thus, in fundamental opposition to Rawls, he states that reason and reasonable consensus should be subordinate to truth: "the pursuit of truth makes consensus possible, keeps public debate logical, honest and accountable, and ensures the unity which vague notions of integration simply cannot achieve."[37]

A PHILOSOPHICAL FAITH IN REASON

Does Rawls show any sensitivity to Pope Benedict's argument about the fundamental connection between reason and truth? In an important section of *Political Liberalism*, Rawls dwells upon what he admits to be a fundamental paradox of public reason: "Why should citizens in discussing and voting on the most fundamental political questions honor the limits of public reason? . . . Surely, the most fundamental questions should be settled by appealing to the most important truths, yet these may far transcend public reason!"[38] Ultimately, Rawls's claim that citizens should nonetheless not trespass the limits of public reason rests on the idea that, as democratic citizens, they pursue the ideal of democratic citizenship—that is, their duty is to explain to one another their principles and policies in terms each could reasonably be expected to endorse as consistent with the principles of freedom and equality. The pursuit of this ideal is in turn supported by the comprehensive doctrines that reasonable people affirm, so that the paradox of public reason disappears: "Citizens affirm the ideal of public reason, not as a result of political compromise, as in a modus vivendi, but from within their own reasonable doctrines."[39] In particular, the duty of civility requires people not to vote purely on the basis of their subjective preferences and interests, since democracy cannot be identified with simple majority rule, implying that a majority can do as it wishes. Nor should they vote on the basis of what they see as right and true according to their comprehensive doctrines. In sum, the duty of civility goes hand in hand with the ideal of a well-ordered, democratic society, which "fashions a climate within which its citizens acquire a sense of justice inclining them to meet their duty of civility."[40] By referring to this ideal and its corresponding duty of civility, Rawls tries to describe the idea of public reason in such a way that it is less liable to being ideologically perverted and remaining spatiotemporally and culturally short sighted, and thus counters the objection made by Pope Benedict. Indeed, he considers this duty, which intrinsically is a moral (not a legal) one, to be one of the main innovations in his account of public reason.

Although the issue of the adequacy of public reason as a common ground for a democratic society is a major point of disagreement between Pope Benedict and Rawls, I think that the distance separating them is less than it seems at first sight. Whereas Pope Benedict cannot reasonably substantiate his claim that Rawls's position inevitably results in reducing overlapping consensus to that of a contingent majority, Rawls cannot accuse Pope Benedict of dogmatically imposing a (Catholic) view of the whole truth upon contemporary pluralist society. Although obviously stemming from quite different backgrounds, Rawls's ideal of democratic citizenship, which qualifies consensus as a reasonable one and as consistent with the principles of freedom and equality, and Pope Benedict's idea of wisdom, which extends to various religious and secular traditions and therefore does not attribute "the whole truth" to the Catholic Church, both try to solve the paradox of reason and truth in a democratic society. Of course, there remains a major difference between their solutions: Rawls's ideal of citizenship relies on citizens' understanding and acceptance of it, which gives it a more "deliberative," democratic character, whereas Pope Benedict's idea of wisdom relies less on the citizens actually understanding and accepting it but offers a much more robust defense against ideological perversion by admitting insights about "the good life" from religious and secular traditions that have proved their truth over time. In short, one might say that the difference between Rawls and Pope Benedict comes down to that between a more "horizontal" ideal of moral and political normativity, which eventually rests on a faith in reason, and a more "vertical" one, which rests on a faith in God's Logos that is present in the world as a purifying force for reason.

It is worth further exploring Rawls's and Pope Benedict's ideas about the need of a moral and political normativity, because they take us to the heart of the metaphysical questions that I mentioned above. It must be emphasized that the "metaphysics" involved—implicitly in Rawls's case, explicitly in Pope Benedict's—is not of a precritical or dogmatic kind that would claim to have a positive, quasi-scientific knowledge of the supersensible. Rather, it is a metaphysics in Kant's sense, a metaphysics of finite reason:[41] that is, as *metaphysics*, it examines the reality of the highest ideas of reason, God, freedom, and immortality,[42] but, as a metaphysics of *finite reason* it also recognizes that the use of reason in this respect can only be hypothetical, and not apodictic. It can never *prove* the truth of these ideas, because they are only adopted as hypotheses, and therefore we can think about them only problematically, by accepting them as a never-ending task of reason.[43]

In order to show that this metaphysics of finite reason indeed plays an important role in both Rawls's and Pope Benedict's thinking, I shall comment on their use of the notion of philosophical or reasonable faith. Rawls refers to this notion in order to give a philosophically substantiated, positive answer to the question of the possibility of a reasonably just political society: "In trying to do these things political philosophy assumes the role Kant gave to philosophy generally: the defense of reasonable faith. . . . [I]n our case this becomes the defense of reasonable faith in the possibility of a just constitutional regime."[44] Although for Rawls this faith concerns only the coherence and unity of reason,[45] it must be noted that, for Kant, this unity is never solely a faith of reason in its own capacities, but is also a purposive one, that is, a belief that, on a fundamental level, reasonableness is not merely a human invention, but is also inherent in reality itself. At the level of theoretical reason, this can be only a problematic idea, which by directing "the understanding towards a certain goal upon which the routes marked out by all its rules converge . . . serves to give to these concepts of the understanding the greatest possible unity combined with the greatest possible extension."[46] But at the level of practical reason, one must accept the effective reality of the highest good as a postulate of practical reason, since it is essential for orientating oneself in moral and political matters. Kant calls this attitude a "reasonable faith," that is, a belief "which is based on no other data than those which are inherent in *pure* reason":[47] it consists in the subjective conviction of the truth of the highest good on purely reasonable grounds, while at the same time being aware that its truth cannot be demonstrated objectively. Phrased more technically, a reasonable faith is a conviction of truth that is subjectively adequate but consciously regarded as objectively inadequate. It thus holds an intermediary position between an opinion—considering something to be true on objective grounds that are nevertheless consciously regarded as inadequate—and knowledge—considering something to be true on objective grounds that are also consciously regarded as adequate. Hence, Kant concludes, "a pure reasonable faith is the signpost or compass by means of which the speculative thinker can orientate himself on his reasonable wanderings in the field of supersensible objects."[48] Rawls agrees with Kant's views on "the role of philosophy as apologia: the defense of reasonable faith," defining this faith as "that of showing the coherence and unity of reason, both theoretical and practical, with itself; and of how we are to view reason as the final court of appeal, as alone competent to settle all questions about the scope and limit of its own authority."[49] Moreover, he identifies this role with "the defense of the possibility of a just constitutional democratic regime."[50] This shows that for Rawls, just as for Kant, reasonable faith refers not only to the unity of reason, but also to the possibility of its ultimate purpose, a just constitutional democratic regime. Obviously, like Kant, Rawls must insist that the finitude of reason means that the reality of this purpose cannot be demonstrated. But by referring to this ultimate purpose, he nevertheless introduces a metaphysical element that points beyond the sphere of reason. For a reasonable faith not only concerns a belief in reason and its unity; it also involves a faith in the possibility of a just constitutional democratic regime as the normative, orientating purpose of reason.

Interestingly, in one publication Pope Benedict also refers to Kant's idea of a reasonable faith in order to propose a solution to the problem of moral and political normativity. He defines this problem as the tendency to shape human affairs purely on the basis of subjective preferences, whether they are part of a consensus or not, a tendency that manifests a lack of orientation or of a perspective transcending the here and now. His solution is an intriguing, and controversial, proposal to secular society. He first refers to Kant's postulates of practical reason as the object of reasonable faith and an orientating principle in moral issues, thereby applying to the moral and political domain the idea of wisdom considered above. This leads Pope Benedict to the bold suggestion that a secular person "who does not succeed in finding the path to accepting the existence of God ought nevertheless try to live and to direct his life *veluti si Deus daretur*, as if God did indeed exist."[51] This means reversing one of the most basic axioms of the Enlightenment. According to Hugo Grotius, in order to keep essential moral values free of contradiction and to base them on grounds independent of the divisions and uncertainties of the various religions and philosophies of life, and thus to secure peaceful coexistence, these values must be defined in such a way as to be valid *etsi Deus non daretur*.[52] Why does Pope Benedict boldly propose that secular people reverse this principle? It is not to convert them to Christianity, but to solve the problem of moral normativity, which religious and secular people have in common. For he proposes not a religious but a reasonable faith, consisting in the idea that in all human beings' ways of life there is a perspective that transcends the here and now and puts their lives in a broader perspective: "This does not impose limitations on anyone's freedom; it gives support to all our human affairs and supplies a criterion of which human life stands sorely in need."[53] Hence, living as if God exists must be interpreted here as employing God as a symbolic representation of universal moral and political normativity, which is prior to consensus building. Living as if God exists means that all people, religious and secular, should be prepared to let their lives be orientated by this

Really? Ble it feel like, "tell my language."

normativity. But by phrasing God's existence in a conditional way, as an "as if," Pope Benedict also enables secular people to interpret this *How?* normativity in a different way from Christianity. In short, living as if God exists serves to concretize wisdom as an existential, orientating kind of knowledge that is a common ground for all people, but that also allows for plurality. Only if we are prepared to live in this way, Pope Benedict claims, can "we become capable of that genuine dialogue of cultures and religions so urgently needed today."[54]

The fact that both Rawls and Pope Benedict refer to a reasonable faith offers an interesting perspective on their views on moral and political normativity. In Rawls's case, introducing this notion helps him to provide his search for a reasonable foundation for democratic society with an ultimate purpose, albeit one that cannot be demonstrated objectively. In Pope Benedict's case, proposing that people live as if God exists is a way of introducing a common ground among religious and secular people, which also allows for plurality among them. Hence, the *Again, yikes.* Christian doctrine is not presented as "the whole truth," but as "an encouragement towards truth," a call to the idea of truth or wisdom.[55]

PLURALITY VERSUS REASONABLE PLURALISM

If we accept the conclusion that, at a fundamental level, an ultimate, orientating purpose is necessary for reason, one can justly ask if this does not jeopardize the very idea of reasonable pluralism as a basic fact of democratic society. This is the critical question that Rawls's perspective poses to Pope Benedict's defense of truth.

As shown above, the main reason for Rawls to oppose the notion of (religious) truth as the basis of public justification is that it excludes other comprehensive doctrines and claims an a priori superiority over the reasonable political values of a constitutional democracy. Pope Benedict, for his part, agrees with Rawls's critique of such religious exclusivism, but claims that Christianity adopts an "inclusivism" toward other faiths.[56] However, he also admits that this term is inadequate, since it suggests that all religions and secular worldviews can be absorbed by a single one. What is needed instead, he claims, is "an encounter of various religions, in a unity that transforms pluralism in plurality."[57] This "encounter," or dialogue, model of religious plurality is based on the conviction that cultures and religions are not completely inaccessible to each other, because they are united by the faith that the Logos is present in all of them.

How does Pope Benedict's view of religious plurality relate to Rawls's idea of reasonable pluralism? Rawls defines reasonable pluralism as "the fact that a plurality of conflicting reasonable comprehensive doctrines, religious, philosophical, and moral, is the normal result of a culture of free institutions," because "a public and shared basis of justification that applies to comprehensive doctrines is lacking in the public culture of a democratic society."[58] This means that reasonable pluralism must be distinguished from pluralism as such, that is, a simple variety of doctrines and views, often the result of peoples' understandable tendency to view the political world from a limited standpoint. If this were the only kind of pluralism, then the deliberative character of democracy and an overlapping consensus between free and equal citizens would be impossible. The constitutive parts of reasonable pluralism—namely, comprehensive doctrines, covering the major religious, philosophical, and moral aspects of human life—must rather be reasonable themselves. Rawls also claims that a reasonable comprehensive doctrine "normally belongs to, or draws upon, a tradition of thought and doctrine. . . . It tends to evolve slowly in the light of what, from its point of view, it sees as good and sufficient reasons."[59] Rawls concludes that in a society whose permanent condition is reasonable pluralism, such that the differences between citizens arising from their comprehensive doctrines may be irreconcilable, "the idea of the reasonable is more suitable as part of the basis of public justification for a constitutional regime than the idea of moral truth."[60]

From this perspective, Pope Benedict's view on religious plurality poses a fundamental problem. He sees the idea of wisdom as a common ground for all religious and secular traditions, just as the ideal of reason serves as a common ground for all reasonable consensus in Rawls's philosophical project. But the idea of wisdom does not only provide a formal common ground, as Rawls's idea of public reason does. It also contains all kinds of specific ideas about man's nature and destiny, which serve as principles for his orientation in life and which run counter to Rawls's reasonable pluralism. In other words, besides offering a formal common ground for interreligious dialogue, the idea of wisdom also serves as a substantive point of convergence for the plurality of religions and secular worldviews. In this crucial respect, the model of convergence proposed by Pope Benedict differs essentially from Rawls's reasonable pluralism, which is based on accepting religious and moral divergence as a fundamental reality.

Pope Benedict deals more explicitly with the issue of pluralism in his debate with Jürgen Habermas. He begins by observing that cultural pluralism is the most important feature of our times, and that considering the intercultural dimension is therefore absolutely essential for reflecting on the basic questions of contemporary human existence.[61] Pope Benedict therefore does not long nostalgically for the return of any premodern cultural or religious uniformity. But in order to be productive at all, he is convinced that pluralism needs to be based on a more fundamental relatedness, in a way similar, but not identical, to Rawls's sense that simple pluralism needs to be based on reasonable pluralism. For Pope Benedict, relatedness means that "the cultures of mankind, each of which together with its religion forms a whole, are not just unrelated blocks standing side by side or in opposition to each other."[62] The question for him, then, is whether and how one can overcome pluralism and have it replaced by relatedness. As I have shown above, he defines secular and religious comprehensive doctrines as traditions of wisdom, and on the basis of this common frame of reference, he claims that reason and faith are able to purify and heal each other of their respective pathologies. As a first step in this mutual learning process, he states that it is

> important to include the other cultures in the attempt at a polyphonic relatedness, in which they themselves are receptive to the essential complementarity of reason and faith, so that a universal process of purifications (in the plural!) can proceed. Ultimately, the essential values and norms that are in some way known or sensed by all men will take on a new brightness in such a process, so that which holds the world together can once again become an effective force in mankind.[63]

This means that Pope Benedict accepts that "the rational or ethical or religious formula that would embrace the whole world and unite all persons . . . is unattainable at the present moment. This is why the so-called 'world-ethos' remains an abstraction."[64] At the same time, however, he is confident that an interaction between the Christian faith and Western rationality as well as with and among other, non-Western cultural traditions will lead to a purification of all of them, so that ultimately a true common ground, based on essential values and norms, will be an effective force for the whole of humanity. From a Rawlsian perspective, this hope for a growing interaction between cultural traditions, like the idea of convergence that underlies it, is not sufficient. For it fails to fully acknowledge the existence of conflicting yet reasonable comprehensive doctrines as a basic fact of any democratic society.

CONCLUSION

The preceding analysis leaves us with an aporia. Is an interaction between secular rationality and the great religious traditions possible in terms of the idea of wisdom as their common ground? The current situation of (reasonable) pluralism does not bode well in this respect. The predicament of modern societies seems to be one of needing ideas of human dignity and political justice as substantive points of reference, but being utterly unable to reach an overlapping, reasonable consensus even as to their minimal content. This is especially so on a global level. The current controversies about the universality of the Universal Declaration of Human Rights of 1948 and, on a more fundamental level, about whether there indeed are universal human values are telling examples. The reasonableness of reasonable pluralism is therefore profoundly in question. Referring again to Kant, one can phrase this aporia as follows: we require an orientating principle and an ultimate purpose to purify religion and reason of their respective pathologies, but the reasonableness of this principle must itself be determined, since "one should never deny reason the prerogative . . . to be the ultimate criterion of truth."[65]

Notes

1. *PL* (exp.) xxxvii. See also *IPRR* 458.

2. Joseph Ratzinger served as the prefect of the Sacred Congregation for the Doctrine of the Faith from 1981 until his election as Pope in 2005. He resigned in 2013.

3. Some examples of this approach, from which I draw in this chapter, are Joseph Ratzinger, *Truth and Tolerance: Christian Belief and World Religions* (San Francisco:

Ignatius Press, 2004), in which he discusses the truth claims of Christian religion from the perspectives of the history of religion and philosophy; Ratzinger, *Christianity and the Crisis of Cultures* (San Francisco: Ignatius Press, 2006), in which he gives a philosophical analysis of the ambivalence of contemporary culture and the legacy of the Enlightenment; Ratzinger, "That Which Holds the World Together: The Pre-Political Moral Foundations of a Free State," in *The Dialectics of Secularization: On Reason and Religion*, by Jürgen Habermas and Joseph Ratzinger (San Francisco: Ignatius Press, 2006), 53–80, in which he discusses the need for a prepolitical, moral common ground in a free, global society; Pope Benedict XVI, *Faith, Reason and the University* (Vatican City: Libreria Editrice Vaticana, 2006), in which he presents a historical investigation of the relation between faith and reason and stresses the importance of reason as a way to belief in God; Pope Benedict XVI, *Lecture by the Holy Father at the University of Rome "La Sapienza"* (Vatican City: Libreria Editrice Vaticana, 2008), in which he defends the truth and reasonableness of Christian faith in a philosophical discussion of Rawls's and Habermas's ideas; and Pope Benedict XVI, *Address by the Holy Father on the Occasion of a Meeting with the Civil and Political Authorities and with the Members of the Diplomatic Corps* (Vatican City: Libreria Editrice Vaticana, 2009), in which he argues that true freedom and basic ethical consensus presuppose the search for truth.

4. "The Pre-Political Moral Foundations of a Free State" is the subtitle of Pope Benedict's contribution in his debate with Habermas.

5. *PL* (exp.) 49.

6. *IPRR* 440–41.

7. See *PL* (exp.) 48ff.

8. See Ratzinger, *Truth and Tolerance*, 249ff.

9. *PL* (exp.) 135.

10. Ratzinger, *Truth and Tolerance*, 253; Benedict XVI, *Lecture at "La Sapienza,"* 10; Ratzinger, "That Which Holds the World Together," 60.

11. Whereas the link between the reasonable, the just, and the humane is evident throughout Pope Benedict's work, it is less explicit in Rawls's. Nevertheless, when he specifies the reasonable, he associates it with two virtues of persons, namely, "first, with the willingness to propose and honor fair terms of cooperation, and second, with the willingness to recognize the burdens of judgment and to accept their consequences." Moreover, in making this connection between the reasonable and the idea of a person, he does not appeal to theology, but to an interpretation of Kant's practical philosophy, according to which "reasonable people take into account the consequences of their actions on others' well-being." *PL* (exp.) 48–49n1.

12. This speech was not delivered, due to the fierce protests of some faculty and students.

13. Benedict XVI, *Lecture at "La Sapienza,"* section 3.

14. Ibid., section 4. Pope Benedict might have had in mind Rawls's remark that religious comprehensive doctrines use nonpublic reasons, which belong to the

"background culture" of civil society. Because of their reasonableness they are "intelligible to the educated common sense of citizens generally." *PL* (exp.) 14; see also 220ff.

15. Benedict XVI, *Lecture at "La Sapienza,"* section 4.

16. *IPRR* 463.

17. Benedict XVI, *Lecture at "La Sapienza,"* section 11.

18. Ratzinger, *Christianity and the Crisis of Cultures*, 47ff.

19. *IPRR* 465.

20. *IPRR* 463.

21. *MR* 264.

22. *MR* 263.

23. *MR* 265.

24. *MR* 267.

25. *PL* (exp.) 243.

26. *MR* 267.

27. Anthony Carroll gives an in-depth analysis of how the modern antagonistic view of the relation between faith and reason is the result of a Protestant interpretation that originates precisely in the idea of a voluntarist God. See Anthony Carroll, "A Catholic Programme for Advanced Modernity," in *Towards a New Catholic Church in Advanced Modernity*, ed. S. Hellemans and J. Wissink (Zurich: Lit Verlag, 2012), 57–58.

28. Benedict XVI, *Faith, Reason and the University*, section 7; Ratzinger, *Christianity and the Crisis of Cultures*, 47.

29. *PL* (exp.) xxxvii (italics mine), 135.

30. Andreas Speer, "Weisheit," in *Historisches Wörterbuch der Philosophie*, 13 vols., ed. J. Ritter, K. Gründer, and G. Gabriel (Darmstadt: Wissenschaftliche Buchgesellschaft, 2004), 12:371.

31. Ratzinger, *Christianity and the Crisis of Cultures*, 77.

32. See Speer, "Weisheit," 371.

33. See Plato, *Phaedrus*, in *Complete Works*, ed. J. M. Cooper (Indianapolis: Hackett, 1997), 278d; and Plato, *Symposium*, in *Complete Works*, 204a.

34. See 1 Corinthians 1:20.

35. Benedict XVI, *Lecture at "La Sapienza,"* section 10.

36. See Ratzinger, *Truth and Tolerance*, 253.

37. Benedict XVI, *Address by the Holy Father*, 2.

38. *PL* (exp.) 216.

39. *PL* (exp.) 218.

40. *PL* (exp.) 252.

41. I draw my interpretation of Kant's philosophy as a metaphysics of finite reason from Georg Picht, *Kants Religionsphilosophie* (Stuttgart: Klett-Cotta, 1985), 594–605.

42. As Kant puts it, "Metaphysics has as the proper object of its enquiries three ideas only: *God, freedom*, and *immortality*. . . . Any other matters with which this science may deal serve merely as a means of arriving at these ideas and their reality.

It does not need the ideas for the purposes of natural science, but in order to pass beyond nature. Insight into them would render *theology* and *morals*, and, through the union of these two, likewise *religion*, and therewith the highest ends of our existence, entirely and exclusively dependent on the faculty of speculative reason." Kant, *Critique of Pure Reason* (London: Macmillan, 1978), B 395n.

43. Kant, *Critique of Pure Reason*, B 674–75.

44. *PL* (exp.) 172.

45. See *PL* (exp.) 101.

46. Kant, *Critique of Pure Reason*, B 672.

47. Immanuel Kant, "What Is Orientation in Thinking?," in *Political Writings*, ed. H. Reiss (Cambridge: Cambridge University Press, 1977), 244, translation modified. I have translated *Vernunftglaube* as "reasonable faith" rather than "rational belief" because this is Rawls's term and because the distinction between the "reasonable" and the "rational" is crucial for the present discussion.

48. Kant, "What Is Orientation in Thinking?," 245.

49. *PL* (exp.) 101. Here Rawls may have in mind Kant's statement that "reason is always the ultimate touchstone of truth." Kant, "What Is Orientation in Thinking?," 244.

50. Ibid.

51. Ratzinger, *Christianity and the Crisis of Cultures*, 51.

52. Hugo Grotius, *Prolegomena to "On the Law of War and Peace"* (Indianapolis: Bobbs-Merrill, 1957), paragraph 11.

53. Ratzinger, *Christianity and the Crisis of Cultures*, 52.

54. Benedict XVI, *Faith, Reason and the University*, section 16.

55. Benedict XVI, *Lecture at "La Sapienza,"* section 11.

56. Ratzinger, *Truth and Tolerance*, 80–81.

57. Ibid., 83.

58. *IPRR* 441; *PL* (exp.) 61.

59. *PL* (exp.) 59.

60. *PL* (exp.) 129.

61. Ratzinger, "That Which Holds the World Together," 73.

62. Ratzinger, *Truth and Tolerance*, 81. He considers this relatedness to be synonymous with the nonmonolithic form of "inclusivism" mentioned above.

63. Ibid., 79–80.

64. Ibid., 76.

65. Kant, "What Is Orientation in Thinking?," 249.

10

Islamic Politics and the Neutral State

A FRIENDLY AMENDMENT TO RAWLS?

ABDULLAHI A. AN-NA'IM

It may be helpful to begin with a brief explanation of two aspects of my title. First, by "Islamic politics," I refer simply to the Islamic dimension in the politics of various communities of Muslims, whether these constitute a so-called majority or a minority of the population. All politics is of course specific and contextual to the time and place, socioeconomic conditions, and so forth of a particular population. The term "Islamic politics" refers to how Islamic values and concepts are deployed in the political discourses, negotiations, and strategies of local or national Muslim communities in their particular contexts. I do not believe that there is a distinctively "Islamic politics" that is peculiar to Muslims and shared by all of them, historically and across the world today. In my view, the Islamic politics of Muslims in India today may have more to do with the "Hindu politics" of their neighbors than with Islamic politics in Senegal. It is in relation to this conception of Islamic politics that I discuss the need for a religiously neutral state in this chapter.

The second aspect of my title to explain is that what I am proposing is a real "amendment" to John Rawls's view of religion and not simply a shift in terminology. When Rawls and other North American and

European political theorists speak of religion, they mean Christianity as they know it. This is appropriate and necessary for them, but it is wrong to assume or expect their thinking to apply to other religions in drastically different contexts. With all due respect, the issue is not one of simply waiting for believers in other religions to "catch up" with North American and European Christians in framing the issues of religion, state, and politics in the terms that Rawls or other theorists of those regions propose. Whatever Muslims need to do, they must do it in terms of their own religion and context.

Yet, my proposed amendment is nonetheless friendly in that it respects and draws upon Rawls's theory and related ideas in examining the issues regarding Islamic politics *on its own terms* and *in its own context.* In making my claims, however, I do not engage with or refer to critics of Rawls who adopt a North American or European view of Christianity similar to his, for the same reason that I think his theory must be amended in relation to Islamic politics. Instead, I seek to develop and apply a theory of Islam, state, and politics that draws on Rawls's thought without being bound or limited by it or its critics.

With these clarifications in place, I now turn to my argument. The question famously posed by John Rawls is, "How is it possible for those affirming a religious doctrine that is based on religious authority . . . also to hold a reasonable political conception that supports a just democratic regime?"[1] However, as I expect Rawls would have accepted, it is not reasonable to raise this question without considering the nature of the religion and doctrine in question, that is, without understanding the nature and formation of religious authority and how a view comes to be a "religious doctrine" for those who affirm it. Reasonable answers to these questions vary from Christianity to Islam, for instance, as well as within each of these two sets of religious traditions. The manner in which certain religious doctrines become entrenched in Catholic Christianity—like those regarding contraception or abortion, for instance—differs from the corresponding doctrines in one Protestant denomination or another. Differences in the nature and formation of religious authority are also found in the Islamic traditions—religious authority in the Sunni traditions (in the plural) is different from that among Shia traditions (also in the plural).[2] In my view, it is unreasonable to assume that one understands what "a religious doctrine that is based on religious authority" is for all religious traditions, or how believers in any religion in every context would react to political authority on the basis of their religious belief. And as I will briefly explain, even the distinction between the so-called religious and secular domains does not apply to all religious traditions.

My underlying concern about Rawls's view of religion, then, is that it adopts an essentialist understanding of religion and religious discourse. Regarding Islam, for instance, there is already a lot of what Rawls would qualify as "public reason" in Islamic religious reasoning, unless that is automatically deemed to be disqualified because it comes from a "comprehensive doctrine." To begin with, the Qur'an always gives accessible and comprehensible reasons for its normative claims and encourages Muslims to reflection and rational reasoning.[3] Indeed, the Qur'an states that reflection and understanding are the purpose of the revelation of the Qur'an itself.[4] Early Muslim scholars and jurists did not simply postulate that some conduct is a sin or not, but gave reasons for their ruling that are comprehensible and reasonable to any person, believer or not. One may not agree with an Islamic jurist's conclusion, but that would not be for lack of effort on the part of the jurists to be persuasive beyond simply asserting a religious rationale.

What Rawls is concerned about—and with this I fully agree—is that purely and categorically religious reasons ought not to be the primary justification of public policy or legislation, as, for example, when a state penalizes conduct simply because it is a sin. The same conduct may be a sin and a crime (for instance, theft), but being a sin should not be the reason for its being a crime. The reasons and process of reasoning for the two are entirely different and should not be conflated into a single process: the reasons and reasoning for penalizing some conduct should never be simply "because God said so," since other citizens may not accept my God or may disagree with me about the meaning of what God said. As I will explain, this is the rationale of my call for the religious neutrality of the state, and also the reason for my fundamental agreement with Rawls's premises and theory.

In this light, what I mean by "a friendly amendment to Rawls" in my title is that the meaning of Rawls's question and the range of reasonable responses to it are relative to a particular religious tradition (not "religion" in the abstract) and to the context in which believers are responding to the question. Part of that context is the postcolonial predicament that African and Asian Muslims share with their non-Muslim neighbors in former colonies, including a profound suspicion of universalizing assertions emanating from North Atlantic societies—about the conception of political authority in this instance—that are supposed to apply to all human societies. Assertions about what is required for any democratic model of governance, anywhere in the world, are too reminiscent of the "civilizing mission" of European colonialism to be taken at face value. This deep and complex suspicion makes Rawls's notion of arguing from conjecture from what other people believe—to show them, as he puts it, that "despite what they might think, they can still endorse a reasonable conception that can provide a basis for public reasons"[5]—totally unpersuasive. Since persuasion is the aim of public reason, the question should be how to achieve that in practice and in terms of a shared view of political authority, which is difficult to imagine succeeding with me, as a religious believer, if my religious discourse is excluded from the domain of public reason.

The question mark in my title is intended to indicate the possibility that what I am proposing may not be an amendment to Rawls after all, if he did allow for what I am stipulating. It may be true, as Tom Bailey and Valentina Gentile indicate in their introduction to this volume, that Rawls accepts the possibility of reasons based on comprehensive doctrine being employed in support of a shared conception of political authority, and also that such reasons may be employed in public deliberations.[6] But, whether this is a correct reading of Rawls's views or not, my purpose is to uphold the right of each member of the relevant community to support a shared conception of political authority for whatever religious, secular, or other reasons he or she chooses. What I find objectionable is the stipulation of what qualifies as "public" reason in one setting or another. Whether citizens have a shared conception of political authority is a legitimate concern, but it is not a requirement that they must have or develop for preconceived, stipulated reasons. If the reasons that citizens advance and their manner of reasoning actively undermine a shared conception of political authority, then that is a separate inquiry to pursue, without insisting on a blanket rejection of one type of reason or another.

So, I am not suggesting that Rawls's question should not be raised in a Muslim context, but only that the meaning of this question and the reasonable response to it are significantly different from what Rawls and his critics have conceived in their respective contexts. In particular, the normative system of Islam, Sharia,[7] is an integral part of the common understanding of Islam among Muslims, and its implications for political life are complex and contingent. On the one hand, although Sharia norms cannot be enforced as positive law of the state as such, as I will explain, they are binding on Muslims in great detail and with very strong religious sanction. A pious Muslim must justify at a personal religious level any departure from what Sharia prescribes, whether it is an obligation to act or to refrain from action. On the other hand, there is a wide diversity of opinion among Muslim jurists on every conceivable issue and each Muslim has a choice among competing views, as his or her individual consciousness dictates. It may be true that the majority of Muslims prefer to conform to the practice of their local communities rather than exercise individual choice in practice. Still, for Muslims maintaining the right and duty to seek Sharia justification is integral to their right to religious self-determination.

Still, Muslims everywhere share their states with non-Muslim citizens, and share the world with the rest of humanity. Muslims' views and behavior regarding Sharia, the state, and politics affect people around them, and are subjects of legitimate concern for non-Muslims. Even among Muslims, whether they constitute a majority or a minority of the population, there is much disagreement on what Sharia means and entails for public affairs. One aspect of this is what I call the "contingency" of the role of Islam in the politics of any Muslim society, even within the same region.[8]

As can be seen in the cases of Northern Nigeria and Senegal, for instance, there can be significant differences in the role of Islam in public life, even in societies that identify with the same school of legal thought—in these cases, the Maliki School of Sunni jurisprudence.[9] Whatever one may think of the relationship of Islam to the state and politics in one place or another, there is no doubt that it is contingent and contested everywhere. With such a wide range of possible outcomes of dynamic factors, and in view of the nature of Sharia and its relationship to state law, for any theory to be appropriate in an Islamic context, it must account for Sharia in ways that Muslims accept as legitimate. This is one dimension that Rawls did not and could not have considered properly.

In my view, there are ways of benefiting from Rawls's views in theorizing the relationship between Islam and the state in Africa and Asia, provided the application of those views in an Islamic context is not expected or assumed to be the same as in a North American or West European context. Whenever I present my model of a secular state for a religious society, I frequently get questions or comments to the effect that since my concept of "civic reason," as I will explain, is so similar to Rawls's concept of "public reason," my proposal must mean this or that or suffer from this or that weakness, depending of what the person thinks of Rawls's theory. My plea is that what I am proposing in the Islamic context may be good or bad, fail or succeed, but that will not be because I am faithfully following or departing from Rawls's theory. This is not the case not only because Islam is not Christianity and the Muslim world is not Christendom, but also because there are too many theological, historical, and contextual differences within each religion and region to speak of any of them in monolithic terms.

In the first and second parts of this chapter, I will first present an overview of my understanding of the relationship between Islam, the state, and politics. This is an understanding that attempts to take Sharia seriously on its own terms, and can be summarized in the following propositions.[10] First, the premise of my argument is that any understanding of Sharia is the product human interpretation and as such is not immutable. Since what Muslims of any community accept as a Sharia norm is the product of human interpretation, it can change through human interpretation, as internalized by Muslims through an internal discourse to promote consensus around the new interpretation, as happened with the earlier norm-formation process. Second, the notion of an Islamic state to enforce Sharia as state law is a postcolonial idea that has no basis in Islamic political thought or practice prior to the 1940s. Third, while Islam and the state should be institutionally separated, Islam and politics cannot and should not be separated. Since Muslims will act politically according to their religious beliefs, it is better to acknowledge and regulate that reality than to ignore or exclude it. Fourth, the tensions raised by separating Islam from the state while acknowledging its impact on politics can be defused through what I call "civic reason,"[11] which is a nonprescriptive view of what Rawls calls "public reason."

In the third part of this chapter, I will briefly consider this view of Islamic politics in relation to common perceptions of Rawls's theory on political authority, public reason, and related views. What I suspect a possible "friendly amendment" might relate to is the difference between the theological history and political context of Rawls's thinking and that of Islamic politics in postcolonial Africa and Asia. I will then conclude with some reflections on whether these two perspectives can accept or support a general theory of religion, the state, and politics.

ISLAM, SHARIA, AND THE MODERN STATE

Early Muslim scholars developed the structure and methodology known as *usul al-fiqh*, through which Muslims can comprehend and implement Islamic precepts as conveyed in the Qur'an and Sunna (also known as Hadith: reports of what the Prophet is believed to have said or did). In its original formulations, this field of human knowledge sought to regulate the interpretation of these foundational sources in light of the historical experience of the first generations of Muslims. It also defines and regulates the operation of such juridical techniques as consensus (*ijma*), reasoning by analogy (*qiyas*), and juridical reasoning (*ijtihad*). Although these techniques are commonly taken simply as methods for specifying Sharia principles, rather than substantive sources as such, consensus and juridical reasoning in fact had a much more foundational role. Indeed, in my view, it is this role that can form the basis of a more dynamic and creative development of Sharia now and in the future.

It can also be said that the consensus of generations of Muslims from the beginning of Islam that the text of the Qur'an is in fact accurately contained in the written text known as *al-Mushaf* is the underlying reason for the text's acceptance by Muslims. The same is true of what Muslims in general accept as authentic reports of what the Prophet said and done—namely, the Sunna—although that took longer to establish and is still controversial among many Muslims. In other words, our knowledge of the Qur'an and Sunna is the result of intergenerational consensus since the seventh century. This is not to say or imply that Muslims manufactured these sources through consensus, but simply to note that we know and accept these texts as valid because generation after generation of Muslims has taken them to be so. Moreover, consensus is the basis of the authority and continuity of *usul al-fiqh* and all its principles and techniques because this interpretative structure is always dependent on its acceptance as such among Muslims in general from one generation to the next. In this sense, consensus is the basis of the acceptance of the Qur'an and Sunna themselves, as well as the totality and detail of the methodology of their interpretation.

Furthermore, Muslims refer to the Qur'an and the Sunna for religious guidance through the structure and methodology that they have been raised to accept, and normally within the framework of a particular school of thought (*madhhab*) and its established doctrine and methodology. Muslims do not normally approach religious texts in a fresh and original manner, without preconceived notions of how to identify and interpret the relevant texts. In other words, whenever Muslims consider the Qur'an and Sunna, they do so through the filters not only of layers of experience and interpretation by preceding generations, but also of an elaborate methodology that determines which texts are deemed to be relevant to any subject and how they should be understood. Human agency is therefore integral to any approach to the Qur'an and Sunna at multiple levels, ranging from centuries of accumulated experience and interpretation to the seeking of religious opinion on specific issues (*fatwa*) from local religious leaders or via the Internet. As Bernard Weiss puts it, "Although the law is of divine provenance, the actual construction of the law is a human activity, and its results represent the law of God *as humanly understood*. Since the law does not descend from heaven ready-made, it is the human understanding of the law—the human *fiqh* [literally, understanding] that must be normative for society."[12] There is consequently an underlying paradox in Muslims' treatment of authority. On the one hand, being a Muslim is founded on the strict individual responsibility of each and every Muslim to know and comply with what is required of him or her by Sharia. That this fundamental principle of individual and personal responsibility can never be abdicated or delegated is one of the recurring themes of the Qur'an.[13] On the other hand, Muslims have always tended to seek and rely on the advice of scholars and religious leaders they trust, which means that both the advisor and the advisee are responsible for the advisee's actions. Over time, the individual tendency to seek advice has in some cases evolved into some degree or form of institutionalization of religious authority, contrary to the original theological premise of individual responsibility.

The lack of theological support for institutionalized religious authority in Islamic traditions may sometimes lead to problematic outcomes, as when extremist groups challenge the traditional authority of established scholars and institutions of learning to propose radical views of aggressive jihad. This risk not only is unavoidable in view of the nature of Islamic religious authority, but is in my view preferable to limiting that authority to certain designated persons or institutions, which would thereby cause the right of other believers to disagree with their views to be forfeited. Legitimate Islamic religious authority cannot be monopolized or institutionalized because it is premised on religious knowledge, piety, and interpersonal trust that cannot be quantified or verified for institutional application.

The separation of Islam from the state and the regulation of its political role through constitutionalism and the protection of human rights that I propose are necessary to ensure freedom and security for Muslims to participate in proposing and debating fresh interpretations of those foundational sources. For any understanding of Sharia is always the product of juridical reasoning in the general sense of reasoning and reflection by human beings as ways of understanding the meaning of the Qur'an and Sunna of the Prophet. Since determinations about whether or not any text of the Qur'an or Sunna applies to an issue, as well as whether or not it is categorical, who can exercise *ijtihad*, and how, are all matters that can only be decided by human reasoning and judgment, imposing prior censorship on such efforts violates the premise of how Sharia principles can be derived from the Qur'an and Sunna.

It is illogical to say that *ijtihad* cannot be exercised regarding a specific issue or question because that determination itself is the product of human reasoning and reflection. It is also dangerous to limit the ability to exercise *ijtihad* to a restricted group of Muslims who are supposed to have specific qualities, because that will depend in practice on those human beings who set and apply the criteria of selecting who is qualified to exercise *ijtihad*. To grant this authority to any institution or organ, whether it is believed to be official or private, is dangerous because that power will certainly be manipulated for political or other reasons. Since knowing and upholding Sharia are the permanent and inescapable responsibility of every Muslim, no human being or institution should control this process for Muslims. The process of deciding who is qualified to exercise *ijtihad* and how it is to be enjoyed by every Muslim, as a matter of religious belief and obligation, cannot be subject to any prior censorship or control. In other words, any restriction of free debate by entrusting human beings or institutions with the authority to decide which views are to be allowed or suppressed is inconsistent with the religious nature of Sharia itself.

The founding jurists and scholars of Sharia exercised a profound acceptance of the diversity of opinion, while seeking to enhance consensus among themselves and their communities. This was done through the notion that whatever is accepted as valid by consensus (*ijma*) among all jurists—or, according to some jurists, the wider Muslim community—is deemed to be permanently binding on subsequent generations of Muslims.[14] Once again, however, the many practical difficulties of applying this notion were clear from the beginning. For those who wanted to confine the binding force of *ijma* to consensus among a select group of jurists, the problem was how to agree on the criteria for identifying those jurists and how to identify and verify their opinions. If one is to say that the authority of *ijma* is to come from the consensus of the Muslim community at large, the question still remains of how to determine and verify that this has happened on any particular matter. Regardless of whether the consensus is supposed to be of a group of scholars or of the community at large, there is also the further question of why the view of one generation should bind subsequent generations. And, whatever solutions one may find for such conceptual and practical difficulties, these solutions will always themselves be *the product of human judgment*. In other words, Sharia norms cannot possibly be drawn from the Qur'an and Sunna except through human understanding, which necessarily means both the inevitability of differences of opinion and the possibility of error, whether among scholars or the community in general.[15]

In this light, the question becomes that of how and by whom such differences of opinion can be properly and legitimately settled in practice in order to determine which positive law is to be applied in any specific case. The basic dilemma here can be explained as follows. On the one hand, there is the paramount importance of a minimum degree of certainty in the determination and enforcement of positive law for any society. The nature and role of positive law in the modern state also serve to regulate the interaction of a multitude of actors and complex factors in ways that cannot possibly be fully accounted for by an Islamic religious rationale alone. This is particularly true of Islamic societies today, due to their growing interdependence with non-Muslim societies around the world.

On the other hand, a religious rationale is necessary for the binding force of Sharia norms for Muslims. Precisely because Sharia is supposed to be binding on Muslims out of religious conviction, a believer cannot be religiously bound except by what he or she personally believes to be a valid interpretation of the relevant texts of the Qur'an and Sunna. Yet, given the diversity of opinions among Muslim jurists, whatever the state decides to enforce as positive law is bound to be deemed an invalid interpretation of Islamic sources by some of the Muslim citizens of that state. The strong traditional view has always been, as Noel Coulson puts it, that "each individual Muslim was absolutely free to follow the school [of jurisprudence] of his choice and that any Muslim tribunal was bound to apply the law of the school to which the individual litigant belonged."[16] Accordingly, an individual also had the right to change his or her school of law on a particular issue.

This situation continued throughout the Muslim world until the introduction of *Al-Majalla* by the Ottoman Empire during the period 1867–77, and more widely through the enactment of family law codes in most Islamic countries during the first half of the twentieth century. In Coulson's words, "The principle underlying the codes is that the political authority has the power, in the interest of uniformity, to choose one rule from among equally authoritative variants and to order the courts of his jurisdiction to apply that rule to the exclusion of all others; . . . the codes [embody] those variants which were deemed [by the political authority of the state] most suited to the present standards and circumstances of the community."[17]

The drastic transformation in the nature of the states under which Muslims lived, as well as the nature of law and the administration of justice, began with the decline of the Mogul Empire in the Indian subcontinent and the Ottoman Empire in the Middle East.[18] European models of the state were imposed through European colonial rule across the Muslim world, from West Africa to Southeast Asia, and continued through the Russian domination of Islamic Central Asia. Thus, for the first time in the history of Muslims, the state became the exclusive and explicit authority for the making and enforcement of law through the centralized administration of justice.[19]

The European model of the state that has been imposed on Islamic societies through colonialism was a centralized, bureaucratic, and hierarchical organization that comprised institutions, organs, and offices that are supposed to perform highly specialized and differentiated functions through predetermined rules of general application.[20] Moreover, while the state is distinct from other kinds of social associations and organizations in theory, it remains deeply connected to them in practice for its own legitimacy and effective operation. For instance, the state must seek out and work with various constituencies and organizations in performing its functions, such as maintaining law and order and providing educational, health, and transport services.

Therefore, state officials and institutions cannot avoid working relationships with various constituencies and groups who have competing views of public policy and its outcomes in the daily life of societies. These constituencies include nongovernmental organizations, businesses, political parties, and pressure groups, which may or may not be religious and may be so in different ways. These working relationships not only are necessary for the ability of the state to fulfill its obligations, but are also required by the principle of self-determination. The autonomy and distinctive nature of the state are a means to the end of enabling all citizens to participate in their own government, not an end in itself. The state incorporates the participation of such nonstate actors through formal mechanisms of negotiation and representation as well as through informal means of communication and mutual influence.[21] These dynamic interactions between state and nonstate actors raise the risks of conflict and competition on all sides, and can also compromise the autonomy of state actors as each nonstate actor seeks to maximize its influence on state policy and administration. These processes should be moderated and checked through the development of stronger state institutions that can keep their relative autonomy in dealing with diverse groups and their competing demands.

ISLAM, POLITICS, AND CIVIC REASON

In practically every society, religious groups are an important policy constituency on fundamental matters of social life, from education to taxation and from issues of public and private morality to charitable social functions. The negotiations between religion and state with regard to these issues can be viewed as arrangements whereby religious groups are acknowledged as an important political constituency, which is neither taken over by the state nor allowed to take over the state itself or any of its institutions. The religious neutrality of the state as the principle of separation of state and religion helps achieve this delicate balance by providing a framework for securing the legitimacy of the state among religious communities while regulating how their concerns are reflected in public policy with due regard to the concerns and interests of other communities and citizens at large.

Since citizens who are not religious or who do not organize to lobby the state as religious communities are entitled to equal respect for their views and interests, the state and its organs must not fall under the control of one religious community, however large it may be. In fact, the neutrality of the state regarding all religious and non-religious perspectives is more important in relation to dominant groups because the risks of state bias in their favor are greater than in the case of minorities. It should also be noted that perception in such matters can be as important as reality because the appearance of bias tends to undermine public confidence in the neutrality of the state, even if it is not true in fact. The religious neutrality of the state provides a basic structure whereby the state is neither partial nor perceived to be partial to any one religious or nonreligious perspective, while giving due regard to all relevant and legitimate perspectives in the formulation and implementation of public policy.

Moreover, the imperatives of certainty, uniformity, and neutrality in national legislation are now stronger than they used to be in the precolonial era. This is not only due to the growing complexity of the role of the state at the domestic or national level, but also because of the global interdependence of all peoples and their states. Regardless of the relative weakness or strength of some states in relation to others, the realities of national and global political, economic, security, and other relations remain firmly embedded in the existence of sovereign states that have exclusive jurisdiction over their citizens and territories. For Islamic societies, this point has recently been painfully emphasized by the eight years of the Iran-Iraq war of the 1980s and by the composition of the international alliance of Muslim and non-Muslim countries that forced Iraq out of Kuwait in 1991. The governments of Islamic countries on both sides of the latter conflict were acting (and continue to act) as nation-states and not as part of a uniform or united global Islamic community or on behalf of the totality of Muslims at large.

Of course, the nature of the state is not identical in all societies, because the processes of state formation and consolidation vary from one country to another. But there are certain common characteristics that all states need to have in order to be part of the present international system, since membership is conditional upon recognition by other members. For the states of Islamic societies to be and remain accepted as members of the international community, they must comply with a recognizable set of minimum features of statehood in the present sense of the term. In particular, the ability to determine and enforce the law in everyday life is central to the existence of any state, whatever its philosophical or ideological orientation may be. Moreover, as I will now proceed to show, the nature of the state and its present global context preclude the possibility of the application of Sharia as historically understood and as still commonly accepted among Muslims.

I will now reflect on the religious neutrality of the state within the framework of what I call "civic reason," the means for facilitating and regulating the relationships between state, politics, and religion. My view is that the state should be institutionally separate from Islam while recognizing and regulating the unavoidable connectedness of Islam with politics. Despite their obvious and permanent connections, I take the state to be the more settled, operational side of self-governance, while politics is the dynamic process of making choices among competing policy options. The state and politics may be seen as two sides of the same coin, but they cannot and should not be completely fused into each other. It is necessary to ensure that the state is not simply a complete reflection of daily politics because it must be able to mediate and adjudicate among competing views of policy, which require it to remain relatively independent from different political forces in society. Yet, the total independence of the state from politics is not possible because officials of the state will always act politically in implementing their own agenda and maintaining the allegiance of those who support them. This reality of connectedness makes it necessary to strive for the separation of the state from politics, so that those excluded by the political processes of the day can still resort to state institutions for protection against the excesses and abuse of power by state officials.

This balance is achieved through direct as well as indirect negotiations. On the one hand, more or less *direct* negotiations and agreements between the state and the dominant religious tradition (and, to a lesser extent, other religious traditions) reflect historical precedent, the importance of a particular religious tradition as part of a cultural heritage, or the socially beneficial role of religious institutions. It is true that the state may not be entirely impartial in the degree of support it extends to different religions and that state policies may contradict the imperative of neutrality toward religion. But in such direct negotiation, the general principle of separation between religion and state is largely affirmed while the value and role of a dominant religion in public life are also acknowledged. The principle of religious neutrality of the state also operates, within the framework of constitutionalism and human rights safeguards, to enable *indirect* negotiations whereby religious as well as nonreligious actors can play a role in shaping public policy. This possibility is ensured by the state protection of freedoms of association and expression, the right to organize and protest, the right to legal redress, and the use of instruments of commerce, media, and communication, which enable citizens to present their point of view and mobilize resources and public support for their perspective. The freedoms and rights that organize and regulate these processes of indirect or mediated influence on state policy are themselves enshrined as secular principles and protected within secular legal and political frameworks.

In these direct and indirect negotiations between state and religious actors, all sides clearly accept in practice the distinction between the state, religion, and politics. But as the idea of negotiation itself clearly indicates, there are tensions in these interactions and relations between state and religious actors, as well as in the assumptions and

implications of their respective positions. The realities of such tensions and the need to maintain the autonomy of both the state and
religion emphasize the importance of a framework that enables all
social actors, whether individuals or groups, to address the state for
policy objectives without compromising the separation of state and
religion. This framework must enable the widest range of social actors
to compete with one another on a free and fair footing in presenting
their views on policy issues. While there are many requirements and
aspects of these processes, here I would like to focus on the "civic reason" dimension and how it operates within this framework.

The critical need to separate state and religion while regulating the
permanent interconnectedness of religion and politics requires that
proposed policy or legislation must be founded on civic reason. This
comprises two elements. First, the rationale and purpose of public policy and legislation must be based on the sort of reasoning that citizens
generally can accept or reject, and it must be possible to make coun-
terproposals through public debate without being open to charges
of apostasy (heresy) or blasphemy as crimes punished by the state.
Second, such reasons must be publicly and openly debated, rather
than being assumed to follow from the personal beliefs and motivations of citizens or officials. It is not possible of course to control the
inner motivations and intentions of people's political behavior, but
the objective should be to promote and encourage civic reasons and
reasoning, while diminishing the exclusive influence of personal religious beliefs, over time. The requirements of civic reason are critically
important because it cannot be taken for granted that the people who
control the state will be neutral. On the contrary, these requirements
must be the objective of the state's operations precisely *because* people
are likely to continue to act on personal beliefs or justifications. These
requirements are also desirable because they encourage and facilitate
the development of a broader consensus among the population at
large, beyond the narrow religious or other beliefs of various individuals and groups.

The operation of civic reason in the negotiation of the role of religion in public policy and the state should be safeguarded by principles
of constitutionalism, human rights, and citizenship. The consistent
and institutional application of these principles ensures the ability
of all citizens to equally and freely participate in the political process

protects them against discrimination on such grounds as religion or belief. With the protection provided by such safeguards, citizens will be more likely to contribute to the formulation of public policy and legislation. Muslims and other believers can make proposals emerging from their religious beliefs, provided they are also presented to others on the basis of reasons these others can accept or reject. I believe that with such possibilities for expressing religious values through the democratic political process, subject to the safeguards of constitutionalism, human rights, and equal citizenship for all, it is more likely that Muslims (and other believers) will support this model of religious neutrality of the state.

However, I should also emphasize the practical difficulties of maintaining this delicate balance of ensuring the separation of Islam and the state while regulating the connectedness of Islam and politics. I am calling for both aspects of this model not only because it is more likely to motivated Muslims to accept it as legitimate, but also because of the practical difficulty of keeping religion out of politics in any case. Since it is neither possible nor desirable to control the way people make their political choices, it is better to acknowledge the public role of religion while deliberately striving to cultivate people's willingness and ability to provide civic reasons for their choices as much as possible. Civic reason, I believe, can and should be cultivated rather than assumed to be practiced sufficiently or abandoned as too difficult to realize.

To summarize, contestation in the sphere of civic reason can legitimize and regulate social and political pluralism, and protect the capacity of religious dissent to facilitate Islamic reform in response to whatever challenges a society faces at any given point. Such contestation may also reflect increased access to civic reason through processes of democratization, developments in communication, and the like. As access to civic reason becomes more widely available and fairer, public policy choices are likely to be more the product of negotiated consensus than impositions of the majority or ruling elites. The wider consensus that can be achieved around public policy choices through this process is likely to promote the legitimacy of the state among its population and thereby enhance political stability in the country. With greater appreciation for the value and credibility of the civic reasoning process itself, religious believers will have more opportunities to promote their religious beliefs through the regular political process without threatening the human rights and freedoms of those citizens who do not share these beliefs. This balance is likely to be achieved precisely because religious views can be neither coercively enforced by the state nor excluded from any consideration because they are religious. The uniform process that applies to any proposed public policy or legislation is mediated through fair and transparent political contestations and subject to constitutional and human rights safeguards. In this way, any proposed public policy or legislation *stands or falls on whether or not it is constitutional*, not because of its perceived religious or secular origin.

IS THIS AN AMENDMENT TO RAWLS?

The reason for my query about whether what I am proposing entails an amendment to Rawls's theory is that his thinking about religious doctrine and related matters is undertaken from a North Atlantic Christian perspective, even when thinking *for* Muslims through "conjecture." Two significant factors noted above to be recalled here are the impact of Sharia on how Muslims think about these questions and the postcolonial context in which Muslims are considering the issue. My query may therefore be directed to Rawls's definition of public reason and how it is supposed to work in practice: in which settings does public reason apply? to whom? and how is it to be monitored or policed?

But first, I am honored that Rawls cites my book *Toward an Islamic Reformation* as a "perfect example of overlapping consensus,"[22] which was my deliberate strategy also for promoting the universality of human rights from a cross-cultural perspective.[23] But I would argue that what I am proposing should simply be seen as the practice of public reason in an Islamic context. The difference is perhaps in my insistence on the primary role of believers in any religion (Muslims in my case) as equal participants in the practice of what Rawls presents as the purpose of public reason.[24] What Rawls calls a "comprehensive doctrine" may simply be the way Muslim citizens come to consent to political authority and ground their "mutual respect," fairness, reasonability, reciprocity, and other values that Rawls invokes.[25] To indicate this difference, I have opted for the term "civic reason."

To briefly elaborate on the reasons for amending Rawls's position, I first recall here the point I made at the beginning of this chapter, namely, that the relationships between religion, the state, and politics should always be considered in terms of a specific religion in a particular society. It is extremely difficult to conceive of "religion" in terms that are sufficiently inclusive to be applied to all human societies in their varied contexts, and it is only to be expected that, consciously or not, any theorist will develop his or her theory of the relationships between religion, the state, and politics with reference to a specific religion in a particular sociopolitical context. I also noted that differences in the nature and formation of religious authority among and within various religious traditions influence how believers perceive religious authority.

Even the distinction between the so-called religious and secular domains does not apply to all religious traditions. In my experience, Muslims have a positive comprehension and experience of the secular, in the sense of the material and this-worldly, and take it to be integral to their worldview rather than distinct or opposed to it. This inherent consistency and complementarity of the secular and the religious induce Muslims to think of both as entwined: life is all at once religious and secular, spiritual and material, and Islam takes each side of the human experience and both of them combined equally seriously. Defining the secular and religious as opposites or as mutually exclusive is therefore not a workable solution for Muslims. As I have put it elsewhere, "it is misleading to contrast the religious and secular in such binary terms because they are in fact mutually interdependent."[26]

Another definition that has been given for the term "secular" is "the assumption that everything material or abstract derives from human endeavor."[27] While this definition avoids a dependence on the religious that is present in many other definitions, it also omits any indication of the relationship between what is secular and what is religious. From an Islamic perspective, a more serious objection to this notion of the secular is that it simplifies a complex theological and philosophical question of predestination and free will in the relationship between divine and human agency. What does it mean to say something "derives from human endeavor"? Does that necessarily deny any role for divine agency, even for those who believe that divine agency works through human agency?

Noting these differences is not to suggest that Rawls's theory is irrelevant to Muslims in their postcolonial context, but only to raise the question of what such differences entail for that theory. Indeed, in my view, the facts of deeper religious diversity, combined with the realities of an increasingly interdependent world, intensify rather than diminish the need for Rawls's theory. Therefore, while I think that Muslims need to mediate the tensions of Islam, state, and politics in ways that take Sharia seriously on its own terms, as I have attempted to do, this also needs to be done in the intimate company of other believers and nonbelievers, as noted above.

Briefly put, Rawls's basic claim in this regard is that since citizens are unlikely to agree in solving basic political questions, political agreement should be reached by means of "public reason," despite strongly felt moral disagreement. For him, public reason is an exercise of deliberation in conditions of deep moral disagreement, and it relates specifically to "constitutional essentials and questions of basic justice." In other words, it specifies at the deepest level the basic moral and political values that are to determine the relationship of a constitutional democratic government to its citizens and the relationships among citizens themselves. And, crucially, Rawls excludes religion, along with all other "comprehensive doctrines," from public reasoning over these matters.[28]

I share Rawls's concerns about reliance on religious beliefs as the basis of public policy and legislation, and his call for the articulation of reasons that are equally accessible to all citizens without reference to religious belief as such. But I believe it is more realistic and fruitful to acknowledge and regulate the connectedness of religion and politics through the requirements of constitutionalism, human rights, and citizenship than to attempt to separate religion and politics. In my view, it is neither possible nor desirable to exclude religion from *politics*, although religion should nonetheless be kept out of *the state* by various mechanisms and strategies. The political actions of religious believers will always be guided by their religious beliefs, whether this is acknowledged or not, and recognizing and regulating these beliefs as legitimate sources of political reasoning is healthier and more practical than forcing them into a fugitive political domain, thereby constraining or distorting believers' participation in politics. I take this approach to embrace religions in a much broader "political" realm than Rawls's "public" realm allows—indeed, as I have indicated, I take "politics" to encompass all public deliberations over policy, whether by officials or private citizens, as distinct from the more settled, operational aspects of the state.

Critique of Rawls

In particular, I consider Rawls's exclusion of religions from public reason to be mistaken in a number of specific ways, and particularly so when applied to the "constitutional essentials and questions of basic justice" that he focuses on. First, it is simply unfair, or discriminatory, to reject a view or discourse because it is deemed to be religious, regardless of what it actually has to say on the issue at hand. Second, this is also a form of anticipatory censorship, which blocks the exercise of the fundamental human rights of freedom of belief and expression before a presumed harm is proven. Such censorship is not only unjust in principle, but also unfeasible: for how are we to know in advance which claims qualify as "religious" before they have been heard? Third, on my view, all citizens should be encouraged to engage in political debate, on all issues and in all contexts, so as to develop and maintain their civic reasoning over time. It seems to me that Rawls's exclusion of religions would constitute a substantial obstacle to this. Fourth, by excluding religions and other "comprehensive doctrines" from public reasoning, Rawls treats them as if they were isolated and closed and not open to internal contestation, and also as if they could be neatly compartmentalized into "religious" and "secular" categories.[29] Yet, this would be a serious misrepresentation of the nature of Islamic political thinking, which develops by both "internal" and "external" criticism and in complex relations to the nonreligious. Rawls's exclusion of religion thus denies the reality of competing rationalities within comprehensive doctrines, and limits the possibilities of persuasion among believers. Finally, and more generally, Rawls's attempts to accommodate religions in public debate are inadequate. In particular, to emphasize the limited scope of "constitutional essentials and questions of basic justice" is still to exclude religions from debate over these fundamental political questions, and however far Rawls's "proviso" and his notion of "conjecture" accommodate religious reasoning in public debate, they still require it to be ultimately translated into the nonreligious, "public" terms that he thinks citizens ought to share.

In my view, then, the freedom to express religious and other "comprehensive" reasons in politics and to organize politically to promote them should be limited only if it violates the constitutional rights of others, as enforced by the state, and not on the grounds of the kinds of reasons involved, as Rawls's theory insists. By thus distinguishing between the state and politics, as I have proposed from an Islamic perspective, I think that the requirements of civic, or "public," reason can be operationalized more effectively.

To briefly recall that distinction, the critical and delicate role that I attribute to the state is the reason why the distinction between "state" and "politics" is both necessary and difficult to maintain. The state is the institutional continuity of sovereignty, while politics refers to the government of the day. Governments are entitled to use the institutions of the state to implement the policies for which they were elected, but should not do so in ways that diminish the autonomy and continuity of state institutions. In that way, the institutions of the state, such as the Ministry of Education or the Ministry of Foreign Affairs, continue to serve the next government, which may be elected to implement different policies than the preceding one. Admittedly, the distinction between state and politics in any society will not be permanently settled, and will vary depending on the political will of the people to uphold the distinction (not a dichotomy) between the state and politics. This can be done, I believe, through institutional and normative safeguards like constitutionalism, human rights, and citizenship, which provide the essential framework for what I understand as civic reason.[30]

In closing, let me try to briefly describe the practice of what I call "civic reason" in the normal course of life of communities everywhere, as opposed to its being artificially limited to certain subject matters or applicable only in certain segregated functions of government officials and candidates for public office. In the normal course of life of a society, children are socialized within their families, at school, and in various other settings to uphold certain values of social interaction and political behavior. The adult population of the same society not only has been socialized in those ways, but is also constantly reminded of the moral integrity and practical utility of underlying values. Those values are likely to include being truthful and trustworthy in social and economic interaction with others, being respectful of the human dignity of others, and accepting their racial or ethnic identity, as well as their religious and political beliefs, because we need them to respect our dignity, identity, and beliefs. This is not to say that any society is perfect or can ever be perfect in promoting and living by these values, but our experience also confirms that these are "survival" skills for all societies and communities.

My main point is that what Rawls calls "comprehensive doctrines" not only are integral to these processes, but in fact play a leading role in our socialization into the superior humane values we need to promote. Our experience clearly shows that we cannot monitor and police what sort of discourse is conducted in which setting and by whom. Religion, culture, social interaction, and economic activities all prepare us for a healthy, productive, peaceful life, although sometimes we also engage in pathological, destructive, and violent encounters. Whatever it is we are, religion for those who believe in it is integral to who we are and how we live.

Notes

1. *PL* (pbk.) xxxvii.

2. I speak here of Sunni and Shia traditions in the plural to acknowledge the profound historical and contemporary diversity within each of these Islamic traditions.

3. See, for example, the Qur'an, 2:173, 242, 219, 266; 6:50, 151; 16:11, 44; 57:17. The Qur'an is cited by chapter and verse numbers.

4. See, for instance, the Qur'an, 12:2; 43:2.

5. *IPRR* 156.

6. See, in particular, the text accompanying note 7 on page 4 in the introduction.

7. The term "Sharia" refers to God's law in its divine and revealed sense. There is a transcendental dimension of Sharia that is, like God, unknowable and a dimension that is accessible to human understanding (*Fiqh*). As Gordon D. Newby puts it, "[Sharia] is said to be the source from which all properly Islamic behavior derives." Newby, *A Concise Encyclopedia of Islam* (Oxford: Oneworld, 2002), 193–94.

8. Abdullahi Ahmed An-Na'im, *African Constitutionalism and the Role of Islam* (Philadelphia: University of Pennsylvania Press, 2006), 16–27.

9. Ibid., 139–47.

10. For more extended discussion, see An-Na'im, *Islam and the Secular State: Negotiating the Future of Sharia* (Cambridge, Mass.: Harvard University Press, 2008); An-Na'im, "The Future of Shari'ah and the Debate in Northern Nigeria," in *Comparative Perspectives on Shari'ah in Nigeria*, ed. P. Ostien, J. M. Nasir, and F. Kogelmann (Ibadan: Spectrum Books, 2005), 327–57; and An-Na'im, "The Compatibility Dialectic: Mediating the Legitimate Coexistence of Islamic Law and State Law," *Modern Law Review* 73, no. 1 (2010): 1–29.

11. An-Na'im, *Islam and the Secular State*, 7–8.

12. Bernard Weiss, *The Spirit of Islamic Law* (Athens: University of Georgia Press, 1998), 116 (emphasis in original).

13. See, for example, the Qur'an, 5:105; 41:46; 4:79–80; and 53:36–42.

14. Weiss, *The Spirit of Islamic Law*, 120–22.

15. Averroës, *The Decisive Treatise Determining the Connection Between the Law and Wisdom and Epistle Dedicatory* (Brigham: Brigham University Press, 2001), 8–10. This is a translation of Ibn Rushd, *Fasl al-Maqa bayn al-Shar'a wa al-Hikmah min Itsal*.

16. Noel J. Coulson, *Conflicts and Tensions in Islamic Jurisprudence* (Chicago: University of Chicago Press, 1969), 34.

17. Ibid., 35–36.

18. See An-Na'im, *Islam and the Secular State*, 140–50 and 182–96, respectively.

19. See Knut Vikor, *Between God and Sultan: A History of Islamic Law* (Oxford: Oxford University Press, 2005).

20. See Graeme Gill, *The Nature and Development of the Modern State* (New York: Palgrave Macmillan, 2003), 2–4.

21. Ibid., 17.

22. *IPRR* 151n46.

23. See An-Na'im, ed., *Human Rights in Cross-Cultural Perspective: Quest for Consensus* (Philadelphia: University of Pennsylvania Press, 1992).

24. *IPRR* 129–80.

25. *PL* (pbk.) 38, 223.

26. Abdullahi Ahmed An-Na'im, "Islam and Secularism," in *Comparative Secularisms in a Global Age*, ed. L. E. Cady and E. S. Hurd (New York: Palgrave Macmillan, 2010), 218.

27. Lilly Weissbrod, "Religion as National Identity in a Secular Society," *Review of Religious Research* 24, no. 3 (1983): 189.

28. See *PL* (pbk.) 212, 214, and 227–30, and *IPRR* 132–33.

29. See Ashis Nandy, *Talking India: Ashis Nandy in Conversation with Ramin Jahanbegloo* (Delhi: Oxford University Press, 2006), 103–4.

30. See An-Na'im, *Islam and the Secular State*, 89–97.

BIBLIOGRAPHY

Anderson, Elizabeth. "Cohen, Justice, and Interpersonal Justification." *APSA 2010 Annual Meeting Paper* (2010). http://ssrn.com/abstract=1642011.

An-Na'im, Abdullahi Ahmed. *African Constitutionalism and the Role of Islam.* Philadelphia: University of Pennsylvania Press, 2006.

———. "The Compatibility Dialectic: Mediating the Legitimate Coexistence of Islamic Law and State Law." *Modern Law Review* 73, no. 1 (2010): 1–29.

———, ed. *Human Rights in Cross-Cultural Perspective: Quest for Consensus.* Philadelphia: University of Pennsylvania Press, 1992.

———. "The Interdependence of Religion, Secularism, and Human Rights." *Common Knowledge* 11, no. 1 (2005): 65–80.

———. "Islam and Human Rights: Beyond the Universality Debate." *American Society of International Law Proceedings* 94 (2000): 95–101.

———. "Islam and Secularism." In *Comparative Secularisms in a Global Age*, edited by Linell E. Cady and Elizabeth Shakman Hurd, 217–28. New York: Palgrave Macmillan, 2010.

———. *Islam and the Secular State: Negotiating the Future of Sharia.* Cambridge, Mass.: Harvard University Press, 2008.

———. "The Rights of Women and International Law in the Muslim Context." *Whittier Law Review* 9 (1987): 491–516.

———. *Toward an Islamic Reformation: Civil Liberties, Human Rights, and International Law.* Syracuse: Syracuse University Press, 1990.

Arendt, Hannah. "The Crisis in Culture: Its Social and Political Significance." In *Between Past and Future: Eight Exercises in Political Thought.* New York: Penguin, 1961.

———. *Lectures on Kant's Political Philosophy.* Edited by Ronald Beiner. Chicago: University of Chicago Press, 1992.

———. "Understanding and Politics." *Partisan Review* 20 (1953): 377–92.

Arnason, Johann, Shmuel Noah Eisenstadt, and Bjorn Wittrock. *Axial Civilizations and World History*. Leiden: Brill, 2005.

Assmann, Jan. *Herrschaft und Heil: Politische Theologie in Altägypten, Israel und Europa*. München: Hanser, 2000.

Audi, Robert. *Democratic Authority and the Separation of Church and State*. Oxford: Oxford University Press, 2011.

———. "Liberal Democracy and the Place of Religion in Politics." In *Religion in the Public Square*, edited by Robert Audi and Nicholas Wolterstorff, 1–66. Lanham: Rowman and Littlefield, 1997.

———. *Religious Commitment and Secular Reason*. Cambridge: Cambridge University Press, 2000.

———. "Religious Commitment and Secular Reason: A Reply to Professor Weithman." *Philosophy and Public Affairs* 20 (1991): 66–76.

———. "The Separation of Church and State and the Obligations of Citizenship." *Philosophy and Public Affairs* 18 (1989): 259–96.

———. "The State, the Church, and the Citizen." In *Religion and Contemporary Liberalism*, edited by Paul Weithman, 38–75. Notre Dame: University of Notre Dame Press, 1997.

Averroës. *The Decisive Treatise Determining the Connection Between the Law and Wisdom and Epistle Dedicatory*. Translated by Charles E. Butterworth. Brigham: Brigham Young University Press, 2001.

Bader, Veit. "Secularism, Public Reason or Moderately Agonistic Democracy?" In *Secularism, Religion and Multicultural Citizenship*, edited by Geoffrey Brahm Levey and Tariq Modood, 110–35. Cambridge: Cambridge University Press, 2008.

Beerbohm, Eric. *In Our Name: The Ethics of Democracy*. Princeton: Princeton University Press, 2012.

Bellamy, Richard. *Political Constitutionalism: A Republican Defence of the Constitutionality of Democracy*. Cambridge: Polity, 2007.

Benhabib, Seyla. "Deliberative Rationality and Models of Democratic Legitimacy." *Constellations* 1, no. 1 (1994): 26–52.

———. *Dignity in Adversity: Human Rights in Troubled Times*. Cambridge: Polity, 2011.

———. *The Rights of Others: Aliens, Residents, and Citizens*. Cambridge: Cambridge University Press, 2004.

———. "Towards a Deliberative Model of Democratic Legitimacy." In *Democracy and Difference*, edited by Seyla Benhabib, 67–94. Princeton: Princeton University Press, 1996.

Biggar, Nigel. *In Defence of War*. Oxford: Oxford University Press, 2013.

Bilgin, Fevzi. *Political Liberalism in Muslim Societies*. London: Routledge, 2011.

Bird, Colin. "Mutual Respect and Neutral Justification." *Ethics* 107 (1996): 62–96.

Blake, Michael. "Reciprocity, Stability, and Intervention: The Ethics of Disequilibrium." In *Ethics and Foreign Intervention*, edited by Deen K. Chatterjee and Don Sheid, 53–71. New York: Cambridge University Press, 2003.

Boettcher, James. "Public Reason and Religion." In *The Legacy of John Rawls*, edited by Thom Brooks and Fabian Freyenhagen, 124–51. New York: Continuum, 2005.

———. "Respect, Recognition, and Public Reason." *Social Theory and Practice* 33 (2007): 223–49.

———. "Strong Inclusionist Accounts of the Role of Religion in Political Decision-Making." *Journal of Social Philosophy* 36 (2005): 497–516.

Boff, Clodovis. *Theology and Praxis: Epistemological Foundations*. Maryknoll: Orbis, 1987.

Bohman, James. "Deliberative Toleration." *Political Theory* 31, no. 6 (2003): 757–79.

———. "Public Reason and Cultural Pluralism: Political Liberalism and the Problem of Moral Conflict." *Political Theory* 23 (1995): 253–79.

Bohman, James, and Henry Richardson. "Liberalism, Deliberative Democracy, and 'Reasons All Can Accept.'" *Journal of Political Philosophy* 17 (2009): 253–74.

Bornkamm, Günther. *Early Christian Experience*. New York: Harper and Row, 1969.

Bourdieu, Pierre. *The Logic of Practice*. Translated by Richard Nice. Cambridge: Polity, 1990.

Brudney, Daniel. "Community and Completion." In *Reclaiming the History of Ethics: Essays for John Rawls*, edited by Andrews Reath, Barbara Herman, and Christine M. Korsgaard, 388–415. New York: Cambridge University Press, 1997.

Butler, Judith. "Is Kinship Always Already Heterosexual?" *differences: A Journal of Feminist Cultural Studies* 13, no. 1 (2002): 14–44.

Cacioppo, John T., and William Patrick. *Loneliness: Human Nature and the Need for Social Connection*. New York: Norton, 2009.

Campos, Paul F. "Secular Fundamentalism." *Columbia Law Review* 94, no. 6 (1994): 1814–27.

Carroll, Anthony. "A Catholic Programme for Advanced Modernity." In *Towards a New Catholic Church in Advanced Modernity*, edited by Staf Hellemans and Josef Wissink, 51–77. Zurich: Lit, 2012.

Carter, Stephen. "Evolutionism, Creationism, and Treating Religion as a Hobby." *Duke Law Journal* 6 (1987): 977–96.

Casanova, José. *Public Religions in the Modern World*. Chicago: University of Chicago Press, 1994.

Cavanaugh, William T. "The City: Beyond Secular Parodies," In *Radical Orthodoxy: A New Theology*, edited by John Milbank, Catherine Pickstock, and Graham Ward, 182–200. London: Routledge, 1999.

Cavell, Stanley. *Cities of Words*. Cambridge, Mass.: Harvard University Press, 2005.

———. *The Claim of Reason*. 2nd ed. Oxford: Oxford University Press, 1999.

———. *Conditions Handsome and Unhandsome*. Chicago: University of Chicago Press, 1990.

Chambers, Clare. "The Marriage-Free State." *Proceedings of the Aristotelian Society* 113, no. 2 (2013): 123–143.

Chambers, Simone. "Secularism Minus Exclusion: Developing a Religious-Friendly Idea of Public Reason." *Good Society* 19, no. 2 (2010): 16–21.

Clanton, J. Caleb. "Democratic Deliberation *After* Religious Gag Rules." In *The Ethics of Citizenship: Liberal Democracy and Religious Convictions*, edited by J. Caleb Clanton, 365–92. Waco, Tex.: Baylor University Press, 2009.

Clivaz, Clare. "L'analyse narrative signale-t-elle l'arrivée du *muthos* en exégèse? Histoire et Poétique autour d'Ac 17, 28." In *Analyse narrative et bible*, edited by Camille Focant and André Wénin, 483–96. Leuven: Peeters, 2005.

Cicero, Marcus Tullius. *On Moral Ends*. Edited by Julia Annas. Translated by Raphael Woolf. Cambridge: Cambridge University Press, 2001.

Cohen, G. A. *Finding Oneself in the Other*. Edited by Michael Otsuka. Princeton: Princeton University Press, 2013.

———. *If You're an Egalitarian, How Come You're So Rich?* Cambridge, Mass.: Harvard University Press, 2000.

———. *Karl Marx's Theory of History: A Defence*. Expanded ed. Princeton: Princeton University Press, 2001.

————. "Reason, Humanity, and the Moral Law." In *The Sources of Normativity*, by Christine M. Korsgaard, with G. A. Cohen, Raymond Geuss, Thomas Nagel, and Bernard Williams, edited by Onora O'Neill, 167–88. Cambridge: Cambridge University Press, 1996.

————. *Rescuing Justice and Equality*. Cambridge, Mass.: Harvard University Press, 2008.

————. *Self-Ownership, Freedom, and Equality*. Cambridge: Cambridge University Press, 1995.

————. *Why Not Socialism?* Princeton: Princeton University Press, 2009.

Cohen, Joshua. "Deliberation and Democratic Legitimacy." In *The Good Polity*, edited by Alan Hamlin and Philip Pettit, 17–34. Oxford: Blackwell, 1989.

————. "Minimalism About Human Rights: The Most We Can Hope For?" *Journal of Political Philosophy* 12 (2004): 190–213.

Cohen, Joshua, and Charles Sabel. "Extra Rempublicam Nulla Justitia?" *Philosophy and Public Affairs* 34, no. 2 (2006): 147–75.

Coles, Romand. *Beyond Gated Politics: Reflections for the Possibility of Democracy*. Minneapolis: University of Minnesota Press, 2005.

Congregation for the Doctrine of the Faith. *Dominus Iesus: On the Unicity and Salvific Universality of Jesus Christ and the Church*. 2000. www.vatican.va/roman_curia/congregations /cfaith/documents/rc_con_cfaith_doc_20000806_dominus-iesus_en.html.

Conly, Sarah. *Against Autonomy: Justifying Coercive Paternalism*. Cambridge: Cambridge University Press, 2012.

Connolly, William E. *Why I Am Not a Secularist*. Minneapolis: University of Minnesota Press, 1999.

Conzelmann, Hans. *Die Apostelgeschichte*. Tübingen: Mohr, 1972.

Cott, Nancy. *Public Vows: A History of Marriage and the Nation*. Cambridge, Mass.: Harvard University Press, 2000.

Coulson, Noel J. *Conflicts and Tensions in Islamic Jurisprudence*. Chicago: University of Chicago Press, 1969.

Cuneo, Terence, and Christopher J. Eberle. "Religion and Political Theory." In *Stanford Encyclopedia of Philosophy*, edited by Edward N. Zalta. October 2, 2008. http://plato.stanford. edu/entries/religion-politics.

Curran, Charles. "Abortion: Its Moral Aspects." In *Abortion: The Moral Issues*, edited by Edward Batchelor Jr., 115–28. New York: Pilgrim, 1982.

Darwall, Stephen. "Two Kinds of Respect." *Ethics* 88 (1977): 36–49.

DeWitt, Norman. *Epicurus and his Philosophy*. Westport, Conn.: Greenwood, 1976.

Dibelius, Martin. *Paulus auf dem Areopag*. Heidelberg: Winter, 1939.

Dombrowski, Daniel A. *Rawls and Religion: The Case for Political Liberalism*. New York: SUNY Press, 2001.

Doppelt, Gerald D. "Beyond Liberalism and Communitarianism: Towards a Critical Theory of Social Justice." In *Universalism vs. Communitarianism*, edited by David Rasmussen, 39–60. Cambridge, Mass.: MIT Press, 1990.

Dunn, James D. G. *The Theology of Paul the Apostle*. Grand Rapids, Mich.: Eerdmans, 1998.

Dworkin, Ronald. *Is Democracy Possible Here?* Princeton: Princeton University Press, 2006.

————. *Life's Dominion: An Argument About Abortion, Euthanasia, and Individual Freedom*. New York: Knopf, 1993.

Dyzenhaus, David. "Liberalism After the Fall: Schmitt, Rawls and the Problem of Justification." *Philosophy and Social Criticism* 22, no. 3 (1996): pp. 9–37.

Eagleton, Terry. *The Meaning of Life*. Oxford: Oxford University Press, 2007.

Eberle, Christopher J. "Basic Human Worth and Religious Restraint." *Philosophy and Social Criticism* 35, nos. 1–2 (2009): 151–81.

———. "God and War: Some Exploratory Questions." *Journal of Law and Religion* 28, no. 1 (2012–13): 1–46.

———. "Religion, Pacifism and the Doctrine of Restraint." *Journal of Religious Ethics* 34, no. 2 (June 2006): 203–24.

———. *Religious Conviction in Liberal Politics.* Cambridge: Cambridge University Press, 2002.

———. "Religious Reasons in Public." *St. John's Journal of Legal Commentary* 22 (2007): 431–43.

———. "What Does Respect Require?" In *Religion in the Liberal Polity*, edited by Terence Cuneo, 173–94. Notre Dame: University of Notre Dame Press, 2005.

———. "What Respect Requires—and What It Does Not." *Wake Forest Law Review* 36 (2001): 305–51.

Eisenstadt, Shmuel Noah, ed. *The Origins and Diversity of Axial Age Civilizations.* New York: SUNY Press, 1986.

Elshtain, Jean Bethke. *Sovereignty: God, State, and Self.* New York: Basic Books, 2008.

Estlund, David. *Democratic Authority.* Princeton: Princeton University Press, 2008.

Fadel, Mohammad. "Public Reason as a Strategy for Principled Reconciliation: The Case of Islamic Law and International Human Rights Law." *Chicago Journal of International Law* 8, no. 1 (2007): 1–20.

———. "The True, the Good and the Reasonable: The Theological Roots of Public Reason in Islamic Law." *Canadian Journal of Law and Jurisprudence* 21, no. 1 (2008): 5–69.

Ferrara, Alessandro. *The Force of the Example: Explorations in the Paradigm of Judgment.* New York: Columbia University Press, 2008.

Fish, Stanley. "Mission Impossible: Settling the Just Bounds Between Church and State." *Columbia Law Review* 97, no. 8 (1997): 2255–333.

———. "Mutual Respect as a Device of Exclusion." In *Deliberative Politics: Essays on Democracy and Disagreement*, edited by Stephen Macedo, 88–102. New York: Oxford University Press, 1999.

Forst, Rainer. *The Right to Justification: Elements of a Constructivist Theory of Justice.* New York: Columbia University Press, 2012.

Fotion, Nicholas. *War and Ethics: A New Just War Theory.* New York: Continuum, 2007.

Fraser, Nancy. "Rethinking the Public Sphere." In *Habermas and the Public Sphere*, edited by Craig Calhoun, 109–42. Cambridge, Mass.: MIT Press, 1992.

Freedman, Jane. "Secularism as a Barrier to Integration? The French Dilemma." *International Migration* 42, no. 3 (2004): 5–27.

Freeman, Samuel. "Public Reason and Political Justification." *Fordham Law Review* 72, no. 5 (2004): 2021–72.

Gadamer, Hans-Georg. "On the Scope and Function of Hermeneutical Reflection." In *Philosophical Hermeneutics*, translated and edited by David E. Linge, 18–43. Berkeley: University of California Press, 1977.

———. *Truth and Method.* Translated by Joel Weinsheimer and Donald G. Marshall. 2nd rev. ed. New York: Continuum, 1989.

Galston, William. *Liberal Pluralism: The Implications of Value Pluralism for Political Theory and Practice.* Cambridge: Cambridge University Press, 2002.

Garsten, Bryan. *Saving Persuasion: A Defense of Rhetoric and Judgment.* Cambridge, Mass.: Harvard University Press, 2006.

Gaus, Gerald. *Justificatory Liberalism*. Oxford: Oxford University Press, 1996.

———. "The Place of Religious Belief in Public Reason Liberalism." In *Multiculturalism and Moral Conflict*, edited by Maria Dimovia-Cookson and Peter M. R. Stirk, 19–37. London: Routledge, 2009.

———. "Review of Christopher Eberle, *Religious Conviction in Liberal Politics*." *Notre Dame Philosophical Reviews*, March 8, 2008. http://ndpr.nd.edu/review.cfm?id=1214.

Gaus, Gerald, and Kevin Vallier. "The Roles of Religious Conviction in a Publicly Justified Policy: The Implications of Convergence, Asymmetry, and Political Institutions." *Philosophy and Social Criticism* 35, nos. 1–2 (2009): 51–76.

George, Robert P., and Christopher Wolfe, eds. "Law, Democracy, and Moral Disagreement." *Harvard Law Review* 110, no. 7 (1997): 1388–406.

———. *Natural Law and Public Reason*. Washington, D.C.: Georgetown University Press, 2000.

———. "Public Reason and Political Conflict: Abortion and Homosexuality." *Yale Law Journal* 106, no. 8 (1997): 2475–504.

Gibbard, Alan. *Wise Choices, Apt Feelings*. Oxford: Oxford University Press, 1990.

Gill, Graeme. *The Nature and Development of the Modern State*. New York: Palgrave Macmillan, 2003.

Girgis, Sherif, Ryan T. Anderson, and Robert P. George. *What Is Marriage? Man and Woman: A Defense*. New York: Encounter Books, 2012.

Gledhill, James. "Procedure in Substance and Substance in Procedure: Reframing the Rawls-Habermas Debate." In *Habermas and Rawls: Disputing the Political*, edited by James Gordon Finlayson and Fabian Freyenhagen, 181–99. New York: Routledge, 2011.

Graham, Keith. "Self-Ownership, Communism and Equality." *Proceedings of the Aristotelian Society*, supp. vol. 64 (1990): 45–61.

Greenawalt, Kent. *Private Consciences and Public Reasons*. New York: Oxford University Press, 1995.

———. *Religious Convictions and Political Choice*. New York: Oxford University Press, 1988.

Gregory, Brad S. *The Unintended Reformation: How a Religious Reformation Secularized Society*. Cambridge, Mass.: Harvard University Press, 2012.

Griffin, Leslie C. "Good Catholics Should Be Rawlsian Liberals." *Southern California Interdisciplinary Law Journal* 5, no. 3 (1997): 297–371.

Grotius, Hugo. *De jure belli ac pacis*. Oxford: Clarendon Press, 1625.

———. *Prolegomena to On the Law of War and Peace*. Translated by F. W. Kelsey. Indianapolis: Bobbs-Merrill, 1957.

Gutmann, Amy, and Dennis Thompson. *Democracy and Disagreement*. Cambridge, Mass.: Harvard University Press, 1996.

———. "Moral Conflict and Political Consensus." *Ethics* 101 (1990): 64–88.

Habermas, Jürgen. "An Awareness of What Is Missing." In *An Awareness of What Is Missing: Faith and Reason in a Post-Secular Age*, 15–23. Cambridge: Polity, 2010.

———. *Between Facts and Norms: Contributions to a Discourse Theory of Law and Democracy*. Translated by William Rehg. Cambridge: Polity, 1996.

———. "The Boundary Between Faith and Knowledge: On the Reception and Contemporary Importance of Kant's Philosophy of Religion." In *Between Naturalism and Religion*, translated by Ciaran Cronin, 209–47. Cambridge: Polity, 2008.

———. "Discourse Ethics: Notes on a Program of Philosophical Justification." In *Moral Consciousness and Communicative Action*, translated by Christian Lenhardt and Shierry Weber Nicholsen, 116–94. Cambridge: Polity, 1990.

———. "From Kant's 'Ideas' of Pure Reason to the 'Idealizing' Presuppositions of Communicative Action: Reflections on the Detranscendentalized 'Use of Reason.'" In *Truth and Justification*, translated by Barbara Fultner, 83–130. Cambridge: Polity, 2003.

———. "A Genealogical Analysis of the Cognitive Content of Morality." In *The Inclusion of the Other: Studies in Political Theory*, edited by Ciaran Cronin and Pablo De Grieff, 3–46. Cambridge: Polity, 1999.

———. "The German Idealism of the Jewish Philosophers." In *Philosophical-Political Profiles*, translated by Frederick G. Lawrence, 21–43. Cambridge, Mass.: MIT Press, 1983.

———. "The 'Good Life'—a 'Detestable Phrase': The Significance of the Young Rawls's Religious Ethics for his Political Theory." *European Journal of Philosophy* 18 (2010): 443–54.

———. "Individuation Through Socialization: On George Herbert Mead's Theory of Subjectivity." In *Postmetaphysical Thinking*, translated by William Mark Hohengarten, 149–204. Cambridge: Polity, 1992.

——— *On the Logic of the Social Sciences*. Translated by Shierry Weber Nicholsen and Jerry A. Stark. Cambridge: Polity, 1988.

———. "'The Political': The Rational Meaning of a Questionable Inheritance of Political Theology." In *The Power of Religion in the Public Sphere*, edited by Eduardo Mendieta and Jonathan VanAntwerpen, 15–33. New York: Columbia University Press, 2011.

———. "Pre-Political Foundations of the Constitutional State?" In *Between Naturalism and Religion*, translated by Ciaran Cronin, 101–13. Cambridge: Polity, 2008.

———. "'Reasonable' Versus 'True,' or the Morality of Worldviews." In *The Inclusion of the Other: Studies in Political Theory*, edited by Ciaran Cronin and Pablo De Grieff, 75–101. Cambridge: Polity, 1999.

———. "Reconciliation Through the Public Use of Reason." In *The Inclusion of the Other: Studies in Political Theory*, edited by Ciaran Cronin and Pablo De Grieff, 49–74. Cambridge: Polity, 1999.

———. "Reconciliation Through the Public Use of Reason: Remarks on John Rawls' *Political Liberalism*." *Journal of Philosophy* 92, no. 3 (1995): 109–31.

———. "The Relationship Between Theory and Practice Revisited." In *Truth and Justification*, translated by Barbara Fultner, 277–92. Cambridge: Polity, 2003.

———. "Religion in the Public Sphere." *European Journal of Philosophy* 14 (2006): 1–25.

———. "Religion in the Public Sphere: Cognitive Presuppositions for the 'Public Use of Reason' by Religious and Secular Citizens." In *Between Naturalism and Religion: Philosophical Essays*, trans. Ciaran Cronin, 114–47. Cambridge: Polity, 2008.

———. "Transcendence from Within, Transcendence in this World." In *Religion and Rationality: Essays on Reason, God, and Modernity*, edited by Eduardo Mendieta, 67–94. Cambridge: Polity, 2002.

———. "The Unity of Reason in the Diversity of its Voices." In *Postmetaphysical Thinking*, translated by William Mark Hohengarten, 115–48. Cambridge: Polity, 1992.

———. *Zwischen Naturalismus und Religion*. Frankfurt: Suhrkamp, 2005.

Hampshire, Stuart. "Liberalism: The New Twist." *New York Review of Books* 40, no. 14 (1993): 43–47.

Hampton, Jean. *Hobbes and the Social Contract Tradition*. Cambridge: Cambridge University Press, 1986.

Hauerwas, Stanley. "The Democratic Policing of Christianity." In *Dispatches from the Front: Theological Engagements with the Secular*, 91–106. Durham: Duke University Press, 1994.

Hertzberg, Benjamin. "Both Citizen and Saint: Religious Integrity and Liberal Democracy." PhD diss., Duke University, 2011.

Hollenbach, David. *The Common Good and Christian Ethics*. Cambridge: Cambridge University Press, 2002.

Honig, Bonnie. *Emergency Politics: Paradox, Law, Democracy*. Princeton: Princeton University Press, 2009.

——— *Political Theory and the Displacement of Politics*. Ithaca, N.Y.: Cornell University Press, 1993.

Honneth, Axel. *Kampf um Anerkennung: Zur moralischen Grammatik sozialer Konflikte*. Frankfurt: Suhrkamp, 1994.

———. *Unsichtbarkeit: Stationen einer Theorie der Intersubjektivität*. Frankfurt: Suhrkamp, 2003.

Horton, John. "Rawls, Public Reason and the Limits of Liberal Justification." *Contemporary Political Theory* 2, no. 1 (2003): 5–23.

Hurka, Thomas. "Proportionality in the Morality of War." *Philosophy and Public Affairs* 33, no. 1 (2005): 34–66.

Insole, Christopher J. *The Politics of Human Frailty: A Theological Defense of Political Liberalism*. Notre Dame: University of Notre Dame Press, 2005.

Jensen, Jeppe. "Revisiting the Insider-Outsider Debate: Dismantling a Pseudo-Problem in the Study of Religion." *Method and Theory in the Study of Religion* 23, no. 1 (2011): 29–47.

Kahl, Werner. "Paulus als kontextualisierender Evangelist beim Areopag." In *Der eine Gott und die fremde Kulte: Exklusive und inklusive Tendenzen in den biblischen Gottesvorstellungen*, edited by Eberhard Bons, 73–94. Neukirchen: Neukirchener, 2011.

Kant, Immanuel. *Critique of Pure Reason*. Translated by Norman Kemp Smith. London: Macmillan, 1978.

———. "What Is Orientation in Thinking?" In *Political Writings*, edited by Hans Reiss and translated by H. B. Nisbet, 237–49. Cambridge: Cambridge University Press, 1977.

Kelly, Erin, and Lionel McPherson. "On Tolerating the Unreasonable." *Journal of Political Philosophy* 9 (2001): 38–55.

King, Martin Luther, Jr. "Letter from Birmingham Jail." In *Why We Can't Wait*, 76–95. New York: Penguin, 1964.

———. *A Testament of Hope: The Essential Writings and Speeches of Martin Luther King, Jr.*, edited by James Melvin Washington. New York: Harper, 1991.

Klauck, Hans-Josef. *The Apocryphal Acts of the Apostles: An Introduction*. Waco, Tex.: Baylor University Press, 2008.

Knowles, Dudley. *Routledge Philosophy Guidebook to Hegel and the Philosophy of Right*. London: Routledge, 2008.

Kuitert, Harry. "Hebben christenen het recht om zichzelf te doden?" *Concilium* 21, no. 3 (1985): 93–98.

Kymlicka, Will. *Multicultural Citizenship: A Liberal Theory of Minority Rights*. Oxford: Oxford University Press, 1996.

———. "Two Models of Pluralism and Tolerance." *Analyse und Kritik* 14, no. 34 (1992): 33–55.

Lane, Linda L. "The Parental Rights Movement." *University of Colorado Law Review* 69 (1998): 825–50.

Larmore, Charles. *The Autonomy of Morality*. Cambridge: Cambridge University Press, 2008.

———. "The Moral Basis of Political Liberalism." *Journal of Philosophy* 96, no. 12 (1999): 599–625.

———. *The Morals of Modernity*. Cambridge: Cambridge University Press, 1996.

———. *Patterns of Moral Complexity*. Cambridge: Cambridge University Press, 1987.

————. "Political Liberalism." *Political Theory* 18, no. 3 (1990): 339–60.

———— "Public Reason." In *The Cambridge Companion to Rawls*, edited by Samuel Freeman, 368–93. Cambridge: Cambridge University Press, 2003.

————. "Respect for Persons." *Hedgehog Review* 7, no. 2 (Summer 2005): 66–76.

Lassman, Peter. "Political Theory as Utopia." *History of the Human Sciences* 16, no. 1 (2003): 49–62.

Lawrence v. Texas. 2003. 539 U.S. 558.

Levine, Andrew. *The General Will: Rousseau, Marx, Communism.* Cambridge: Cambridge University Press, 1993.

Locke, John. *A Letter Concerning Toleration.* London: Routledge, 1991.

————. *Two Treatises of Government, and a Letter Concerning Toleration.* Edited by Ian Shapiro. New Haven: Yale University Press, 2004.

Losonczi, Péter. "Religion, Pluralism, and Politics: A Case for an Inter-Contextual Study on Europe and India." In *Secularism, Religion and Politics: India and Europe*, edited by Péter Losonczi and Walter van Herck. New York: Routledge, 2014.

Lott, Micah. "Restraint on Reasons and Reasons for Restraint." *Pacific Philosophical Quarterly* 87 (2006): 75–95.

Love, Nancy S. "Rawlsian Harmonies: Overlapping Consensus Symphony Orchestra." *Theory, Culture and Society* 20, no. 6 (2003): 121–40.

Lüdemann, Gerd. *Paul: The Founder of Christianity.* New York: Prometheus Books, 2002.

Luhmann, Niklas. *Die Gesellschaft der Gesellschaft.* 2 vols., Frankfurt: Suhrkamp, 1998.

————. *Dar Recht der Gesellschaft.* Frankfurt: Suhrkamp, 1995.

————. *Die Religion der Gesellschaft.* Frankfurt: Suhrkamp, 2000.

————. *Die Wissenschaft der Gesellschaft.* Frankfurt: Suhrkamp, 1990.

Macedo, Stephen, ed. *Deliberative Politics: Essays on Democracy and Disagreement.* New York: Oxford University Press, 1999.

————. "In Defense of Liberal Public Reason: Are Slavery and Abortion Hard Cases?" *American Journal of Jurisprudence* 42, no. 1 (1998): 1–29. Reprinted in *Natural Law and Public Reason*, edited by Robert George and Christopher Wolfe, 11–49. Washington, D.C.: Georgetown University Press, 2000.

————. "Liberal Civic Education and Religious Fundamentalism: The Case of God v. John Rawls?" *Ethics* 105 (1995): 468–496.

————. "Why Public Reason? Citizens' Reasons and the Constitution of the Public Sphere." (August 23, 2010). http://ssrn.com/abstract=1664085.

MacIntyre, Alasdair. *After Virtue: A Study in Moral Theory.* Notre Dame: University of Notre Dame Press, 1981.

Maffettone, Sebastiano. *Rawls: An Introduction.* Cambridge: Polity, 2010.

March, Andrew F. *Islam and Liberal Citizenship: The Search for an Overlapping Consensus.* Oxford: Oxford University Press, 2009.

————. "Is There a Right to Polygamy? Marriage, Equality and Subsidizing Families in Liberal Public Justification." *Journal of Moral Philosophy* 8, no. 2 (2011): 244–70.

————. "What Lies Beyond Same-Sex Marriage? Marriage, Reproductive Freedom and Future Persons in Liberal Public Justification." *Journal of Applied Philosophy* 27, no. 1 (2010): 39–58.

Marshall, T. H. *Citizenship and Social Class, and Other Essays.* Cambridge: Cambridge University Press, 1950.

Marx, Karl. "The Communist Manifesto." In *Karl Marx: Selected Writings*, edited by David McLellan, 245–72. 2nd ed. Oxford: Oxford University Press, 2000.

———. "On the Jewish Question." In *Karl Marx: Selected Writings*, edited by David McLellan, 46–70. 2nd. ed. Oxford: Oxford University Press, 2000.

Mattox, John Mark. *Saint Augustine and the Theory of Just War*. New York: Continuum, 2006.

McConnell, Michael. "Five Reasons to Reject the Claim that Religious Arguments Should Be Excluded from Democratic Deliberation." *Utah Law Review* 3 (1999): 639–57.

——— "Secular Reason and the Misguided Attempt to Exclude Religious Argument from Democratic Deliberation." *Journal of Law, Philosophy and Culture* 1, no. 1 (2007): 159–74.

McGraw, Bryan T. *Faith in Politics: Religion and Liberal Democracy*. Cambridge: Cambridge University Press, 2010.

McMahan, Jeff. "Just Cause for War." *Ethics and International Affairs* 19, no. 3 (2005): 55–75.

Mead, George Herbert. *Mind, Self, and Society*. Chicago: University of Chicago Press, 1934.

Mendieta, Eduardo. "A Postsecular World Society? On the Philosophical Significance of Postsecular Consciousness and the Multicultural World Society: An Interview with Jürgen Habermas." Translated by Matthias Fritsch. *The Immanent Frame*, February 3, 2010. http://blogs.ssrc.org/tif/2010/02/03/a-postsecular-world-society.

Metz, Tamara. *Untying the Knot: Marriage, the State and the Case for Their Divorce*. Princeton: Princeton University Press, 2010.

Milbank, John. *Theology and Social Theory: Beyond Secular Reason*. Oxford: Blackwell, 1990.

Mill, John Stuart. *On Liberty, and Other Essays*. New York: Oxford University Press, 1991.

Moon, J. Donald. *Constructing Community: Moral Pluralism and Tragic Conflicts*. Princeton: Princeton University Press, 1993.

Mouffe, Chantal. "Deliberative Democracy or Agonistic Pluralism?" *Social Research* 66, no. 3 (1999): 745–58.

Mulhall, Stephen. "Perfectionism, Politics and the Social Contract: Rawls and Cavell on Justice." *Journal of Political Philosophy* 2, no. 3 (1994): 222–39.

———. "Promising, Consent, and Citizenship: Rawls and Cavell on Morality and Politics." *Political Theory* 25, no. 2 (1997): 171–92.

Mulhall, Stephen, and Adam Swift. *Liberals and Communitarians*. 2nd ed. Cambridge: Blackwell, 1996.

———. "Rawls and Communitarianism." In *The Cambridge Companion to Rawls*, edited by Samuel Freeman, 460–87. Cambridge: Cambridge University Press, 2003.

Murray, John Courtney. "Natural Law and the Public Consensus." In *Natural Law and Modern Society*, edited by John Cogley, Robert Hutchins, and John Murray, 48–81. New York: Meridian Books, 1966.

———. *We Hold These Truths: Catholic Reflections on the American Propositions*. New York: Sheed and Ward, 1961.

Nagel, Thomas. "Moral Conflict and Political Legitimacy." *Philosophy and Public Affairs* 16 (1987): 215–40.

———. "The Problem of Global Justice." *Philosophy and Public Affairs* 33, no. 2 (2005): 113–47.

Nandy, Ashis. *Talking India: Ashis Nandy in Conversation with Ramin Jahanbegloo*. Delhi: Oxford University Press, 2006.

National Association of Evangelicals. *An Evangelical Declaration Against Torture: Protecting Human Rights in an Age of Terror*, 2007. www.nae.net/government-relations/endorsed-documents/409-an-evangelical-declaration-against-torture-protecting-human-rights-in-an-age-of-terror.

Neal, Patrick. "Does He Mean What He Says? (Mis)understanding Rawls's Practical Turn." *Polity* 27, no. 1 (1994): 77–112.

———. "Is Political Liberalism Hostile to Religion?" In *Reflections on Rawls: An Assessment of His Legacy*, edited by Shaun P. Young, 153–77. Farnham, Vt.: Ashgate, 2009.

———. "Is Public Reason Innocuous?" *Critical Review of International Social and Political Philosophy* 11, no. 2 (2008): 131–53.

Neuhouser, Frederick. *Rousseau's Theodicy of Self-Love*. Oxford: Oxford University Press, 2008.

Newby, Gordon D. *A Concise Encyclopedia of Islam*. Oxford: Oneworld, 2002.

Nock, Arthur. *Essays on Religion and the Ancient World*. Oxford: Clarendon Press, 1986.

Norden, Eduard. *Agnosthos Theos: Untersuchungen zur Formengeschichte Religiöser Rede*. 1912; Darmstadt: Wissenschaftliche Buchgesellschaft, 1974.

Norris, Pippa, and Ronald Inglehart. *Sacred and Secular: Religion and Politics Worldwide*. Cambridge: Cambridge University Press, 2004.

Nussbaum, Martha. *Frontiers of Justice: Disability, Nationality, Species Membership*. Cambridge, Mass.: Harvard University Press, 2006.

———. *Liberty of Conscience*. New York: Basic Books, 2008.

———. "Perfectionist Liberalism and Political Liberalism." *Philosophy and Public Affairs* 39, no. 1 (2011): 3–45.

———. "Veiled Threats." *New York Times Opinionator*, July 11, 2010. http://opinionator.blogs.nytimes.com/2010/07/11/veiled-threats.

Obama, Barack. *The Audacity of Hope: Thoughts on Reclaiming the American Dream*. New York: Three Rivers Press, 2006.

Ostien, Philip Jamila M. Nasir, and Franz Kogelmann, eds. *Comparative Perspectives on Shari'ah in Nigeria*. Ibadan: Spectrum Books, 2005.

Pannenberg Wolfgang. "Wie wahr is das Reden von Gott?" *Evangelische Kommentare* 4, no. 11 (1971): 629–33.

Perry, Michael. "A Critique of the 'Liberal' Political-Philosophical Project." *William and Mary Law Review* 28, no. 2 (1987): 205–33.

———. "Religion as a Basis of Law-Making?" *Philosophy and Social Criticism* 35 (2009): 105–26.

———. "Religious Arguments in Public Political Debate." *Loyola of Los Angeles Law Review* 29 (1996): 1421–58.

———. *Under God?* Cambridge: Cambridge University Press, 2003.

———. "Why Political Reliance on Religious Grounded Morality Is Not Illegitimate in a Liberal Democracy." *Wake Forest Law Review* 36, no. 2 (2001): 217–49.

Pervo, Richard I. *Acts: A Commentary*. Minneapolis: Fortress, 2009.

Pesch, Rudolph. *Die Apostelgeschichte (Apg 13–28)*. Köln: Benziger, 1986.

Picht, Georg. *Kants Religionsphilosophie*. Stuttgart: Klett-Cotta, 1985.

Piettre, René. "Paul et les Épicuriens d'Athènes entre polythéismes, athéismes, et monothéismes." *Diogenes* 205 (2004): 52–68.

Plato. *Five Dialogues*. Translated by G. M. A. Grube. 2nd ed. Indianapolis: Hackett, 2002.

———. *Phaedrus*. In *Complete Works*, edited by J. M. Cooper, 506–56. Indianapolis: Hackett, 1997.

———. "Socrates' verdediging." In *Plato, Feest, Euthyfron, Socrates' verdediging, Kriton, Faidon*. Amsterdam: Atheneum, 2008.

———. *Symposium*. In *Complete Works*, edited by J. M. Cooper, 457–505. Indianapolis: Hackett, 1997.

Plümacher, Eckhard. *Lukas als hellenistischer Schriftsteller: Studien zur Apostelgeschichte.* Göttingen: Vandenhoeck and Ruprecht, 1972.

Pogge, Thomas. *World Poverty and Human Rights: Cosmopolitan Responsibilities and Reforms.* Cambridge: Polity, 2002.

Polikoff, Nancy D. *Beyond (Straight and Gay) Marriage: Valuing All Families Under the Law.* Boston: Beacon, 2008.

Porter, Jean. "Does the Natural Law Provide a Universally Valid Morality?" In *Intractable Disputes About the Natural Law: Alasdair MacIntyre and Critics,* edited by Lawrence Cunningham, 53–95. Notre Dame: University of Notre Dame Press, 2009.

Quine, W. V. O. *Word and Object.* Cambridge, Mass.: MIT Press, 1960.

Quinn, Philip L. "Political Liberalisms and their Exclusions of the Religious." In *Religion and Contemporary Liberalism,* edited by Paul Weithman, 138–61. Notre Dame: University of Notre Dame Press, 1997.

Quong, Jonathan. *Liberalism Without Perfection.* Oxford: Oxford University Press, 2011.

———. "The Rights of Unreasonable Citizens." *Journal of Political Philosophy* 12 (2004): 314–35.

———. "The Scope of Public Reason." *Political Studies* 52 (2004): 233–50.

Ratzinger, Joseph [as Pope Benedict XVI]. *Address by the Holy Father on the Occasion of a Meeting with the Civil and Political Authorities and with the Members of the Diplomatic Corps.* Vatican City: Libreria Editrice Vaticana, 2009.

———. *Faith, Reason and the University.* Vatican City: Libreria Editrice Vaticana, 2006.

———. *Lecture by the Holy Father at the University of Rome "La Sapienza."* Vatican City: Libreria Editrice Vaticana, 2008.

Ratzinger, Joseph. *Christianity and the Crisis of Cultures.* San Francisco: Ignatius, 2006.

———. "That Which Holds the World Together: The Pre-Political Moral Foundations of a Free State." In *The Dialectics of Secularization: On Reason and Religion,* by Jürgen Habermas and Joseph Ratzinger, 53–80. San Francisco: Ignatius, 2006.

———. *Truth and Tolerance: Christian Belief and World Religions.* San Francisco: Ignatius, 2004.

Reder, Michael. "Wie weit können Glaube und Vernunft unterscheiden werden." In *Ein Bewusstsein von dem, was fehlt: Eine Diskussion mit Jürgen Habermas,* edited by Michael Reder and Josef Schmidt, 51–68. Frankfurt: Suhrkamp, 2008.

Reidy, David. "Rawls's Religion and Justice as Fairness." *History of Political Thought* 31, no. 2 (2010): 309–43.

———. "Rawls's Wide View of Public Reason: Not Wide Enough." *Res Publica* 6, no. 1 (2000): 49–72.

Richards, David A. J. "Ethical Religion and the Struggle for Human Rights: The Case of Martin Luther King, Jr." *Fordham Law Review* 72, no. 5 (2004): 2105–52.

Ricoeur, Paul. *The Conflict of Interpretations: Studies in Phenomenology and Existential Philosophy.* Evanston, Ill.: Northwestern University Press, 1992.

———. *The Course of Recognition.* Cambridge, Mass.: Harvard University Press, 2005.

———. "Is a Purely Procedural Theory of Justice Possible?" In *The Just,* translated by David Pellauer, 36–57. Chicago: University of Chicago Press, 2000.

———. *La memoire, l'histoire, l'oubli.* Paris: Seuil, 2000.

———. *Oneself as Another.* Chicago: University of Chicago Press, 1992.

Rodin, David, and Henry Shue, eds. *Just and Unjust Warriors.* Oxford: Oxford University Press, 2010.

Rorty, Richard. "Religion as a Conversation-Stopper." In *Philosophy and Social Hope*, 168–74. New York: Penguin, 1999.

———. "Religion in the Public Square: A Reconsideration." *Journal of Religious Ethics* 31, no. 1 (2003): 141–49.

Rosen, Michael. *Dignity: Its History and Meaning*. Cambridge, Mass.: Harvard University Press, 2012.

Rosenblum, Nancy. "Civil Societies: Liberalism and the Moral Use of Pluralism." In *Civil Society and Democracy*, edited by Carolyn M. Elliott, 106–14. Oxford: Oxford University Press, 2003.

———, ed. *Obligations of Citizenship and Demands of Faith: Religious Accommodation in Pluralist Democracies*. Princeton: Princeton University Press, 2000.

Rosenzweig, Franz. *Star of Redemption*. Translated by William W. Hallo. Notre Dame: University of Notre Dame Press, 1985.

Rousseau, Jean-Jacques. "Discourse on Political Economy." In *The Social Contract, and Other Later Political Writings*, edited by Victor Gourevitch, 3–38. Cambridge: Cambridge University Press, 1997.

———. "Of the Social Contract." In *The Social Contract, and Other Later Political Writings*, edited by Victor Gourevitch, 39–152. Cambridge: Cambridge University Press, 1997.

Sandel, Michael. *Liberalism and the Limits of Justice*. 2nd ed. Cambridge: Cambridge University Press, 1998.

———. "Review of *Political Liberalism* by John Rawls." *Harvard Law Review* 107 (1994): 1765–94.

Scherer, Matthew. "Saint John: The Miracle of Secular Reason." In *Political Theologies: Public Religions in a Post-Secular World*, edited by Hent de Vries and Lawrence E. Sullivan, 341–62. New York: Fordham University Press, 2006.

Schillebeeckx, Edward. *Mensen als verhaal van God*. Baarn: Nelissen, 1989.

———. *Theologisch geloofsverstaan anno 1983*. Baarn: Nelissen,1983.

Schleiermacher, Friedrich. *Hermeneutik*. Edited by Heinz Kimmerle. Heidelberg: Carl Winter, 1974.

Schubert, Charlotte. "Der Areopag. Ein Gerichtshof zwischen Politik und Recht." In *Grosse Prozesse im Alten Athen*, edited by Leonhard Burckhard and Jürgen von Ungern-Sternberg, 50–65. München: Beck, 2000.

Schüller, Bruno. *Die Begründung sittlicher Urteile: Typen ethischer Argumentation in der katholischen Moraltheologie*. Düsseldorf: Patmos, 1973.

———. "Zur Problematik allgemein verbindlicher ethischen Grundsätze." *Theologie und Philosophie* 45 (1970): 1–23.

Schwartzman, Micah. "The Completeness of Public Reason." *Politics, Philosophy and Economics* 3, no. 2 (2004): 191–220.

———. "The Sincerity of Public Reason." *Journal of Political Philosophy* 19, no. 4 (2011): 375–98.

Searle, John. *The Construction of Social Reality*. London: Penguin, 1995.

Shiffrin, Steven. "Religion and Democracy." *Notre Dame Law Review* 74, no. 5 (1999): 1631–56.

Shklar, Judith. *American Citizenship: The Quest for Inclusion*. Cambridge, Mass.: Harvard University Press, 1991.

Shue, Henry. "Torture." *Philosophy and Public Affairs* 7, no. 2 (1978): 124–43.

Solum, Lawrence. "Constructing an Ideal of Public Reason." *San Diego Law Review* 30 (1993): 729–62.

Speer, Andreas. "Weisheit." In *Historisches Wörterbuch der Philosophie*. 13 vols. Edited by Joachim Ritter, Karlfried Gründer, and Gottfried Gabriel, vol. 12, 371–97. Darmstadt: Wissenschaftliche Buchgesellschaft, 2004.

Sterba, James. "Reconciling Public Reason and Religious Values." *Social Theory and Practice* 25 (1999): 1–28.

Stout, Jeffrey. *Democracy and Tradition*, Princeton: Princeton University Press, 2004.

Strawson, P. F. *Freedom and Resentment, and Other Essays*. New York: Routledge, 2008.

Sunstein, Cass. "Ginsburg's Dissent May Yet Prevail." *Los Angeles Times*, April 20, 2007.

———. "It's For Your Own Good!" *New York Review of Books* 60, no. 7 (2013): 53–54.

Sunstein, Cass, and Richard Thaler. "Privatizing Marriage." *Monist* 91, no. 3–4 (2008): 377–87.

Sussman, David. "What's Wrong with Torture?" *Philosophy and Public Affairs* 33, no. 1 (2005): 1–33.

Swaine, Lucas. "Demanding Deliberation: Political Liberalism and the Inclusion of Islam." *Journal of Islamic Law and Culture* 11 (2009): 92–110.

Talisse, Robert. "Dilemmas of Public Reason: Pluralism, Polarization, and Instability." In *The Legacy of John Rawls*, edited by Thom Brooks and Fabian Freyenhagen, 107–23. New York: Continuum, 2005.

Taylor, Justin. *Les actes des deux apôtres*. Paris: Gabalda, 1994.

Torkki, Juhana. "Paul in Athens (Acts 17: 16–34): A Dramatic Episode." In *Lux Humana, Lux Aeterna: Essays on Biblical and Related Themes in Honour of Lars Aejmelaeus*, edited by Antti Mustakallio, 337–63. Göttingen: Vandenhoeck and Ruprecht, 2005.

———. "The Dramatic Account of Paul's Encounter with Philosophy: An Analysis of Acts 17:16–34 with Regard to Contemporary Philosophical Debates." Ph.D. diss., University of Helsinki, 2004.

US National Conference of Catholic Bishops. *The Challenge of Peace: God's Promise and Our Response*. Washington, D.C.: National Conference of Catholic Bishops, 1983.

Vallier, Kevin. "Against Public Reason's Accessibility Requirement." *Journal of Moral Philosophy* 8 (2011): 366–89.

———. "Consensus and Convergence in Public Reason." *Public Affairs Quarterly* 25, no. 4 (2011): 261–79.

———. "Liberalism, Religion and Integrity." *Australasian Journal of Philosophy* 90, no. 1 (2012): 149–65.

Vallier, Kevin, and Fred D'Agostino. "Public Justification." *Stanford Encyclopedia of Philosophy*, edited by Edward N. Zalta. August 3, 2013. http://plato.stanford.edu/entries/justification-public.

Van der Horst, Pieter. "The Altar of the 'Unknown God' in Athens (Acts 17:23) and the Cult of 'Unknown Gods' in the Hellenistic and Roman Period." *Aufstieg und Niedergang der Römischen Welt* 18, no. 2 (1989): 337–63.

———. *De onbekende God*. Utrecht: Wever, 1988.

Van der Toorn, Karel. *Sin and Sanction in Israel and Mesopotamia*. Assen: Van Gorcum, 1985.

Van der Ven, Johannes A. "From Natural Rights to Human Rights: A Cultural War in the Modern Era." *Religion, State and Society* 41, no. 2 (2013): 164–87.

———. *Human Rights or Religious Rules?* Leiden: Brill, 2010.

Vikor, Knut. *Between God and Sultan: A History of Islamic Law*. Oxford: Oxford University Press, 2005.

Vitoria, Francisco de. "On the Law of War." In *Political Writings*, edited by Anthony Pagden and Jeremy Lawrence, 293–327. Cambridge: Cambridge University Press, 1991.

Von Harnack, Adolf. *Ist die Rede des Paulus in Athene ein ursprünglicher Bestandteil des Apostelgeschichte?* Leipzig: Hinrich, 1913.

Vrousalis, Nicholas. "G. A. Cohen's Vision of Socialism." *Journal of Ethics* 14, nos. 3–4 (2010): 185–216.

———. "Jazz Bands, Camping Trips and Decommodification: G. A. Cohen on Community." *Socialist Studies* 8, no. 1 (2012): 1–20.

Waldron, Jeremy. *God, Locke, and Equality: Christian Foundations in Locke's Political Thought.* Cambridge: Cambridge University Press, 2002.

———. "John Rawls and the Social Minimum." In *Liberal Rights*, 250–69. Cambridge: Cambridge University Press, 1993.

———. *Liberal Rights.* Cambridge: Cambridge University Press, 1993.

———. "Religious Contributions to Public Deliberation." *San Diego Law Review* 30 (1993): 817–48.

———. "Secularism and the Limits of Community." In *Globalization Challenged: Conviction, Conflict, Community*, edited by George Rupp, 52–67. New York: Columbia University Press, 2006.

———. "Two-Way Translation: The Ethics of Engaging with Religious Contributions in Public Deliberation." *Mercer Law Review* 63, no. 3 (2012): 845–68.

Walgrave, Jan. "Redelijke geloofsverantwoording." *Tijdschrift voor Theologie* 2, no. 2 (1962): 101–26.

Walzer, Michael. "Drawing the Line: Religion and Politics." *Utah Law Review* 3 (1999): 619–38.

———. *Spheres of Justice.* New York: Basic Books, 1983.

Warner, Michael. *The Trouble with Normal: Sex, Politics, and the Ethics of Queer Life.* Cambridge, Mass.: Harvard University Press, 1999.

Weiss, Bernard. *The Spirit of Islamic Law.* Athens: University of Georgia Press, 1998.

Weithman, Paul. "Deliberative Character." *Journal of Political Philosophy* 13 (2005): 263–83.

———. "John Rawls and the Task of Political Philosophy." *Review of Politics* 71, no. 1 (2009): 113–25.

———, ed. *Religion and Contemporary Liberalism.* Notre Dame: University of Notre Dame Press, 1997.

———. "Religion and the Liberalism of Reasoned Respect." In *Religion and Contemporary Liberalism*, edited by Paul Weithman, 1–37. Notre Dame: University of Notre Dame Press, 1997.

———. *Religion and the Obligations of Citizenship.* Cambridge: Cambridge University Press, 2002.

———. *Why Political Liberalism? On John Rawls's Political Turn.* Oxford: Oxford University Press, 2011.

Williams, Andrew. "The Alleged Incompleteness of Public Reason." *Res Publica* 6, no. 2 (2000): 199–211.

Williams, Bernard. *Moral Luck.* Cambridge: Cambridge University Press, 1981.

Wils, Jean-Pierre. *Hermeneutiek en verlangen: Over godservaring en ethiek in het spoor van Friedrich D. E. Schleiermacher.* Nijmegen: Radboud Universiteit Nijmegen Press, 1997.

———. "Die hermeneutische Signatur der kommunitaristischen Liberalismuskritik." In *Kommunitarismus und Religion*, edited by Michael Kühnlein, 17–38. Berlin: Akademie Verlag, 2010.

———. "Universality of Human Rights and the Need for Parsimony." In *Tensions Within and Between Religions and Human Rights*, edited by Johannes A. Van der Ven and Hans-Georg Ziebertz, 9–26. Leiden: Brill, 2011.

Witherington, Ben. *The Acts of the Apostles: A Social-Rhetoric Commentary*. Grand Rapids, Mich.: Eerdmans, 1998.

Wolterstorff, Nicholas. "Do Christians Have Good Reasons for Supporting Liberal Democracy?" *Modern Schoolman* 78, nos. 2–3 (2001): 229–48.

———. "The Role of Religion in Decision and Discussion of Political Issues." In *Religion in the Public Square: The Place of Religious Convictions in Political Debate*, edited by Robert Audi and Nicholas Wolterstorff, 67–120. Lanham, Md.: Rowman and Littlefield, 1997.

———. "Why Can't We All Just Get Along with Each Other?" In *Religious Voices in Public Places*, edited by Nigel Biggar and Linda Hogan, 17–36. Oxford: Oxford University Press, 2009.

———. "Why We Should Reject What Liberalism Tells Us About Speaking and Acting in Public for Religious Reasons." In *Religion and Contemporary Liberalism*, edited by Paul Weithman, 162–81. Notre Dame: University of Notre Dame Press, 1997.

Young, Iris Marion. *Inclusion and Democracy*. New York: Oxford University Press, 2000.

Zerilli, Linda M. G. "Value Pluralism and the Problem of Judgment: Farewell to Public Reason." *Political Theory* 40, no. 1 (2012): 6–31.

CONTRIBUTORS

ABDULLAHI A. AN-NAʿIM is professor of law at Emory University. His research focuses on human rights in cross-cultural perspectives, Islam and the secular state, and constitutionalism in African and Islamic societies. Besides numerous articles and chapters, he is the author of *What Is an American Muslim?* (Oxford University Press, 2014), *Muslims and Global Justice* (University of Pennsylvania Press, 2011), *Islam and the Secular State: Negotiating the Future of Shari'a* (Harvard University Press, 2008), *African Constitutionalism and the Role of Islam* (University of Pennsylvania Press, 2006), and *Toward an Islamic Reformation: Civil Liberties, Human Rights, and International Law* (Syracuse University Press, 1990), and the editor of *Human Rights Under African Constitutions* (University of Pennsylvania Press, 2006, 2003), *Islamic Family Law in a Changing World: A Global Resource Book* (Zed, 2002), *Cultural Transformation and Human Rights in Africa* (Zed, 2002), and *Human Rights in Cross-Cultural Perspectives: Quest for Consensus* (University of Pennsylvania Press, 1992).

TOM BAILEY teaches philosophy at John Cabot University in Rome, Italy. His research focuses on contemporary political philosophy, ethics, and the history of modern philosophy. His publications in these areas include "Nietzsche the Kantian?" in *Oxford Handbook of Nietzsche*, edited by K. Gemes and J. Richardson (Oxford University Press, 2013), "Analysing the Good Will: Kant's Argument in the First Section of the *Groundwork*," in *British Journal for* the History of Philosophy (2010), and the edited collection *Deprovincializing Habermas: Global Perspectives* (Routledge, 2013).

CHRISTOPHER J. EBERLE is associate professor of philosophy at the U.S. Naval Academy. Besides *Religious Conviction in Liberal Politics* (Cambridge University Press, 2002), he has published numerous articles on religious respect and reasons in politics, including "Respect for Persons and the Doctrine of Religious Restraint" in *Philosophy and Social Criticism* (2009) and "Religious Reasons in Public" in *St. John's Journal of Legal Commentary* (2007), as well as articles on religion, morality, and war, such as "Just Cause and Cyber War" in *Journal of Military Ethics* (2013), "God and War: Some Exploratory Questions" in *Journal of Law and Religion* (2012–13), and "God, War, and Conscience" in *Journal of Religious Ethics* (2007).

VALENTINA GENTILE is vice director of the Center for Ethics and Global Politics at LUISS University in Rome, Italy. Her research focuses on liberal tolerance, reasonable pluralism, and moral stability in divided societies, as well as on justice and recognition. She is the author of *From Identity-Conflict to Civil Society: Restoring Human Dignity and Pluralism in Deeply Divided Societies* (LUISS University Press, 2013), as well as "Secularism in Contemporary India" in *Secularism, Religion and Politics: India and Europe*, edited by P. Losonczi and W. Van Herck (Routledge, 2014), " 'Epistemic Injustice' and the 'Right to Not Be Poor': Bringing Recognition Into the Debate on Global Justice" in *Global Policy* (2013), and "Civil Society in Bosnia After Dayton: The Role of Associations of Victims and Relatives of Missing Persons" in *Conflict Society and Peace-Building: The Role of Human Rights*, edited by R. Marchetti and N. Tocci (Routledge, 2011).

JAMES GLEDHILL is assistant professor of political theory at the University of Hong Kong. His research focuses on the relationship between John Rawls's political thought and that of Jürgen Habermas. His publications include "In Defense of Transcendental Institutionalism" in *Philosophy and Social Philosophy* (2014), "The Basic Structure of the Institutional Imagination" in *Journal of Social Philosophy* (2014)," "Constructivism and Reflexive Constitution-Making Practices" in *Raisons Politiques* (2013), "Rawls and Realism" in *Social Theory and Practice* (2012), and "Procedure in Substance and Substance in Procedure: Reframing the Rawls-Habermas Debate" in *Habermas and Rawls*, edited by J. G. Finlayson and F. Freyenhagen (Routledge, 2011).

PETER JONKERS is professor of philosophy at the Tilburg School of Catholic Theology. He specializes in the philosophy of religion, and his current research focuses on the place of religious truth claims in pluralistic societies. His recent publications in this field include "Redefining Religious Truth as a Challenge for Philosophy of Religion" in *European Journal for Philosophy of Religion* (2012), " 'A Purifying Force For Reason': Pope Benedict on the Role of Christianity in

Advanced Modernity" in *Towards a New Catholic Church in Advanced Modernity*, edited by S. Hellemans and J. Wissink (Lit, 2012), "Hegel on Catholic Religion" in *Hegel's Philosophy of the Historical Religions*, edited by B. Labuschagne and T. Slootweg (Brill, 2012), "Orthopraxis and Being Faithful to One's Tradition" in *Orthodoxy, Liberalism, and Adaptation*, edited by B. Becking (Brill, 2011), "Can Freedom of Religion Replace the Virtue of Tolerance?" in *From Political Theory to Political Theology*, edited by P. Losonczi and A. Singh (Continuum, 2010), "Religious Truth in a Globalizing World" in *Politics and Religion in the New Century*, edited by C. Besseling and P. Quarido (Sydney University Press, 2009), and "Contingent Religions, Contingent Truths?" in *Religions Challenged by Contingency*, edited by Jonkers and D. M. Grube (Brill, 2008).

SEBASTIANO MAFFETTONE is professor of political philosophy and director of the Department of Political Science at LUISS University in Rome. His research focuses on contemporary political philosophy and particularly on the work of John Rawls. He is the author of *John Rawls: An Introduction* (Polity, 2010), along with numerous other publications in this field.

ANDREW F. MARCH is associate professor of political science at Yale University. His work focuses on contemporary liberal and Islamic political philosophy. He is the author of *Islam and Liberal Citizenship: The Search for an Overlapping Consensus* (Oxford University Press, 2009), along with numerous articles, including "Rethinking Religious Reasons in Public Justification" in *American Political Science Review* (2013), "Genealogies of Sovereignty in Islamic Political Theology" in *Social Research* (2013), "Speech and the Sacred: Does the Defense of Free Speech Rest on a Mistake About Religion?" in *Political Theory* (2012), "Theocrats Living Under Secular Law: An External Engagement with Islamic Legal Theory" in *Journal of Political Philosophy* (2011), "Is There a Right to Polygamy? Marriage, Equality and Subsidizing Families in Liberal Public Justification" in *Journal of Moral Philosophy* (2011), "Taking People as They Are: Islam as a 'Realistic Utopia' in the Political Theory of Sayyid Qutb" in *American Political Science Review* (2010), "Reading Tariq Ramadan: Political Liberalism, Islam, and 'Overlapping Consensus'" in *Ethics and International Affairs* (2007), and "Islamic Foundations for a Social Contract in Non-Muslim Liberal Democracies" in *American Political Science Review* (2007).

PATRICK NEAL is professor of political science at the University of Vermont. He specializes in liberal political philosophy and his current research focuses on Rawls and the relationship between religion and liberalism. He is the author of *Liberalism and Its Discontents* (New York University Press, 1997) and numerous articles, including "Habermas, Religion, and Citizenship" in *Politics and Religion* (2014), "Rawls, Abortion, and Public Reason" in *Journal of Church and State* (2014), "Is Political Liberalism Hostile to Religion?" in *Reflections on Rawls*, edited by S. Young (Ashgate, 2009), "The Path Between Value Pluralism and Liberal

Political Order" in *San Diego Law Review* (2009), and "Is Public Reason Innocuous?" in *Critical Review of International Social and Political Philosophy* (2008).

MICAH SCHWARTZMAN is Edward F. Howrey Professor and professor of law at the University of Virginia School of Law. His research focuses on law and religion, liberal political philosophy, and theories of public reason. His publications include "Against Religious Institutionalism" (with Richard Schragger) in *Virginia Law Review* (2013), "What If Religion Is Not Special?" in *University of Chicago Law Review* (2012), "The Sincerity of Public Reason" in *Journal of Political Philosophy* (2011), "Conscience, Speech, and Money" in *Virginia Law Review* (2011), "The Relevance of Locke's Religious Arguments for Toleration" in *Political Theory* (2005), and "The Completeness of Public Reason," in *Politics, Philosophy and Economics* (2004).

ROBERT B. TALISSE is professor of philosophy and political science at Vanderbilt University. His current research focuses particularly on issues of democracy, pluralism, public justification, fanaticism, and social epistemology. His publications in these areas include *Pluralism and Liberal Politics* (Routledge, 2011), *Reasonable Atheism* (with S. Aikin, Prometheus, 2011), *Democracy and Moral Conflict* (Cambridge University Press, 2009), *A Pragmatist Philosophy of Democracy* (Routledge, 2007), and *Democracy After Liberalism* (Routledge, 2005).

JOHANNES A. VAN DER VEN is emeritus professor of empirical science of religion at Radboud University Nijmegen, where he is currently also a research associate in political philsosophy. He has worked extensively on the philosophy and empirical study of religion, and his current research focuses particularly on the relation between religion and human rights. Besides hundreds of scholarly articles, his publications include *Human Rights or Religious Rules?* (Brill, 2009), *Is There a God of Human Rights?* (Brill, 2004), *God Reinvented?* (Brill, 1998), *Ecclesiology in Context* (Eerdmans, 1996), *Practical Theology: An Empirical Approach* (Kampen, 1993), and the coedited collections *Tensions Within and Between Human Rights and Religions* (with H. Ziebertz, Brill, 2012), *Normativity and Empirical Research in Theology* (with M. Scherer-Rath, Brill, 2004), and *Divine Justice and Human Justice* (with J. S. Dreyer, Unisa, 2002).

PAUL WEITHMAN is the Glynn Family Honors Collegiate Professor of Philosophy at the University of Notre Dame. His research focuses on the place of religion in political philosophy and on the work of John Rawls. Besides numerous articles and chapters, he has published *Why Political Liberalism? On John Rawls's Political Turn* (Oxford University Press, 2011) and *Religion and the Obligations of Citizenship* (Cambridge University Press, 2002), and edited *Liberal Faith* (Notre Dame University Press, 2008), *The Philosophy of Rawls* (5 vols., with H. Richardson, Garland, 1999), and *Religion and Contemporary Liberalism* (Notre Dame University Press, 1997).

INDEX

abortion rights: citizenship of women as dependent on, 79, 129n38; as issue of rights of unrepresented entities, 107–8, 116; and liberalism, biased predetermination of debates over, 72n32; pluralism of comprehensive doctrines and, 180, 181t; Rawls on, 72n32, 186; religious reasoning about, 5, 6, 59, 118, 125n5, 179, 184, 186

accessibility of reasons: *vs.* convergence conception of justified coercion, 35, 38, 41–43; defined, 50n7; degree of appeal to revelation or clerical authority and, 34–35, 38–41, 98, 100, 102–3, 104–5, 110, 113, 114; ideal of conscientious engagement and, 60–61, 62–63, 125n5; justificatory liberalism on, 54; and mutual respect, 34–35, 35–38; as overly-simple criterion for evaluation of religious reasons, 98. *See also entries under* common ground; Principle of Religious Insufficiency

accountability of political officials, as privilege of citizenship, 75–76

Acts of the Apostles. *See* Paul's speech to the Athenians (Acts 17:16–34)

advocacy. *See* political advocacy

agapic pacifists: and convergence conception, 45; and duties of citizenship, 74n66; and moral responsibility to obey law, 65, 66–67; and mutual respect, 58–59, 61; principles of, 45

agonistic conception of democracy: and religious reasons, acceptability of, 103, 127n18; response to questions unresolvable by public reason, 103, 118

Al-Majalla, 252

Al Qaeda, 40

animal rights: as problematic, 120–21; as rights of unrepresented entities, 107–8

An-Na'im, Abdullahi, 20–21, 161–62, 242–64

evidentialism, Cliffordian, 73n44
excluded classes, rights and privileges of
citizenship, efforts to secure, 78
exclusivist views on religious reasoning,
7, 76, 81, 86–87, 97, 98, 122n2. *See also*
inclusivism; liberal "standard view" on
justification of state coercion; public
reason
externally-oriented ends in communities,
197–98, 197–99; in Cohen's justificatory
community, 198–99, 202

fairness: and justification of political
authority, 3, 92; reason as guarantee of,
Benedict XVI on, 222–23; as trait associated with reasonableness, in Rawls,
239n11. *See also* justice as fairness
family law codes, enactment in Islamic
countries, 252
feminist critics, on biased predetermination of outcomes in justificatory liberalism, 72n32
First Amendment, and religious pluralism,
Rawls on, 136, 179
freedom: Benedict XVI on, 222; Cohen
on, 202; as fundamental principle of
rational-choice liberalism, 177–78;
justification of state coercion in cases
affecting, 111–14; as liberal value, 1, 3,
5, 53; mutual respect as basis of, 9; in
U.S., defective nature of, 91. *See also*
autonomy; basic liberties
freedom of association, protection of, in
Islamic political theory of An-Na'im, 256
freedom of conscience: Doctrine of
Restraint and, 58, 61; public reason
liberalism as best protection of in
pluralistic society, 146–51
freedom of expression: in Islamic political
theory of An-Na'im, 256; restrictions
on, criteria for acceptable forms of,
111–12, 115
freedom of religion: Rawls on, 227; and
religious pluralism, 34
freedom of speech: and nonpolitical
discussion of religious reasoning, 57, 67;

restrictions on religious reasoning and,
1, 6, 7, 9. *See also* political advocacy;
religious reasons, restrictions on
Freeman, Samuel, 24n25
future persons, rights of, as issue of rights
of unrepresented entities, 116, 118, 120

Gadamer, Hans-Georg: Habermas and,
208–9; model of linguistic intersubjectivity, 208–9
Galston, William, 25n29
games: Cavell on, 218n56; transcending
individual subjectivity in, 208–9
Gaus, Gerald, 49n5, 60, 65, 70n1, 127n18, 158
gender equality: and criteria for acceptability of religious reasons, 121. *See also*
equality
Gentile, Valentina, 1–21, 245
George, Robert, 72n32
Gledhill, James, 18–19, 195–214
God: faith in, reconcilability with public
reason, viii, 181–82; rights of, in Islamic
law, 108; voluntarist conception of in
Rawls, 227–28; will of as grounded in
reason, in Catholic doctrine, 228
good, priority of right over, 10
goodness, Rawls on, 223
Greenawalt, Kent, 72n30
Grotius, Hugo, 185, 234

Habermas, Jürgen: Benedict XVI's criticism of, 237; communicative model
of intersubjectivity, 208–9, 211,
218–19n62; criticism of Rawls, 209–14,
219n63; engagement with religion,
219n63; Gadamer and, 208–9; model
of justificatory community in, 196,
208–14; on Plato and theory, 200;
postmetaphysical philosophy of,
209–14, 219n63; on rationalist *vs.* dialogical approaches to religious faith,
211; restrictions on religious reasons
in, 29
Hadith. *See* Sunna (Hadith)
harm principle, negative freedoms and,
111–12

Vallier, Kevin, 127n18
van der Ven, Johannes A., 17–18, 170–87
Vitoria, Francisco de, 46–47
Voltaire, 215n15
voting, as characteristic function of citizen, 78–79

Waldron, Jeremy, 125n5
war, presumption against coercion and, 30–31. *See also* enemy combatants; Just War Tradition
Weiss, Bernard, 249
Weithman, Paul, 13–14, 15, 75–94
well-ordered society: assurance problem in, 76–77, 82–90; autonomy in, 92–93. *See also* justificatory community; non-well-ordered societies
Why Not Socialism? (Cohen), 199
"wide view," 4, 88–90; and criteria for evaluation of religious reasons, 99; as response to questions unresolvable by

public reason, 103. *See also* inclusivism; proviso of Rawls; public reason
Williams, Bernard, 63–64
Williams, Rowan, 48n1
wisdom, Benedict XVI on: as both common ground and specific convergence point, 236–37; as broader reasonableness, 229; Christianity as nonexclusive path to, 230, 231–32, 235; criticiam of, 236–38; normative value of reasonable faith in, 234–35; practical agreement on, as unlikely, 237–38; *vs.* public reason as normative point of reference for consensus, 224, 225, 226, 228, 229–30, 232; as purifying force for reason, 237–38. *See also* reason; religious beliefs based on revelation or clerical authority; truth
witnessing: of excluded reasons, 8; prophetic, 109
Wolfe, Christopher, 72n32
Wolterstorff, Nicholas, 71n30